SolidWorks 2018

Modeling, Assemblies, and Drafting from Machined Parts to Blobjects

A Project-Oriented Rapid Learning Manual
Beginner to Advanced

By
Stephen M. Samuel, PE
Ashlyn Wright

**Superior Vision Yields
Optimal Products**

ISBN 978-1-935951-13-1

Published by:
Design Visionaries
14934 Camden Ave.
San Jose, CA 95124
info@designviz.com
www.designviz.com
Local Phone: (408) 997 6323

Printed in the United States of America
Published August 2018

DESIGN VISIONARIES

Superior Vision Yields
Optimal Products

Dedication

We dedicate this work to those folks who fight the good fight in classrooms all over the world. Teachers quietly raise our level of civilization and are in many cases under appreciated for it. Teachers are heroes.

About the Authors:

Stephen M. Samuel, PE Founder and President of Design Visionaries, has over 32 years of experience in developing and using high-end CAD tools and mentoring its users. During a ten-year career at Pratt & Whitney Aircraft, he was responsible for implementing advanced CAD/CAM technology in a design/manufacturing environment. He has trained thousands of engineers in Unigraphics/NX, written self-paced courses in UGNX Advanced Modeling and Best Practices, and performed design work for numerous Fortune 500 companies. Stephen is the author of distinctive publications on UGNX, CAD, CAE and Teamcenter Engineering PLM. Stephen holds 2 US patents and lives and works in San Jose, California.

Ashlyn Wright is a student at UC Berkeley who wholeheartedly enjoys the proximity to great food and greater minds as she pursues a degree in Cognitive Science. When not at school, she resides in San Jose with a loving family and a pair of finicky felines. She is incredibly grateful to have had the opportunity to work with the amazing team at Design Visionaries. As someone with firsthand experience learning SolidWorks from a previous incarnation of this textbook, she is excited to have helped bring this updated edition to a new wave of dedicated learners.

Acknowledgements

We would like to thank the following people for their tireless efforts. Without the contributions from each of you this book would be a mere shadow of what it has become:

Michael Samuel, Jeninne Scott, Landon Ritchie

Cover design by: Michael Samuel and Landon Ritchie

What Readers Have to Say About Our Previous Books

"Practical Unigraphics NX Modeling for Engineers was extremely effective and much better than [other] textbooks. I would highly recommend this book to other professors and students alike."

Fred Dyen, Director of St. Louis University's Aviation Maintenance Institute (AMI)

"The UG NX textbook is well organized. Its tutorial style of learning is easy for students to utilize. The practice exercises are essential. From my experience in teaching students to use UG software, I have found that this is the best textbook currently on the market for teaching UG NX."

Dr. Pat Spicer, Professor at Western Illinois University

Preface

Dear Reader,

Thank you for purchasing our SolidWorks 2018 workbook. We have taken great care and pride in writing this book and we hope that you receive a huge benefit from using it. Design Visionaries is an engineering consulting firm that performs many design projects great and small, including industrial design, product design and engineering analysis. Our customers entrust us with the design of medical devices, aerospace components, heavy machinery, consumer products, etc.

The methods outlined in this book go beyond an academic use of the software. They are tricks of the trade that come from thousands of hours of actual use of the software to design some of the most difficult products in the world. In addition, Design Visionaries offers world class on-site training which enables us to develop and evolve our training material so that they provide the maximum benefit.

I hope you enjoy using this text, and we invite you to visit our website – *www.designviz.com/goodies* where you can download all the completed part files of this book, additional free material, and some extra goodies.

Thank you,

Stephen M. Samuel, PE
April 1, 2018

Table of Contents

Exercise Guide

Ex.	Name	Description	Picture
0	Getting Used to the User Interface (Pg.30)	A general look at the SolidWorks User Interface.	
1	Changing Units (Pg. 38)	How to change the units of your part file.	
2	Switching and Viewing Windows (Pg. 39)	How to view and arrange multiple windows for maximum productivity.	
3	How to Make a Basic Sketch (Pg. 41)	How to use the Rectangle tool and place dimensions.	
4	More Sketching (Pg. 47)	Using the Draw tool/ Circle tool and creating basic dimensions.	
5	Constraints 1: Horizontal, Vertical and Midpoint (Pg. 58)	How to use Horizontal and Vertical constraints to define your sketch, and how to create Midpoint constraints.	

6	Constraints 2: Equal (Pg. 61)	How to use the Equal constraint.	
7	Constraints 3: Parallel and Concentric (Pg. 63)	How to use the Parallel and Concentric constraint.	
8	Constraints 4: Concentric and Trim Tool (Pg. 66)	More on the Concentric constraint and how to Trim lines.	
9	Constraints 5: Collinear (Pg. 69)	How to use the Collinear constraint.	
10	Constraints 6: Tangent (Pg. 70)	How to use the Tangent constraint.	
11	Constraints 7: Connect and Angle (Pg. 72)	How to use the Connect constraints and Angle dimension tool.	
12	Extruding (Pg. 75)	How to Extrude.	

13	More Extruding (Pg. 80)	Extruding and learning how to use the Arc command.	
14	Using Global Variables and Equations (Pg. 84)	How to create relationships between dimensions and features using Global Variables and Equations.	
15	Creating Holes (Pg. 89)	How to use the Hole Wizard and its options.	
16	More Holes (Pg. 97)	Creating a Hole on a curved surface.	
17	Cutting (Pg. 104)	How to use the Extruded Cut command.	
18	Revolving (Pg. 109)	How to use the Revolve Boss/Base command.	

19	Revolved Cut with Angled Datum Planes (Pg. 111)	How to use angled datum planes to create an angled hole and Revolved Cut.	
20	Mirror (Pg. 120)	How to Mirror a body.	
21	Draft, Fillet, and Chamfer (Pg. 123)	How to use the Ellipse command with a Draft. Plus, adding Chamfers and Fillets to a body.	
22	Sweep along a Path (Pg. - 128 -)	How to Sweep a section along a path to create a solid body.	
22-B	Sweep along a Path (Pg. 131)	Section driven along a path	
23	Thin Wall (Pg. 134)	How to give a solid body a uniform wall thickness (Shell) by removing material.	
24	Mounting Bosses (Pg. 137)	How to create a Boss.	

25	Loft and Sketch Patterns (Pg. 141)	Using SolidWorks's great feature techniques to create Pattern features on a nice Lofted surface.	
26	Vent Command (Pg. 146)	How to use the Vent command.	
27	Rectangular Hole Pattern and Grouping Features (Pg. 149)	How to create a group of features then pattern them.	
28	Circular Hole Pattern (Pg. 154)	How to create a Circular Pattern of holes.	
29	Curved Pattern (Pg. 159)	How to create a pattern of holes along a path.	
30	Helical Cut: Neural (Pg. 162)	How to use the Helical Cut feature and Circular Pattern tool to create a neural.	
31	Intersections and Varying Dimension Patterns (Pg. 168)	How to intersect bodies and modify patterns on a per instance basis.	

32	Selective Deletion (Pg. 174)	Illustrates how to selectively delete features while leaving their child features untouched.	
33	Text Tool, Wrapping, Normal Cut (Pg. 179)	How to create a Decal on a body exploring new features such as Wrap.	
34	Boundary Surface Through 3 Sketches (Pg. - 183 -)	How to create a Boundary surface.	
35	Boundary Surface with Guide Curves (Pg. - 186 -)	Techniques on how to gain more control over a Boundary surface by using guide curves.	
36	Flatten Surface (Pg. - 189 -)	How to use the Flatten Surface tool.	
37	Converting Surfaces into a Solid (Pg. - 191 -)	Using the Knit and Fill Surface commands to turn surfaces into a solid.	
38	Extrude Surfaces that are Tangentially Connected (Pg. - 195 -)	How to create continuous lofted surfaces and change them into a solid.	

39	Surfacing, Trim, Swept, Extend and Split (Pg. - 201 -)	Exploring several surfacing tools to create and edit a sheet body.	
40	Offset Surfaces (Pg. - 209 -)	Using the revolved surface tool and using Offset Face.	
41	Thickened Cut (Pg. - 214 -)	How to Replace a body with a curved surface.	
42	Replace Sketch Entity (Pg. - 218 -)	How to change a sketch while keeping features that rely on the sketch associative.	
43	Adding Threads (Pg. - 227 -)	How to create a Thread on a cylinder.	
44	Using Direct Editing (Pg. - 235 -)	A look into modeling in the traditional sense and editing faces directly.	
45	Replace Face (Pg. - 238 -)	Using the Replace Face command to replace a feature with a Swept surface.	

46	Instant3D (Pg. - 243 -)	Using Instant3D to edit features in a part.	
47	Textures, Colors, Appearance Settings (Pg. - 248 -)	Applying texture, Color and general Appearance Settings	

Assemblies:

48	Assembly 1 (Pg. - 254 -)	How to put together a simple Assembly – bolt and nut.	
49	Assembly 2: The Lever (Pg. - 260 -)	More practice with assemblies while specifically highlighting the Slot Constraint.	
50	Assembly 3 (Pg. - 266 -)	Exploring more Assembly techniques with several different components.	
51	Assembly 4 - Chain Assembly (Pg. - 275 -)	Assemblies with repeated parts using the Chain Pattern tool.	
52	Assembly 5 - Pipe (Pg. - 278 -)	Assembling a complicated Assembly.	
53	Assembly 6 - "Do Nothing" (Pg. - 284 -)	Assembly creation and Motion Study creation.	

54	Cam Tool "Hurdy Gurdy" (Pg. - 291 -)	Creating another Motion Study	
55	Assembly 7 Top Down Assemblies ID Model (Pg. - 300 -)	Creating Top Down assemblies starting with an ID model	
56	Assembly 8 Product Coordinate Systems (Pg. - 308 -)	Placing components using coordinate systems	
57	Assembly 9 Assembly Level Features (Pg. - 310 -)	Modeling that emulates actual the manufacturing process.	
58	Structural Members (Pg.- 312 -)	Drive profiles along curves to create structures	

Drafting:

59	DimXpert: Annotations and Introduction to Drafting (Pg. - 315 -)	Using DimXpert to create dimensions and a Drawing.	
60	Drafting 1 (Pg. - 326 -)	Beginners guide to drafting - including sections and detailed views.	
61	Drafting 2 - Broken View (Pg. - 333 -)	Using the Broken View command to break a long, slender cylinder in a Drawing.	
62	Drafting 3 - Assemblies (Pg. - 336 -)	Exploding an Assembly and adding it to a Drawing.	
63	Pack and Go (Pg. - 340 -)	Pulling all the files associated with an assembly to a file or zip file	

Sheet Metal

64	Sheet Metal 1 - The Basics (Pg. - 342 -)	The basics of sheet metal, Base Flange and Edge Flange.	
65	Sheet Metal 2 - The Hem and Miter Flange Tools (Pg. - 349 -)	Using the Hem and Miter Flange tools	
66	Sheet Metal 3 - The Jog Tool (Pg. - 352 -)	Use Jog to go up and over or down and under.	
67	Sheet Metal 4 - Lofted Bends (Pg. 354)	How to use the Lofted Bend tool to create sheet metal lofts.	
68	Sheet Metal 5 - Gussets (Pg. 359)	How to add structural support to sheet metal parts in the form of gussets.	
69	Sheet Metal 6 - Sketched Bend (Pg. 363)	Creating bends that are at strange angles and in irregular locations	
70	Sheet Metal 7 - The Forming Tool (Pg. 366)	Use pre-defined geometry to affect a sheet metal body	

71	Sheet Metal 8 - Convert to Sheet Metal (Pg. 373)	Create sheet metal objects from solid models	
72	Sheet Metal 9 - Unfold and Fold (Pg. 376)	Unfold a flange to add a feature or cutout then re-fold it	

Advanced Surfacing:

73	Projected Curve (Pg. 380)	Create a 3D curve using Splines on faces.	
74	Curve on Surface (Pg. 382)	Project a Spline on surface then Trim it.	
75	Scale (Pg. 385)	How to Scale solid models	
76	Curve Through Points (Pg. 388)	Generate a 3D curve using XYZ points then create a Tube.	
77	Spline Control (Pg. 390)	Learn basic Spline control features.	

78	Transition of Surfaces (Pg. 393)	Using a 3D Spline as a guide to Bridge two surfaces.	
79	Equation Driven Curve (Pg. 396)	Create a curve using an equation, then Sweep it.	
80	Curved Surface, Delete Face, Ruled Surface (Pg. 398)	Using different commands to create a curved surface and a Boundary surface.	
81	Surfaces that come to a Sharp Point (Pg. 401)	Using lofts and 3D Splines to create beautiful surfaces.	
82	Difficult Surfaces: Jellyfish (Pg. 404)	Create a Jellyfish using 3D Splines, Boundary surfaces, and Spirals.	

83	Surface Area Reduction (Pg. 408)	Sweep of two profiles, reducing the area along a guide.	
84	Lofts: Two Different Sized Profiles (Pg. 411)	Create a Loft using two different profiles.	
85	Wire Creation (Pg. 413)	Create two wires that are wound together.	
86	Flex Feature Command (Pg. 417)	Using the Flex command to twist a model.	
87	Draft Using a Parting line (Pg. 421)	Using a Parting line to Draft a part in two directions.	
88	Move Face, Offset Surface with Replace Face (Pg. 424)	Using different commands to manipulate faces.	

89	Clam Shell (Pg. 428)	Creating two bodies as a clam shell to illustrate Lip/Groove command.	
90	Offset Face from a Solid (Pg. 434)	Creating Offset surfaces using the Move Face command.	
91	Taper with Sweep (Pg. 436)	Taper a Swept solid using the Sweep command.	
92	Curve Projection and Circular Pattern (Pg. 439)	Project a Circular Pattern onto a curved surface.	
93	Saddle Holes (Pg. 442)	Adding Holes to a saddle	
94	Fit Spline (Pg. 444)	Using the Fit Spline tool to create joined curves.	

95	Knobs (Pg. 446)	Cool techniques to create different Knobs with labels.	
96	The Lizard (Pg. 454)	Creating difficult "free-flowing" geometry.	
97	Hand Sketches into SolidWorks (Pg. 466)	Creating models from imported hand sketches.	
98	More Advanced Curves from Equations (Pg. 478)	Equation driven curves.	
99	Virus Model Using Equations (Pg. 479)	Surfaces driven by equations are used to make a cool model of a virus.	

100	Configurations (Pg. 482)	Making different versions of the same part with configurations.	
101	Simulation Xpress (Pg. 486)	Use SimulationXpress to do preliminary calculations on your model.	
102	Automotive Geometry (Pg.491)	Techniques for creating automotive geometry.	
P1	A Project (Pg.509)	Apply CAD skills to a real-life situation. A drawer assembly.	
P2	Project 2: Marshmallow Gun (Pg. 528)	An awesome "Do-It-Yourself" project to test out your new CAD skills.	

The Book of Do:

When you teach a person how to ride a bike you can talk until you're blue in the face. You can tell them about the complex physics that goes on behind the scenes when they ride it, but let's face it, a person will never be a good bike rider until they spend the time pedaling without training wheels as you run frantically behind them. That sums up the philosophy of this book. In the end, the only way to be a great SolidWorks user is to spend the time working through the exercises. We have put this book together based on decades of experience in industrial and product design. The exercises in this book are designed to exponentially advance your ability to use SolidWorks to its greatest potential.

Guide to the SolidWorks User Interface

In the following pages we will take a look at the SolidWorks user interface and discover the fastest way to navigate the SolidWorks environment.

The following figure displays the screen you will see when first opening SolidWorks. From this screen it is possible to open existing SolidWorks files, create new SolidWorks files, complete some helpful SolidWorks tutorials, and get linked to support from SolidWorks **Online Help** and the **Tutorial** webpages.

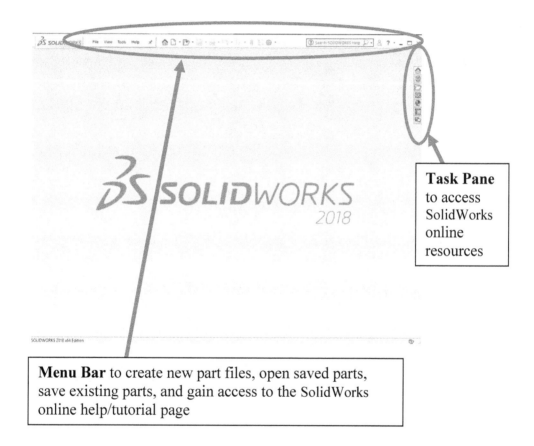

Task Pane to access SolidWorks online resources

Menu Bar to create new part files, open saved parts, save existing parts, and gain access to the SolidWorks online help/tutorial page

Exercise 0: Getting Used to the User Interface

Start by creating a new **Part File** and looking at what's inside the SolidWorks modeling environment. To create a new part, move the cursor over to the SolidWorks icon/name and click on **File/New.**   In the **New SolidWorks Document** Window, you will notice three icons that allow you to select what type of file you want to create. *Note: Most of the parts in this book will be created using the **Part** icon unless otherwise stated.*

Now click on the **Part** icon and select **OK** at the bottom of the window. You will also notice an **Advanced** tab at the bottom left of the new **Part** window. Disregard this for now. It is mostly used for creating parts using saved templates.

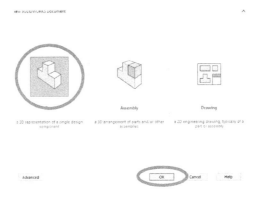

Once the new **Part File** has been created, the modeling environment appears as shown in the following figure. The main areas of SolidWorks are identified below.

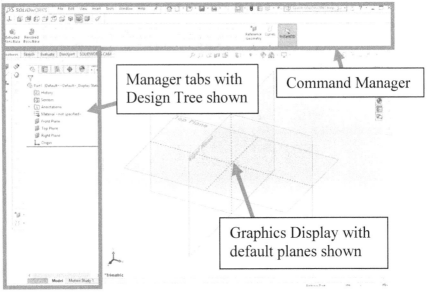

The **Command Manager** area of the screen is where most of the features are found in SolidWorks. Selecting the tabs shown below brings up toolbars such as Features and Sketch. *Note: By right-clicking one of the already present tabs, you can add new tabs from a selection menu. For this book, we recommend adding "Surfaces", "Sheet Metal", and "Direct Editing" to the original four tabs. Explore the tabs to see all the amazing features, most of which we will be covering in this book.*

You'll also notice a small search bar in the top right corner of the Command Manager. This search bar is automatically set to search SolidWorks Help for answers, but by clicking the arrow on the right edge of the bar, it can be configured to help you find commands.

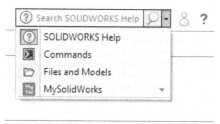

This can be very useful if you are new to a command and don't yet know where it is or if you simply forget where a command is located. Once you search a command, you can use it directly from the command search bar by clicking it, or you can choose to be shown where it is by clicking the eye to the right of the command. This is useful when you want to be able to find the command again and access it without having to search for it every time.

Note: You must have valid geometry on which to use the command or it will appear grey and will not be selectable.

The **Feature Manager** comes to life when modeling. By default, it appears on the left side of the screen. The **Feature Manager Design Tree** provides a summary view of the active part, assembly, or drawing the user creates. The Design Tree, shown below, is dynamically linked to the graphics area, so any feature, sketch, view, or geometry can be selected in either area.

Note: You can right-click on the datum planes or any feature you later create to modify, show/hide, suppress, or even delete the feature.

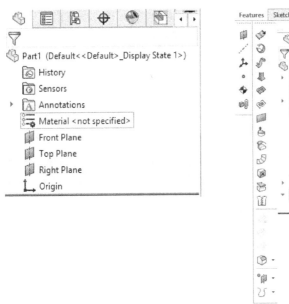

The **Task Pane** is a group of commands used in SolidWorks to access certain features and the SolidWorks community. The figure below is an example of the **Task Pane** with the **Resources** tab shown.

SolidWorks also has a **Help** and **Tutorials** feature. In the **Help** feature, users can search for information on the many features, commands, and tools SolidWorks has to offer. If you have an online account, you can also access their forums page to get more assistance. This help menu can be reached either by clicking **Help** on the top menu bar, or by searching something in the SolidWorks Help search bar mentioned previously.

SolidWorks also contains a Tutorials feature embedded in the software. There are a number of tutorials that may be helpful for you as you learn SolidWorks, but we recommend that you go through this book first before exploring the tutorials section. You won't regret it.

Viewing Stuff

The **Graphics Display** is where you can create, modify and view geometry. To do so efficiently, two hands are better than one. By using a 3D connection space ball or similar product, you can quickly rotate, zoom, and pan around the modeling environment. This will leave the mouse free to click on the modeling detail that you require. If a Space Ball is not available, you may use the viewing tools found under **View/Modify** in the tool bar or simply right-click in the graphics window. These techniques will help you navigate the graphics display.

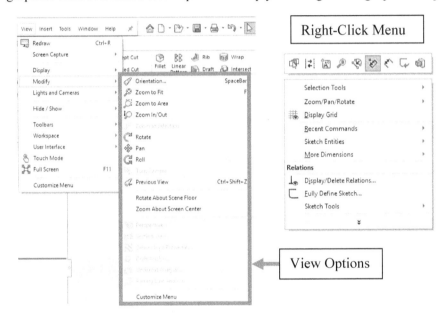

Another great viewing tool is the **Heads-up View Toolbar** located in the Graphics Display. It allows you to control most viewing functions such **as Zoom to Fit, Zoom to Area, Previous View, Section View,** and **Display Style**. Display Style allows you to display your model in shaded (with or without edges), wireframe, and hidden lines views.

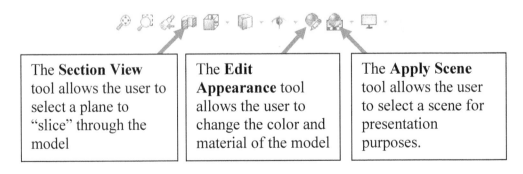

The **Section View** tool allows the user to select a plane to "slice" through the model	The **Edit Appearance** tool allows the user to change the color and material of the model	The **Apply Scene** tool allows the user to select a scene for presentation purposes.

Perhaps the most important view manipulation tools you can use are right on your mouse.

Rotate

To rotate the model, hold the middle mouse button down and drag. As you move the mouse to the left or right the part rotates around the screen Y-axis. As you move the mouse up or down, the part rotates about the screen X-axis. If you want to rotate the model around the screen Z-axis, you can hold down the Alt key while you hold and move the middle mouse button left or right. The model will respond by rotating clockwise or counterclockwise respectively. This is called a "Roll View" in the menu structure.

Zoom

To zoom in and out on the part you can use the middle wheel on your mouse if it has one. You can also zoom by holding down the shift button, then holding down the middle mouse button and moving the mouse up and down. Another option is to zoom out by pressing the Z key and zoom in by pressing the Z key as you hold down the shift button.

Fit

To fit the current view of the model to the screen size, simply press the F key.

Pan

To pan, hold the Ctrl key and middle mouse button down and move the mouse in the direction you want the image to move.

Using the middle mouse button to rotate, zoom and pan is the lion's share of what's necessary to maintain a highly productive modeling session without using a device like a space ball. These techniques will become second nature to you as you spend countless hours practicing your modeling skill.

Modeling Information

Import and Export

Importing and exporting different file types can be critical for applications such as sharing solids and using solids as reference objects. SolidWorks has a ton of different file types to choose from.

To **Export**, select **File/Save As.** When the window appears, name your file and choose a file type. Common file types for sharing solids include parasolids, STEP, IGES, and STL.

To **Import**, select **Insert/Features/Imported** then select the file you wish to import.

Measure and Draft Analysis

Being able to evaluate your model can be critical when analyzing it and saves lots of time that would otherwise be spent trying to dig up the numbers. The **Evaluate Command Manager** has numerous tools that are essential for efficient modeling and viewing.

The **Measure** command can be used to measure lengths of edges, arcs, distances between features, angles, projected distances etc.

The **Draft Analysis** command shows in a color view the faces that have a positive draft, faces that need a draft, and faces that have negative draft. In an intricate model with lots of small faces, this tool can be a life saver.

Exercise 1: Changing Units

During the installation of SolidWorks, the administrator has the decision to make the default units either Millimeters or Inches. To change units from the default, click on the **Tools** tab in the tool bar, then select **Options.**

In the Options window, select the **Document Properties** tab. Locate and click on the **Units** tab, select the appropriate units, and click **OK**. Changing the dimensions will update the model with the new dimensions. *Note: All of the exercises in this book will be created in inches unless otherwise stated.*

Exercise Complete

Exercise 2: Switching and Viewing Windows

In the **Open** tab in the tool bar, you can click on the down arrow and browse between currently open documents or previously opened. It is possible to switch between the open documents by selecting the previewed part in the window. Please try clicking on the **Open** tab.

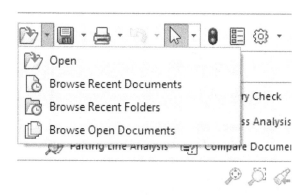

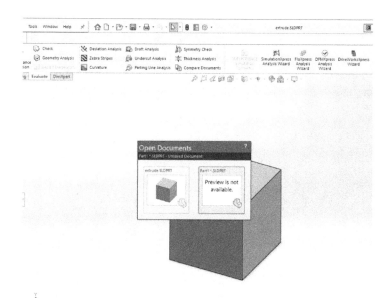

Exercise Complete

Understanding the Basics

The best CAD modelers are able to imagine the shape of what they want to build, and then instinctively know the commands to make that shape appear. In many ways these are the same skills that we learned when we spent hours playing with blocks and things like that as kids. In fact, when I was a young boy my father used to take me to the junk yard and we'd find old mechanisms and take them apart. In this way I gained a great insight into how things were put together and how things worked. In order to be good at SolidWorks you must be able to think of what it would take to make things in real life, then simply emulate those steps using the various commands. Imagine you took a hanger wire, bent it into a perfect square, then submersed it in bubble solution and lifted it up quickly. The shape you would create would be a square column. In SolidWorks this is called an **Extrude** operation. When you use the Extrude command to make a shape, you have to start out with a sketch. The hanger wire is the sketch, the column is the Extrude, and an Extrude is a subset of the **Extruded Boss/Base** menu. If you take the same hanger wire, dip it in the bubble solution, then pull it out in a circular pattern, the geometry you will get will look like a wheel. This is called a **Revolve**. If you take the construction one step further and pull the hanger along some odd snake-like path, you will get a shape that would emulate a flexible molding on the edge of a boat or something similar. In SolidWorks, this is accomplished with a **Sweep.** In each case, the section that you start with is a sketch and the solids that you create emulate the shapes in real life. Since sketching is the rudimentary skill required, in this next chapter we'll learn how to make a sketch. This is one of the most useful and universal entities in solid modeling.

Exercise 3: How to Make a Basic Sketch

Click **New** and select **Part,** as shown in the figure.

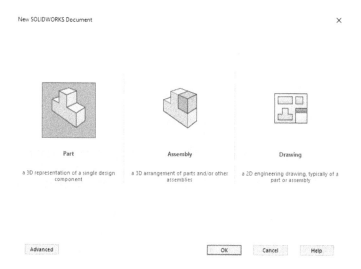

The modeling environment will now be displayed as shown below. This is where geometry can be created. *Note: The planes shown below in blue will not appear when the graphics display appears. They are shown for discussion purposes.*

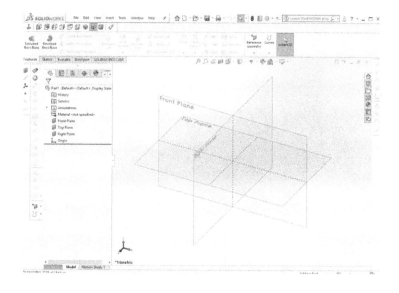

In the **Command Manager**, select the **Sketch** tab as shown below. Then, select the **Sketch** command. A prompt appears asking you to select the datum plane upon which to create your sketch.

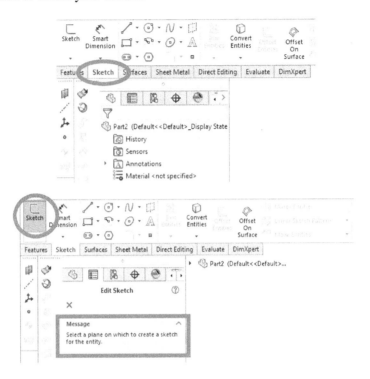

There are three default datum planes available for selection in the graphics display: the Top, Front, and Right planes. For this exercise, select the **Front** plane by clicking on it in the graphics display. The plane will highlight in orange.

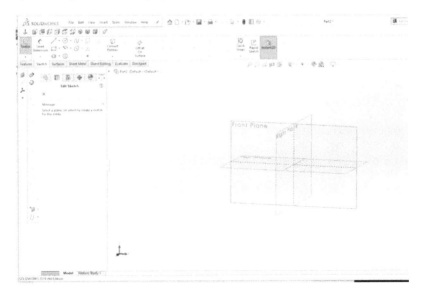

After you select a plane, the sketcher will orient the view so you are looking normal to it. *Note: We changed our background to white for clarity. To change the color of the background select the* **Tools** *tab in the tool bar, select* **Options**. *In the* **System Options** *tab, click on Colors and change the Viewport Background to the desired color.*

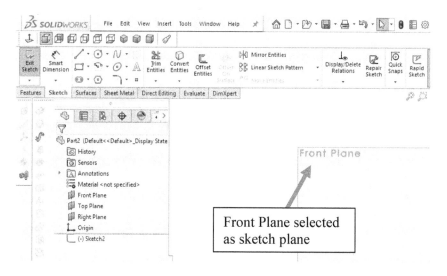

Front Plane selected as sketch plane

To begin sketching, select a tool from the **Draw** options box. For this example, select the **Rectangle** tool circled in the following figure.

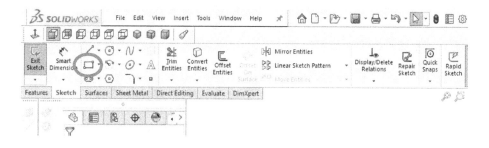

Click on the screen to place the top left corner of the rectangle as shown below. Finish the rectangle by clicking to place the bottom right corner of the rectangle. To deselect the rectangle function, hit ESC on the keyboard or right-click and choose **Select**. *Note: The lines will snap to vertical and horizontal positions. Also note that in this example, the origin is shown in the center of the rectangle.*

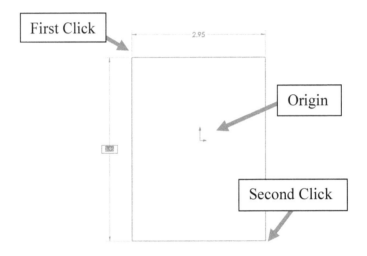

The finished rectangle should look like the following figure.

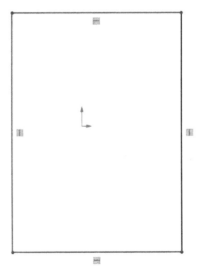

To change the size of the rectangle, click on the **Smart Dimension** tool in the Command Manager.

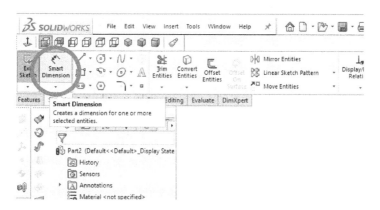

First click on the top line of the rectangle. Then click a second time to place the dimension in a suitable location. To change the value, a **Modify** box will appear. Type in a value of **1in** and hit enter or click **OK** (the green check mark) to apply.

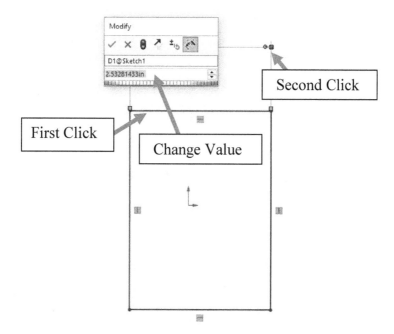

For this exercise, change the horizontal dimension to **1 in** and the vertical dimension to **1.618 in**, as shown in the following figure.

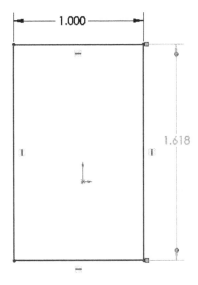

To complete the sketch, click either **Exit Sketch** in the Command Manager, or the sketch symbol with a blue arrow in the **Confirmation Corner** in the Graphics Area.

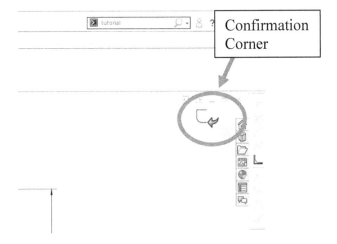

The ratio of 1 to (approximately) 1.618 is called the golden rectangle. There are many examples in architecture, such as the United Nations building, where the golden rectangle is used. The proportions come from a very cool formula that ensures that if you draw a 45 degree line from one corner to one of the vertical lines, then draw a horizontal line at that intersection point, the resulting smaller rectangle has the same proportions as the original golden rectangle. The pattern goes on infinitely.

Exercise Complete

Exercise 4: More Sketching

Create a new **Part File**. Using the **Line** tool located in the Sketch Command Manager, draw the figure below.

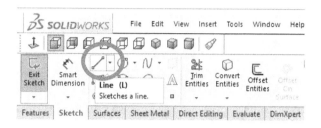

Note: The line tool will create a continuous chain of lines as you continue to click endpoints.

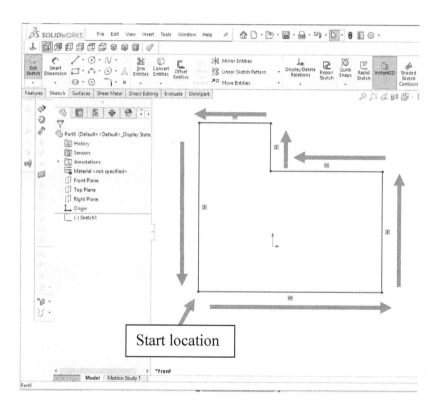

Select the **Circle** tool, shown below.

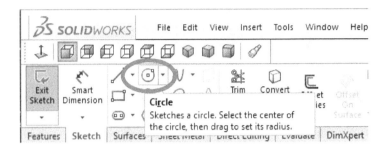

Click on the screen roughly in the location shown in the following figure. Move the cursor away from the center of the circle to choose its approximate size and click to confirm.

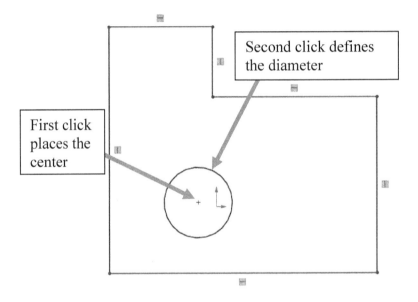

Using the **Smart Dimension** tool in the Dimension options box, add dimensions to the sides and diameter as shown below.

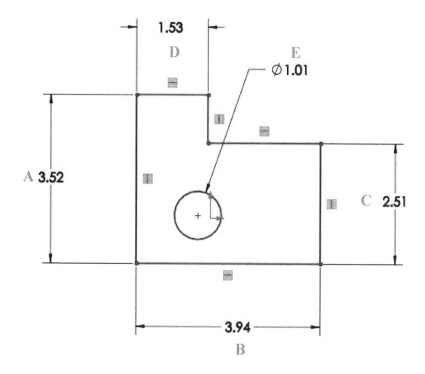

To change the value of the dimensions, double click the dimensions, and change the value in the menu as shown in Exercise 3. Dimension the sketch as shown in following figure using the **Smart Dimension** tool.

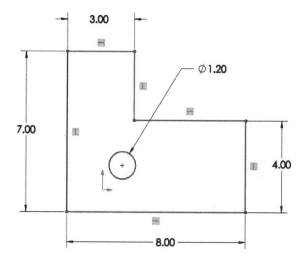

To move the circle to the correct position, use the **Smart Dimension** tool again. Click on the **4 in** vertical line, and move the mouse over the edge of the circle so that the center point appears. When you click on the center point, the horizontal dimension will appear. Create the second dimension using the same technique to relate the circle and the **8 in** side.

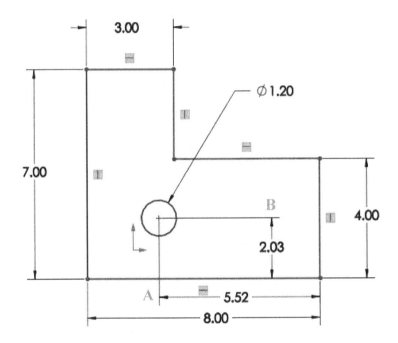

Change the values to: A = 4 and B = 2

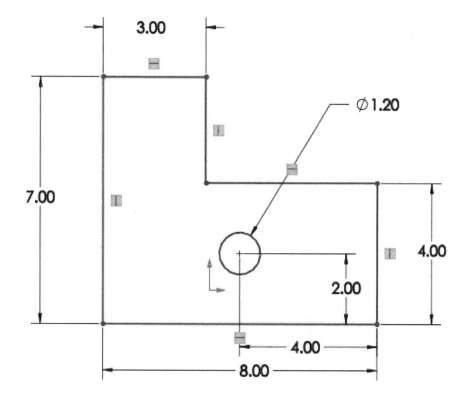

As you can imagine, there are a number of other dimensions you can place on a sketch, including angular, radial, horizontal and vertical dimensions. Most of these are adequately achieved using the automatic selections made by the **Smart Dimension** tool.

Exercise Complete

Constraints

It is extremely important to understand constraints as opposed to dimensions when you are creating a sketch. A constraint is an operator that forces geomety to conform to a rule. It's different from a dimension because it doesn't have an associated numerical value. When you are using constraints to their fullest potential you use them to capture the design intent of the geometry that you are creating. For example, in the figure below there are two large rectangles with smaller rectangles inside of them. The rectangle on the left-hand side is dimensioned so that the inner rectangle and the outer rectangle are centered. The rectangle on the right hand side is centered using a vertical command on the midpoints of the horizontal top segments. The design intent is for the inner rectangles to remain centered no matter what change is made to the overall width.

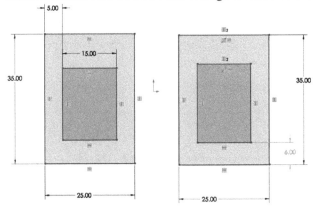

As you can see, as soon as the width of the rectangle is reduced the pair of rectangles on the left are no longer centered. The rectangles on the right remain centered because the constraint scheme has truly captured the design intent.

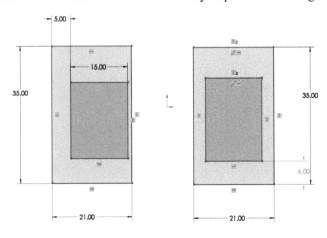

A partial list of the kinds of constraints that you will want to be familiar with includes horizontal, vertical, collinear, parallel, equal, fix, perpendicular, parallel, coradial, tangent, concentric, midpoint, coincident, and merge. By using these constraints along with dimensions, you can get most shapes to behave properly. The following images and exercises will help you familiarize yurself with these constraints.

Below, each constraint is explained and illustrated with Before and After screenshots. *Note: Any constraint shown in the following examples using circles can be used with arcs as well.*

Select two lines to use the **Collinear** constraint. Since the line on the right was already constrained to be horizontal, the line on the left conforms to the line on the right.

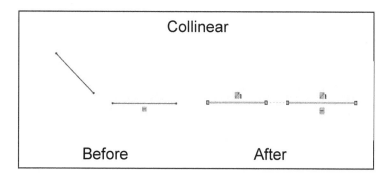

To make lines parallel, select the two lines and apply the **Parallel** constraint.

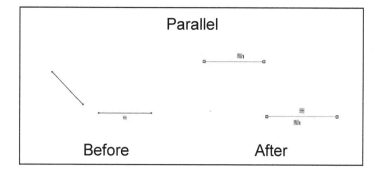

To make two lines equal in length, select them and apply the **Equal** constraint. The **Equal** constraint can also be used on the radii of circles.

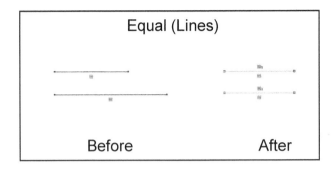

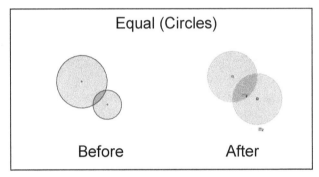

To make two lines perpendicular, select them and apply **Perpendicular** constraint.

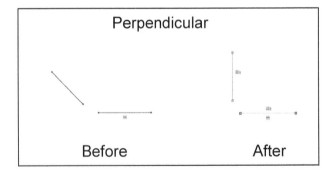

If you select two line endpoints you can get them to touch using the **Merge** constraint.

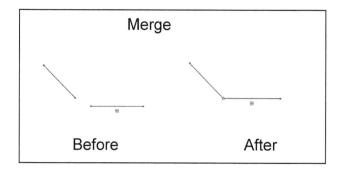

Merge

Before   After

Two circles will become concentric and have equal radii if you use the **Coradial** constraint.

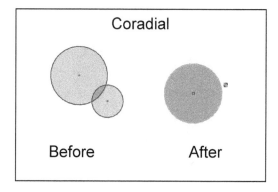

Coradial

Before   After

Select two circles or a circle and a line and you can apply the **Tangent** constraint.

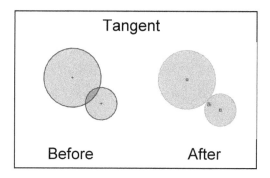

Tangent

Before   After

The **Concentric** constraint ensures that two circles of any radius will be aligned at their center points.

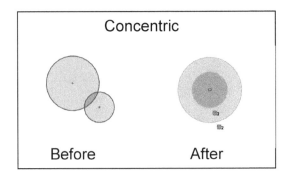

The **Midpoint** constraint connects the end point of a line to the midpoint of another line.

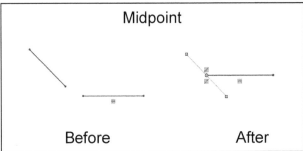

When the end point of a line is coincident to another line it means that the end point is forced to take a position along the infinite extension of that line. The **Coincident** constraint also works with points and circles.

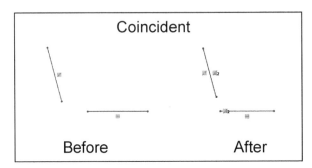

A Note About Selection

When applying constraints, it is important to know how to select the various entities. When you are trying to select a line entity, be careful not to click right on the end because that will select the line's endpoint instead. Should you desire to select the midpoint of a line, you need to select the line by right-clicking it. A menu will appear with the option to "Select Midpoint."

When in the general sketch environment, entities will only select one at a time. Clicking another entity will deselect the previous one. To select more than one entity, hold down the Shift or Ctrl key as you click.

Exercise Complete

Exercise 5: Constraints 1 - Horizontal, Vertical and Midpoint

Create a new **Part File** and create a **Sketch** on the **Front Plane**. Using the **Line** tool, create a shape that looks like the figure below.

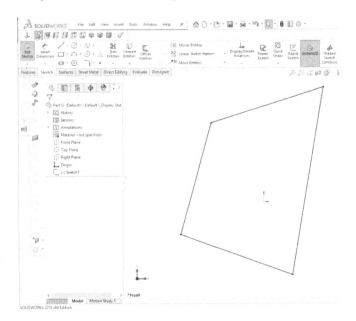

In the Command Manager, click on the dropdown arrow of the **Display/Delete Relations** tool, then click **Add Relation**.

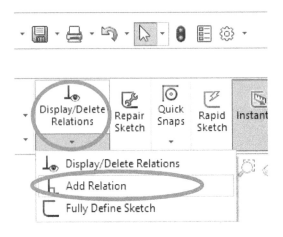

When in the **Add Relation** tool, you can select multiple entities sequentially without having to hold down the Shift or Ctrl key. Select the two near-vertical lines and choose the **Vertical** constraint. Now, click on the two near-horizontal lines and click **Horizontal**. Click **OK** to continue.

With two sides constrained:

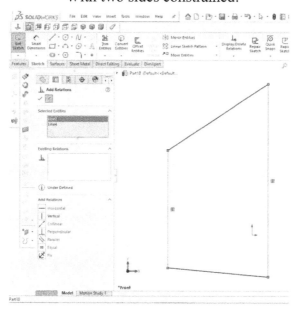

With all sides constrained:

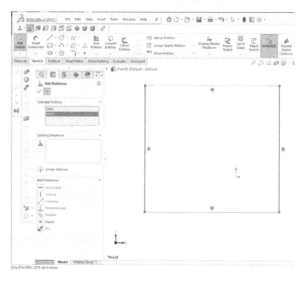

To center the rectangle on the datum plane, it is helpful to **Show** the planes. In the Design Tree, click on each plane and click on the eye symbol that appears.

Next, click on the arrow under the **Display/Delete Relations** tool and select **Add Relations** again. Hover the cursor over a Horizontal edge of the rectangle, then right click. Find and choose "Select Midpoint" from the menu that appears. Finally, select the **Right** plane. In the **Add Relations Manager**, you will notice the **Coincident** relation is shown. Click on it and, like magic, the horizontal line will become centered to the origin. Perform the same operation on a vertical edge of the rectangle to make it coincident with the **Top** plane.

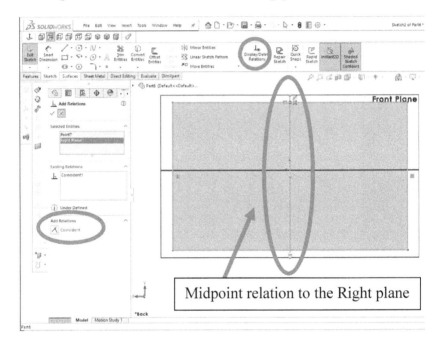

Midpoint relation to the Right plane

Exercise Complete

Exercise 6: Constraints 2 - Equal

Create a new **Part File**. Create a sketch using the **Line** tool that looks like the figure shown below.

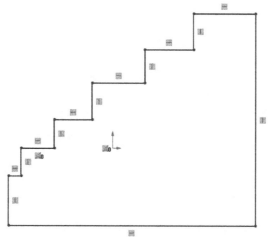

Select each line of each "step" while holding down the Shift key. The Properties Manager will appear automatically. In the Add Relations bar towards the bottom, click on **Equal**.

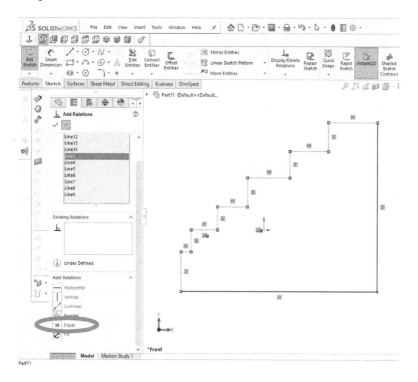

The **Equal** tool will make selected lines equal in length or selected curves equal in radius. The finished sketch should look like the following figure.

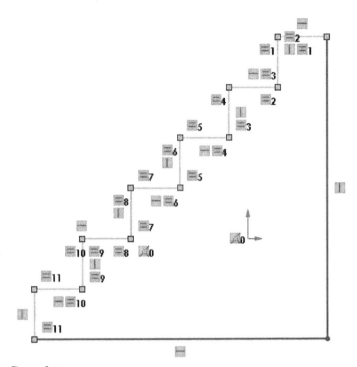

Exercise Complete

Exercise 7: Constraints 3 - Parallel and Concentric

In a new **Part File**, create a sketch using the **Line** tool and the **3 Point Arc** tool that looks like the figure shown below. Then click on the two lines shown below.

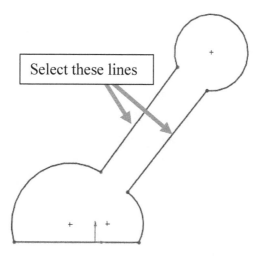

Choose the **Parallel** Command from the **Add Relations** bar in the Display/Delete Relations Manager shown in the figure below.

Now click on the 2 lower arcs as shown in the following figure.

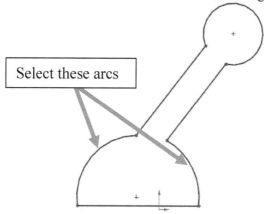

Click on the **Concentric** relation.

Note: if the figure goes a little crazy, don't panic. Sometimes the software does not calculate the change the way you may have predicted. It is usually possible to CTRL+Z (Undo).

Use the **Line** command to create a line between the centers of the lower arc and the upper arc, as shown below. Click on the line and change the line to **For Construction** in the Line Properties Manager.

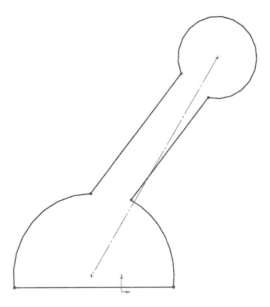

Create a **Parallel** relation between the two lines and the construction line as shown in the figure below.

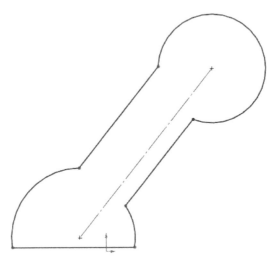

Click on the **Smart Dimension** command in the **Sketch** Command Manager

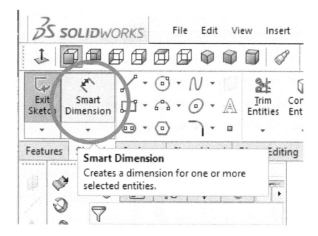

Add the dimensions as shown in the following figure.

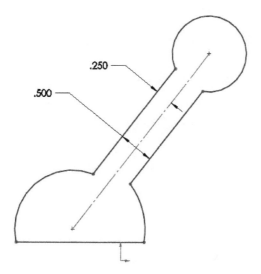

Exercise Complete

Exercise 8: Constraints 4 – Concentric and Trim Tool

Create a new **Part File**. Create a sketch using the **Circle** command in the Sketch Manager that looks like the figure shown below.

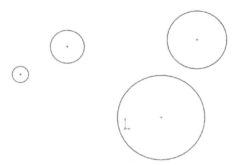

Click on the **Add Relations** command in the **Display/Delete Relations** command manager. Select all the circles. then click on the **Concentric** relation.

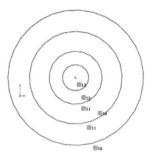

With the **Line** tool draw 2 lines as shown below.

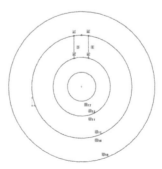

Click on the **Trim Entities** tool in the Sketch Command Manager.

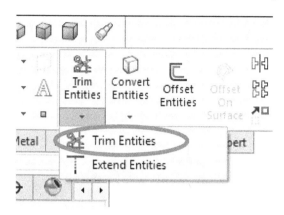

The **Trim** tool can be used in a couple of ways, but of the most useful tools are **Trim to Closest,** and **Power Trim.**

To use the **Trim to Closest** tool, click on a line to be erased. **Power Trim** is similar to drawing with a pencil. Click and drag the cursor over a segment to be deleted.

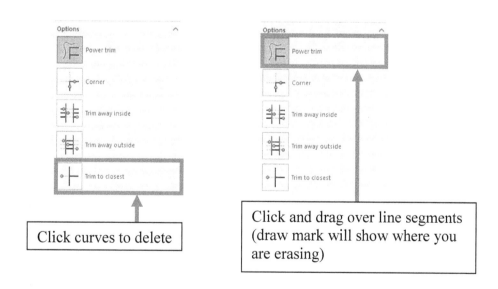

Choose one of the trim tools to delete the segments indicated below.

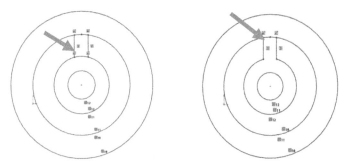

The sketch should now look like the following figure.

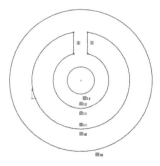

Exercise Complete

Exercise 9: Constraints 5 - Collinear Tool

Create a new **Part File**, and create a sketch that looks like the figure shown below.

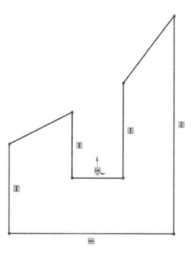

While holding the Shift or Ctrl key select the two top lines as shown in the following figure. Then click on the **Collinear** tool in the **Add Relations** Command Manager.

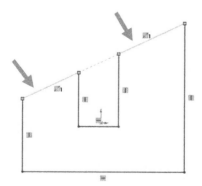

Exercise Complete

Exercise 10: Constraints 6 - Tangent

Create a new **Part File,** then use the **Line** and the **3 Point Arc** tool to create a sketch that looks like the figure shown below.

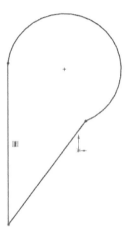

While holding the Shift or Ctrl key, select the one of the lines and the arc. The Properties Manager will appear. Now click on the **Tangent** Relation. Make the arc tangent to both lines. The sketch should now look like the following figure.

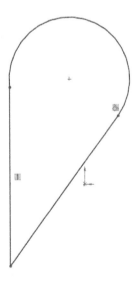

In the Sketch Command Manager, click on **Mirror Entities.** Select the arc and the lower right line. Both entities should appear in the **Entities to Mirror** box. Now click on the **Mirror About** box and select the left line. The arc and line will be mirrored as shown below. Don't you just *love* this tool?

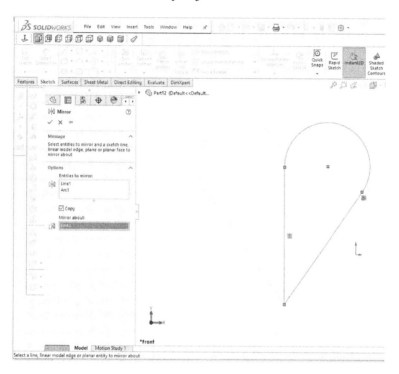

Exercise Complete

Exercise 11: Constraints 7 - Merge and Angle

In a new **Part File**, use the **Line** and **3 Point Arc** tools to create a sketch that looks like the figure shown below.

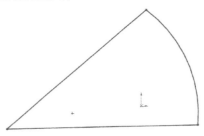

To move the center mark of the arc to the point shown above, select both the center of the arc and the endpoint of the line while holding the Shift or Ctrl key. The Properties Manager will appear. Click on **Merge** in the **Add Relations** box.

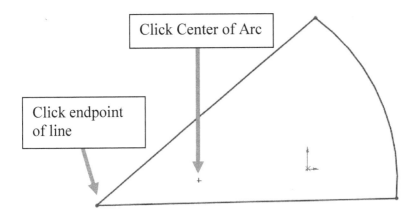

The sketch should now look like the following figure.

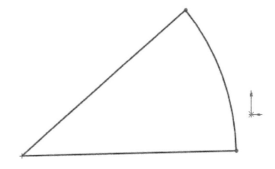

To change the angle (A) between the two lines, click on the **Smart Dimension** tool in the Sketch Command Manager and select both of the lines as shown below.

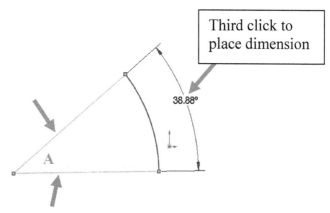

Third click to place dimension

38.88°

A

Change the angle to **20°**

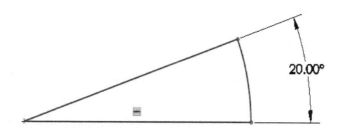

20.00°

Exercise Complete

Creating Solids

Once you have mastered the art of sketching, you are ready to create solid geometry. One of the easiest ways to do this is by using the **Extrude** command. The **Extrude** command emulates that act of filling up a play dough machine, pressing the handle and watching the dough come out in the perfect shape of what ever template you put in the front. The **Revolve** command is simililar, but it requires a center line to swing the sketch around. The **Sweep** is a similar command that allows you to drive one sketch along another. For example, if you were making a model of the molding that runs along the edge of a sail boat, you would create a sketch of the cross section of the molding on a plane that is perpendicular and at the end of the drive curve that represents the boat edge. You would then drive the sketch all the way along the edge.

When you use the **Sweep** command, the cross section is called the profile and the drive curve is called the path.

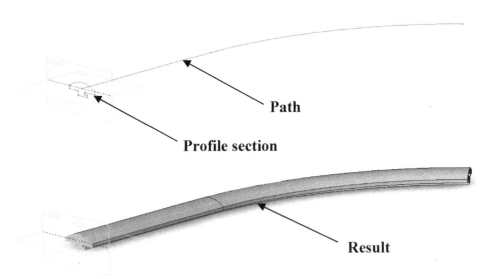

Yet another way to create solid geomety is by creating a set of surfaces that form a closed shape, then instucting SolidWorks to consider them all a solid body with solid material inside. In SolidWorks you may accomplish this by using the **Knit Surface** command with the "Create Solid" option selected.

The following few exercises will introduce you to all of these techniques and more.

Exercise 12: Extruding

Create a new **Part File** and select **Extruded Boss/Base** under **Features** in the Command Manager

The first step is to select a sketch plane. Pick the **Front Plane**, as shown in the following figure to begin sketching.

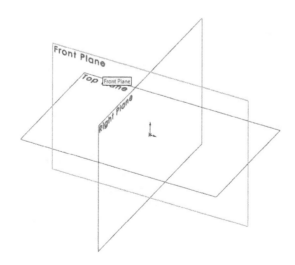

Use the **Line** tool to draw a shape similar to the one shown in the following figure.

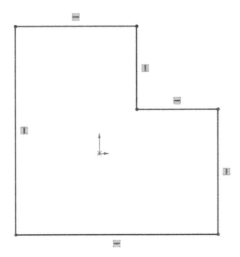

Dimension the shape using the **Smart Dimension** tool with the values shown in the figure below.

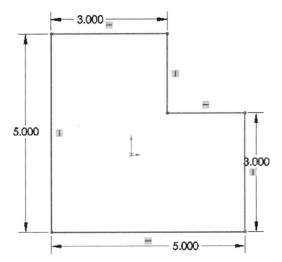

Once you're satisfied with the sketch, click the **Exit Sketch** button.

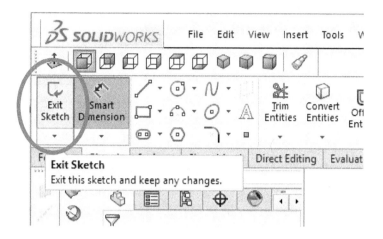

The screen should now look like the following figure. Notice the **Extrude** options in the menu on the left.

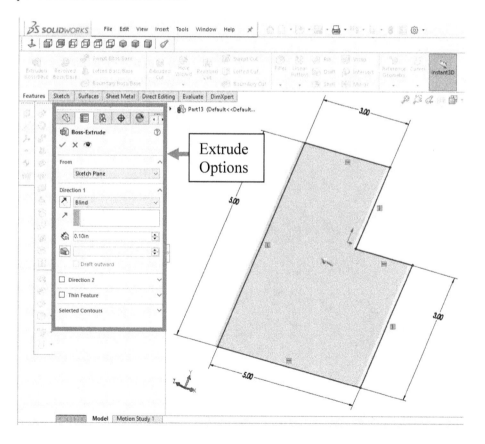

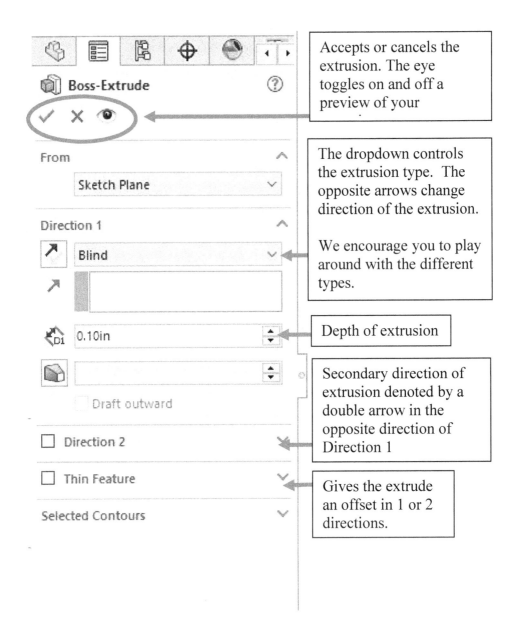

Accepts or cancels the extrusion. The eye toggles on and off a preview of your

The dropdown controls the extrusion type. The opposite arrows change direction of the extrusion.

We encourage you to play around with the different types.

Depth of extrusion

Secondary direction of extrusion denoted by a double arrow in the opposite direction of Direction 1

Gives the extrude an offset in 1 or 2 directions.

Enter **1** into the **Depth** box. Preview will update to show a depth of **1 in**. Then specify the direction of the extrude. Accomplish this by clicking the arrows next to the box that contains the word **Blind.** This switches the direction of the extrusion so that it extends below the plane instead. *Note: You can also double click on the arrow shown on the part itself and change the depth or direction manually.*

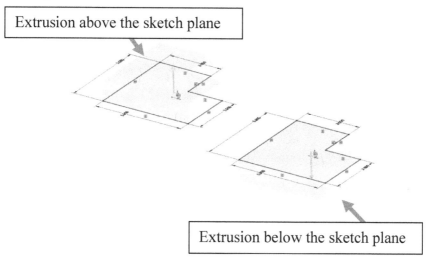

Extrusion above the sketch plane

Extrusion below the sketch plane

The screen should look like the figure shown below.

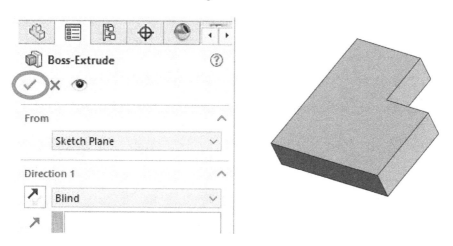

Click **OK** (circled above) to complete the **Extrude**.

Exercise Complete

79

Exercise 13: More Extruding

Start a new **Part File**. Click the **Extruded Boss/Base** button in the Features Command Manager and select a plane to sketch on.

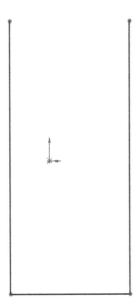

Using the **Line** tool, draw a shape similar to the one shown above.

In the Sketch Command Manager, select the **Arc** dropdown menu and select the **Tangent Arc** Command.

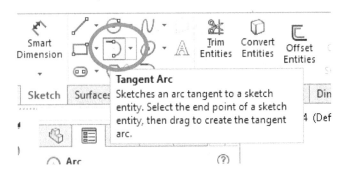

Click on the starting point indicated in the following figure to begin the arc.

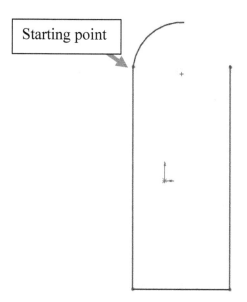

Starting point

Now here's where it gets tricky to create the curve as desired. Drag the cursor straight up and to the right. *Note: Follow the desired shape as if you were actually drawing it with a pencil. This will help create the correct arc.*

Once the tangency is achieved, click to define the end point as shown in the following figure.

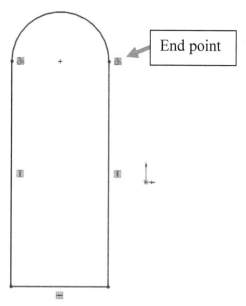

End point

It is also possible to create an arc like this using the **Arc by 3 Points** Command. See previous exercise if you've forgotten how to use it.

To create the overall height dimension, use the **Smart Dimension** command. While in Smart Dimension mode, hover the cursor over the arc and right click. Then choose '**Select Midpoint**'. Now select the bottom line and click to create the dimension. Type in **8in** as shown in the figure below.

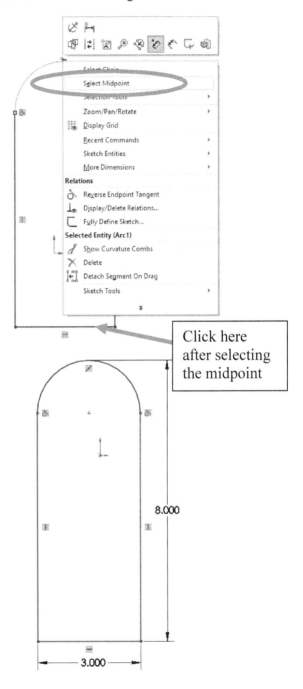

Click here after selecting the midpoint

Now that the sketch is dimensioned, close the sketch with the **Exit Sketch** Command as done in the previous exercise.

The next is to type **0.5in** into the depth box. By default, the sketch plane is selected. Click **OK** to apply.

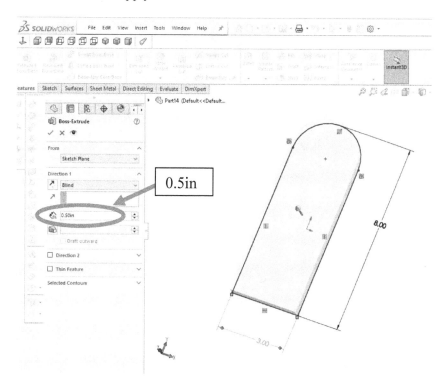

Your model should now look like the following figure.

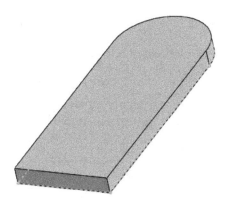

Exercise Complete

Exercise 14: Using Global Variables and Equations

In a new **Part File,** create the following sketch using the **Line** tool and add the dimensions shown below

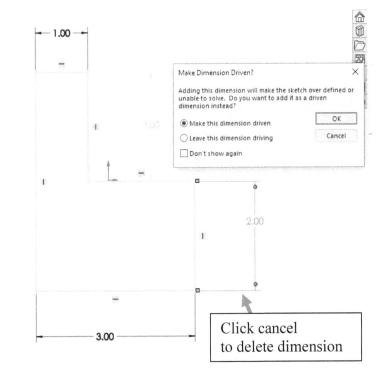

Note: When a sketch is over dimensioned any redundant dimensions bring up the prompt shown next to the sketch and the sketch will appear in yellow. To resolve the issue, you can make the dimension driven or click cancel to delete it.

In the following section we will learn how to create relationships between dimensions using Global Variables. Double-click on the **4 in** dimension. The **Modify** window will appear. First, type = into the modify window to indicate to SolidWorks that you are ready to enter an equation or define a variable. For this exercise, we will be using "A" as shown in the following figure.

Note: You must include the = before "A" if you wish to keep the dimension related to it. That way if you change the value of "A" your dimensions will update accordingly!

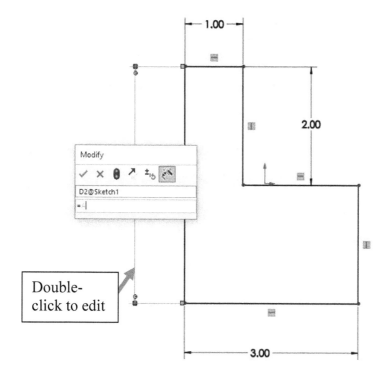

Click **OK.** You will now be shown a prompt asking if you want to define a new global variable called "A". Click **Yes.**

You'll notice that there is now an Equations folder in your part's design tree that contains your new variable. We will be utilizing this later in the exercise.

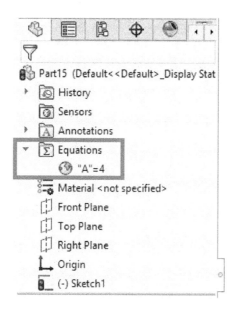

85

Double-click on the **2 in** dimension and in the **Modify** window, enter = again to indicate that you will be entering an equation. Add the equation "A"/2, making sure to include quotation marks around the variable name. The variable will not be recognized without them. Click **OK.**

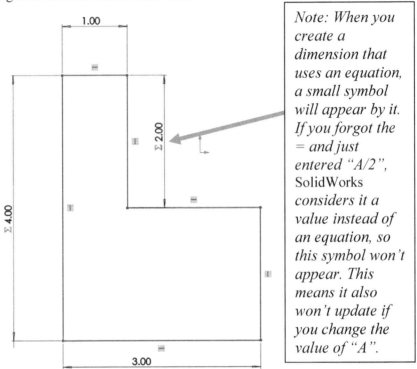

Note: When you create a dimension that uses an equation, a small symbol will appear by it. If you forgot the = and just entered "A/2", SolidWorks considers it a value instead of an equation, so this symbol won't appear. This means it also won't update if you change the value of "A".

Remember the Equations folder mentioned earlier in this lesson? Right click it and choose Manage Equations. You'll see a window like the one below. From here you can edit all of your existing variables and equations or create new ones.

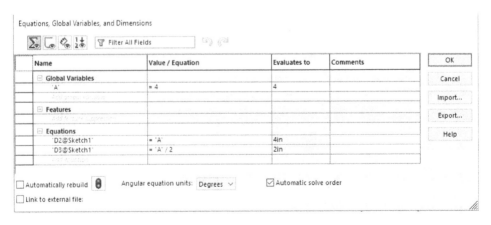

Check the box that says Automatically Rebuild. This will update your dimensions automatically when you change something so that you don't have to do it yourself.

Change the value of "A" so that it equals 8 instead of 4. Click **OK.** Your sketch should update to look like the following example.

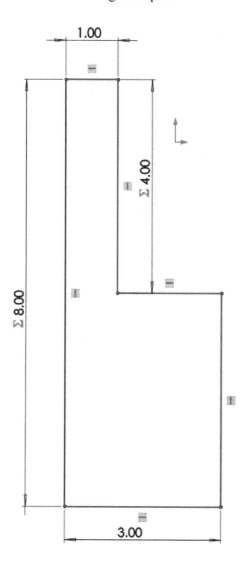

In addition to relating sketch dimensions, this feature can also be used to relate feature dimensions. Exit your sketch and click **Extruded Boss/Base.**

Extrude to a value of "A"*2. Again, don't forget the equal sign and quotation marks! You should get the following part.

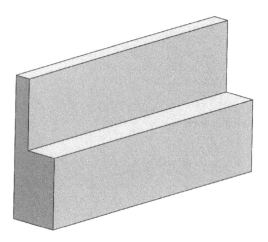

Now head back over to the Equations folder and bring up the Manage Equations window again. Change the value of "A" back to 4. Both your sketch and extrude feature will update to look like the following part.

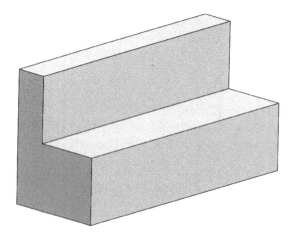

Try playing around with this technique some more. It can be very useful for relating the various features and dimensions of a part.

Exercise Complete

Exercise 15: Creating Holes and Mirroring a Body

As an engineer or designer, you are or will become quite familiar with holes. They are essential for fastening multiple parts together, reducing weight, or even designing for aesthetic appeal. Whatever the case may be, creating them in SolidWorks is quite simple.

Create a new **Part File**. Click the **Extruded Boss/Base** button in the Features Command Manager and select the Front Plane. Create a sketch similar to the sketch below. *Note: Dimensions are not important in this exercise.*

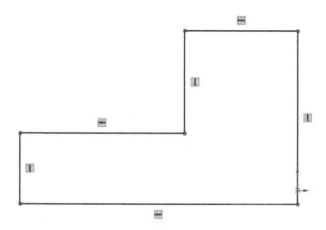

Now draw a circle on the right side of the half-model. Try to get the cursor somewhere in the middle, SolidWorks will automatically snap to the midpoint. Create the circle shown below.

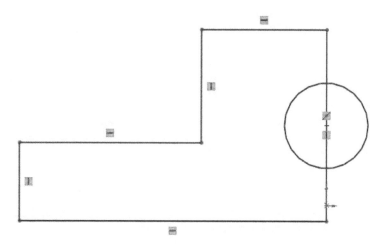

Now, using the **Trim** tool, trim the model as shown. *Note: Trimming a midpoint relation (i.e. for a circle) may bring up a prompt window. Click "Yes" to continue.*

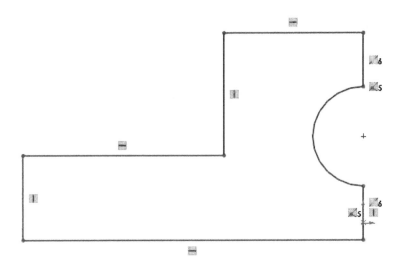

Close the sketch, using the **Exit Sketch** button in the Command Manager.

Once you've exited the **Sketch**, you are still in the **Extrude** Command. Now the model is ready to be extruded. Set the extrude depth to **2 in** and change the direction to **Mid Plane.** Click **OK**. The feature should resemble the one below.

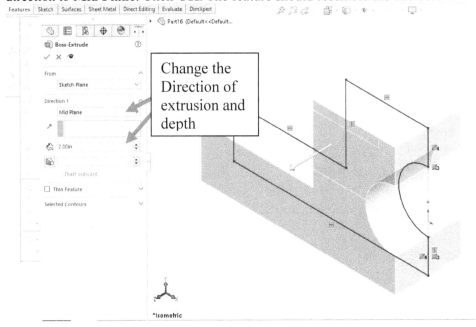

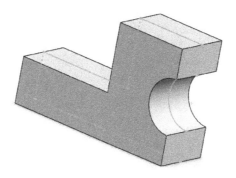

You will now mirror the body. Accomplishing this is quite straightforward. In the Features Command Manager, select **Mirror** as shown below. The **Mirror** tool can also be found in **the Linear Pattern** drop-down menu.

The **Mirror** Properties Manager appears as shown below.

Select the Face/Plane to mirror

To mirror the model, click on the face shown. A preview of the mirrored feature will appear in the graphics area.

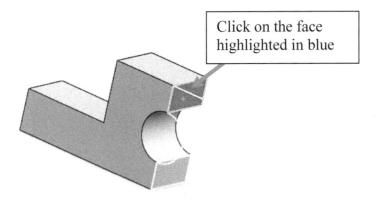

Click on the face
highlighted in blue

Click **OK** to accept the change. The model should now resemble the figure below.

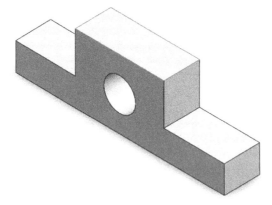

What you did above was one way to create a hole. In the following exercises, you will be creating holes in other ways. SolidWorks has a **Hole Wizard** which can create a number of different types of holes such as a **Counterbore**, **Countersink**, and **Tapped** holes. Let's take a look at how to create two simple through holes on this block.

In the Features Manager, click on the **Hole Wizard**. You can also find the **Hole Wizard** in **Insert / Features / Hole Wizard.** The **Hole Wizard** Properties Manager appears as shown below.

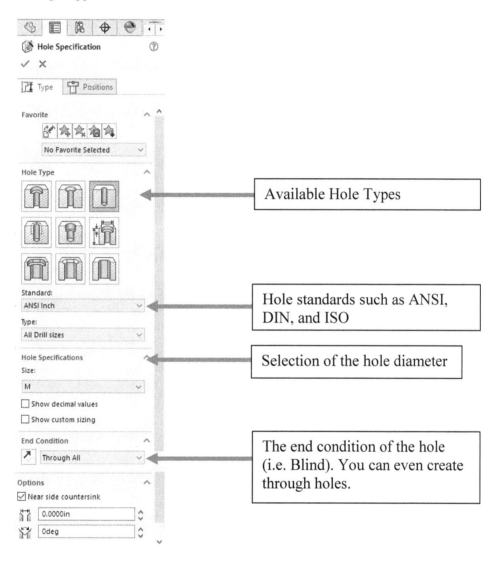

Available Hole Types

Hole standards such as ANSI, DIN, and ISO

Selection of the hole diameter

The end condition of the hole (i.e. Blind). You can even create through holes.

To create some holes, go ahead and select the Hole Type to be **Hole**. In the Hole Specifications box with 'Show Custom Sizing' checked, type in **0.5 in** for the Hole Diameter and leave the Angle at the bottom alone. In the End Condition box, select **Through All**. Once you've done that, click on the Positions tab up at the top of the Hole Wizard Properties Manager.

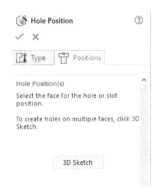

We want to create the holes on the two highlighted surfaces shown below. In order to do that, we need to change the view.

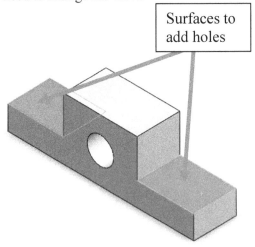

To change the view, go to the Heads-up View Toolbar. Click on the **View Orientation** drop down window, click on **Top** as shown below.

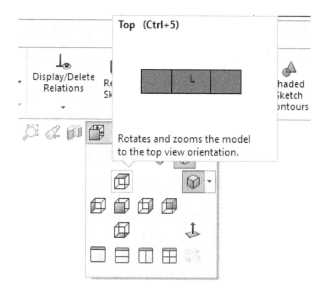

The model is now orientated in the view where you will be adding the two holes.

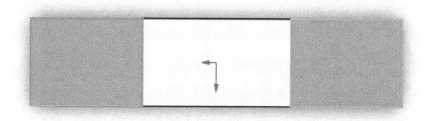

While still in the Positions tab, left click anywhere on the right surface to add a hole. A preview of the hole appears.

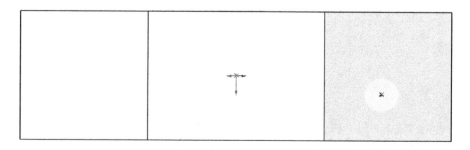

Now, you're probably asking yourself *How can I get this hole in the position I want?* Easy! Use the Smart Dimension Command.

Add the dimensions using the center of the hole as shown below.

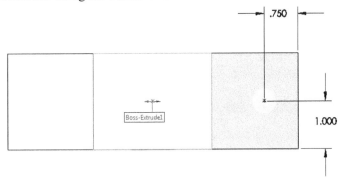

Now, deselect the Smart Dimension Command by clicking **OK**. While still in the Positions Command, click the left surface of the model to add a hole there as well. Using the **Smart Dimension** Command, add some dimensions. Once complete, accept the holes by clicking **OK**. In the Heads Up View Toolbar, click on **Isometric** view. Does your model look like the one below?

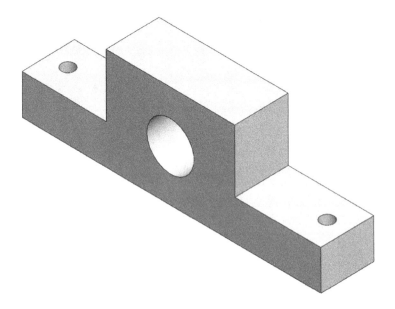

Now, have some fun. Find symmetric models throughout your home, classroom, or workspace and have at it. You now have the tools to create some amazing features using the **Mirror** and **Hole Wizard** Commands!

Exercise Complete

Exercise 16: More Holes

In this exercise, you're going to create a cylindrical model with a Counterbored hole. Create a new **Part File**. In the **Extrude Boss/Base** Command, go ahead and create the cylinder shown by first sketching the circle with a diameter of **2in**. *Note: To keep things in order, sketch the circle with the midpoint at the center of the origin.*

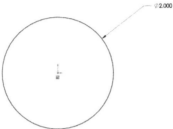

Extrude to a depth of **3 in** with the direction set to Mid Plane.

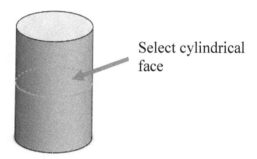

Select cylindrical face

To create the hole, we need to create a reference plane tangent to the surface of the cylinder. In the Features Manager, select **Reference Geometry.** Then, in the dropdown menu click on **Plane.**

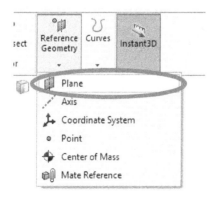

In the **Plane** Properties Manager, you have a few choices on how to create a plane on the surface of the cylinder. Click on the surface of the cylinder. You will notice that it becomes the first reference with a **Tangent** relation. To fully define the plane, you need a second reference. In the Design Tree Property Manager, which is accessible from the dropdown menu in the top left corner of the Graphics Window, select the **Front** Plane. Now the second reference is selected. Click on **Parallel** as the relation. The plane added should look like the following figure.

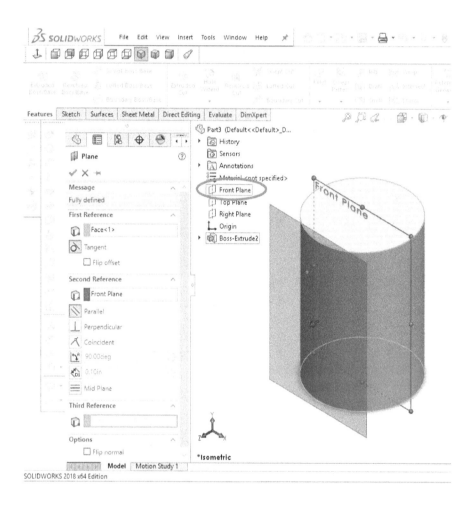

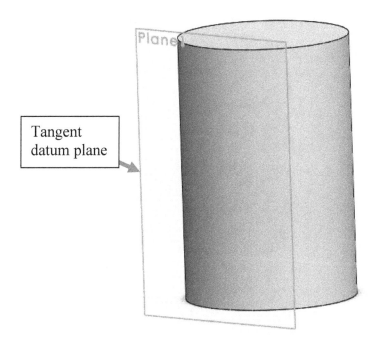

Tangent
datum plane

Now we need to create another reference to center the hole on the cylinder. Select the **Point** tool in the **Reference Geometry** dropdown menu.

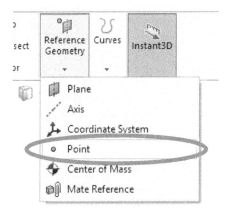

The Point Property Manager is similar to the Plane Manager in that you need to select references. In this case, two references are needed: the Plane you just created and the center of the origin (again found in the Design Tree Property Manager). Do you recall sketching the circle at the origin and extruding the cylinder at the Mid Plane? This ensured that the origin is exactly in the center of the cylinder. Accept the new point.

The Point Reference should now be visible on the plane you created earlier.

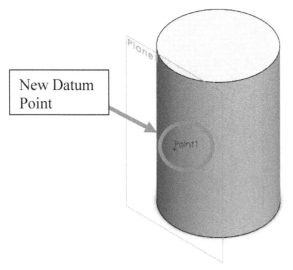

New Datum
Point

Now let's create that Counterbore hole! Click on **Hole Wizard** in the Features Manager.

In the Hole Type section, select the **Counterbore** hole which is the first icon shown. Leave the Standard section at the default, which should be ANSI inch. *Note: ANSI is only the default if you are working in inches.*

The type is a Heavy Hex Bolt. See the following figure to fill in the rest of the specifications. There is lots to do, but that's what makes the **Hole Wizard** so amazing and functional.

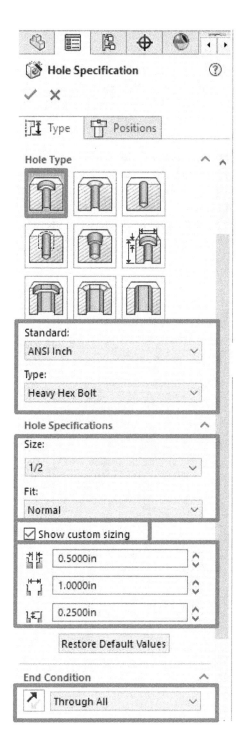

Fill in the all the sections as shown

Next, click on the Positions tab in the Hole Property Manager. The next steps are rather crucial but should be straightforward.

Click on the surface of the cylinder to select it. A preview of the hole should appear. Don't worry about the orientation just yet, simply click again to place the hole's midpoint. Next, right click and click on Select or tap ESC on the keyboard to exit the function.

Now, left-click and drag the midpoint of the hole toward the datum point you created. You will notice a yellow-dashed rectangle. Snap onto the point, and release the mouse. A green coincident constraint should appear when the points are aligned. If you are having trouble placing the point, it may be helpful to add an 'On Surface' constraint with the face of the cylinder or to reorient the views to help you place it. Click **OK** to create the Hole.

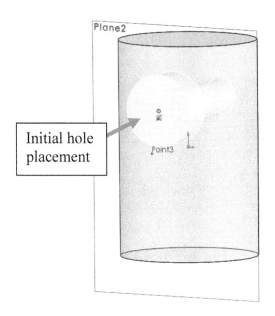

Initial hole placement

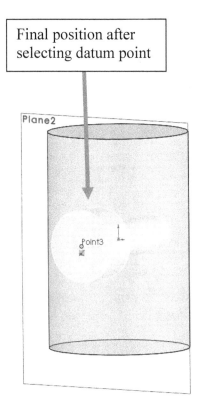

Final position after selecting datum point

Your model should resemble the figure below, with the hole centered on the cylinder.

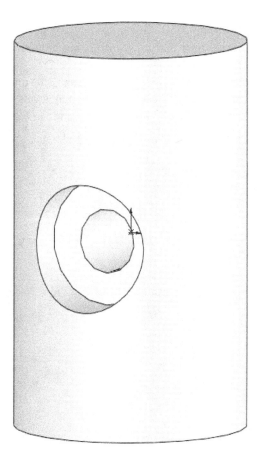

Exercise Complete

Exercise 17: Cutting

Cutting is another great tool in SolidWorks. A Cut is the reverse of an Extrude. Instead of creating material, you are removing it. Take a second to think of all those real life examples where cutting would come in handy.

To proceed with this exercise, open a new **Part File** and click the **Extruded Boss/Base Command** button. Create a sketch that looks like the figure shown below. Feel free to be creative with the dimensions. *Note: Recall the Mirror Entities Command?*

Exit the sketch and **Extrude** to a thickness of **0.25in**.

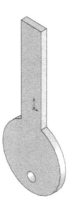

Click the **Extruded Cut** button in the Features Command Manager and select the front face to sketch on. See the figure below.

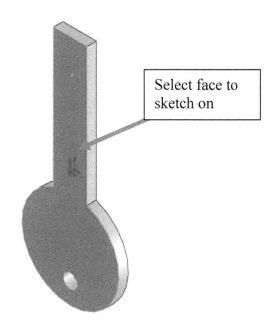

Select face to sketch on

Create a sketch that looks similar to the following figure. Be creative.

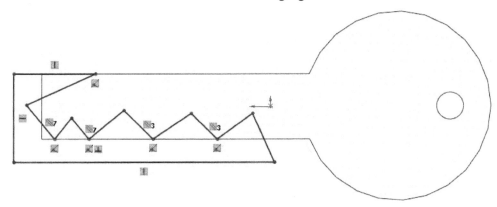

Exit the Sketch.

You are now in the **Extruded Cut** Properties Manager. Set the Direction to **Through All**.

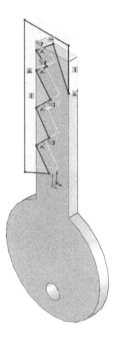

Click **OK**, and the part should now look like the following figure.

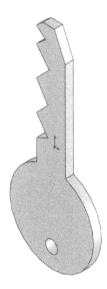

Now let's create another **Cut**. Create a sketch on the front surface that looks like the figure below.

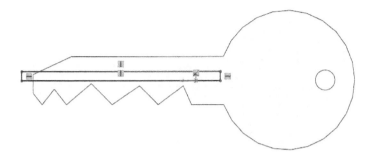

Exit the Sketch. In the Extruded Cut Manager, select **Blind** for the Direction with a Depth of **.100 in**. The direction should be towards the back of the key. See the arrow on the part.

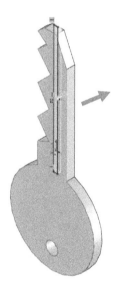

Click **OK**.

`

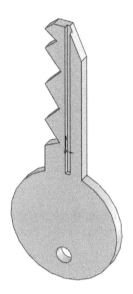

Exercise Complete

Exercise 18: Revolving

The **Revolve** tool, is a great way to efficiently and quickly model cylindrical geometry. It is incredibly useful for creating everything from bolts and cups to shafts and gears.

To try it out, create a new **Part File.** Click the **Revolved Boss/Base** button in the Features Command Manager. Sketch on the Front Plane. *Note: Notice the line to the right of the sketch? That is the Axis of Revolution where your revolved feature will be generated from. The reference line is the entity that informs the revolve command where the axis of rotation will be.*

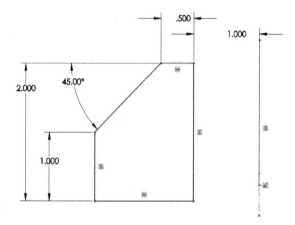

Now exit the sketch and, by default, the shape will be revolved around the reference line. However, you may select any other line in the sketch or some previously created datum axis.

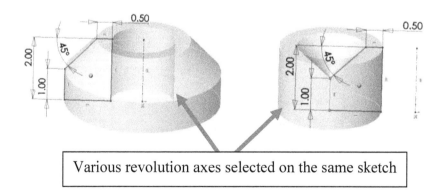

Various revolution axes selected on the same sketch

109

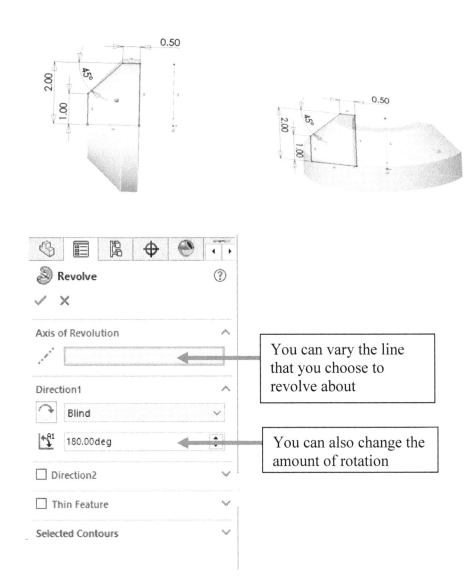

Now finish this exercise by creating the shape below.

Exercise Complete

Exercise 19: Revolved Cut with Angled Datum Planes

Create a new **Part File**. Make a sketch using the **Rectangle** tool that looks like the figure shown below on the **Right** plane. Constrain the midpoints of the sides with the **Right** and **Top** planes to center the sketch as shown in Exercise 5. Exit the sketch and extrude **4 in** with the direction set to Mid Plane.

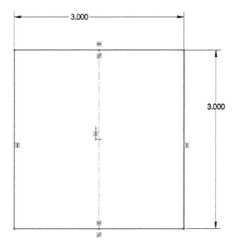

Your model should resemble the figure below. *Note: Planes have been shown for perspective.*

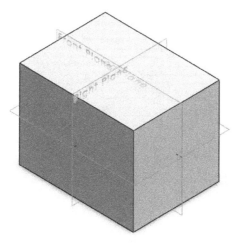

In order to create an angled datum, recall the Reference Geometry Command in the Features Command Manager. You first want to create two axes that are perpendicular to the Front and Right Planes respectively.

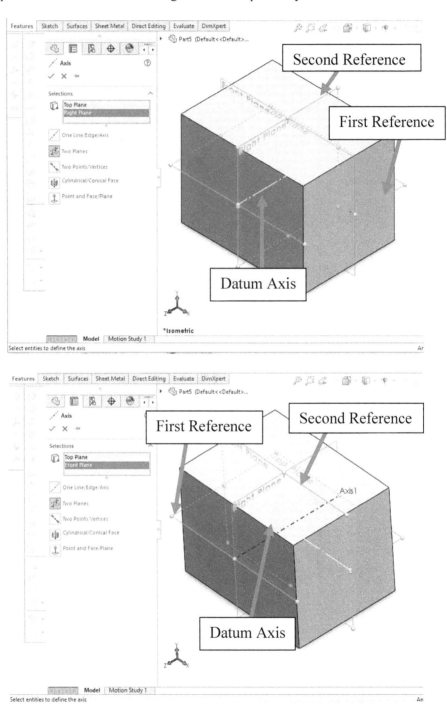

Now that you have the datum axis, you can create the datums that will be the "work surface" for an angled revolved cut. Create a datum parallel to the Right Plane but set at an angle of **20 degrees**. Follow the figures below.

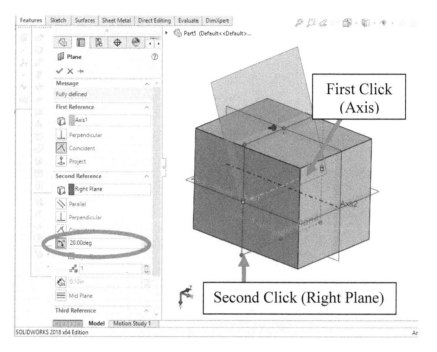

Create another plane, now parallel to the Front Plane and angled at **10 degrees**.

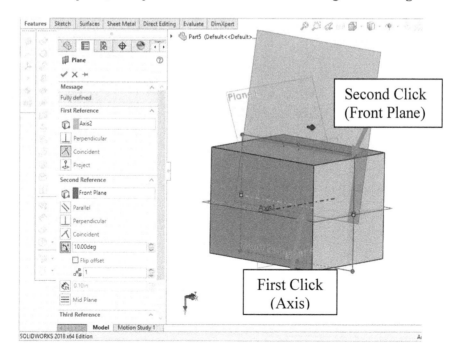

Your model should resemble the figure below. *Note: For clarity, you can change the size of the datum as seen in the figure just by clicking on the datum and dragging one of the points that appears on the edge to stretch it out.*

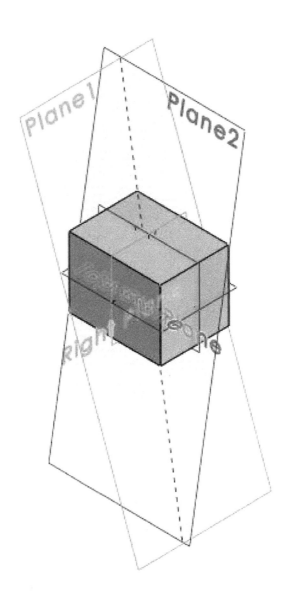

To hide any reference geometry, you can right click on it, locate the eye icon and click to hide/show.

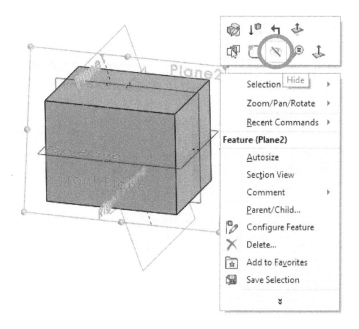

Hide the Front, Top and Right Planes if they are showing.

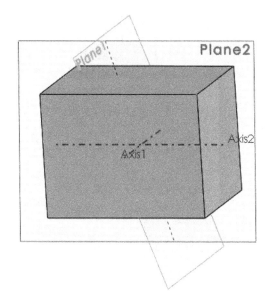

The next step is to create the Sketch for our revolved cut. However, you first need a datum axis that intersects the new planes you created. Start by Selecting the **Reference Geometry** Command and choosing **Axis**. In the Axis Properties box, select the two new planes. Now the new datum axis is the intersect point of those two planes.

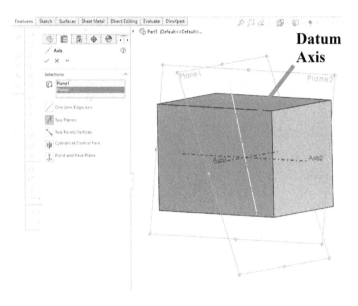

Go ahead and create a **Sketch** that looks like the figure below on the second new plane.

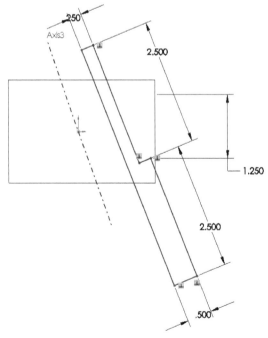

Select the **Display/Delete** Relations and **Add Relations**. Select the near-vertical line shown in the figure below and rotate the model to view that new axis that intersects the two planes. Select the **Collinear** relation and accept.

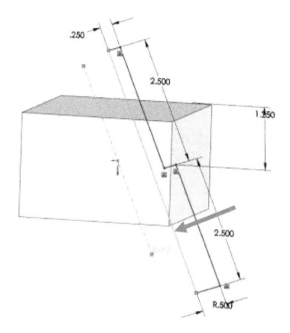

Click on the longest line of the sketch and the intersection line as shown below.

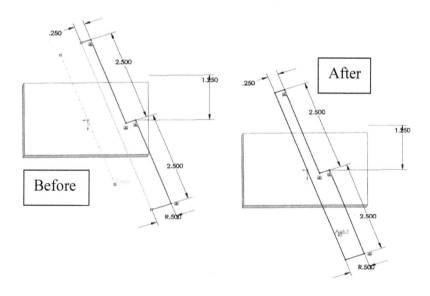

Close the Sketch.

Click **Revolved Cut** in the Command Manager. Select the new intersect axis as the line of revolution and leave the angle at **360 degrees**. Rotate and preview the model.

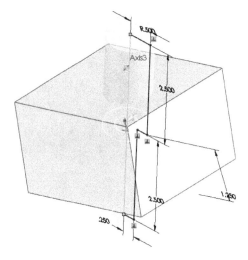

Click **OK**.

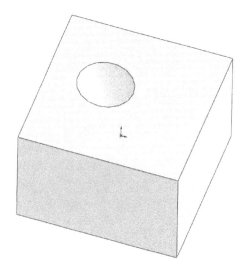

Now, in the Heads Up Tool bar, change the view to Wireframe as shown below.

Wireframe
Displays all edges of the model.

Your model should resemble the figure below.

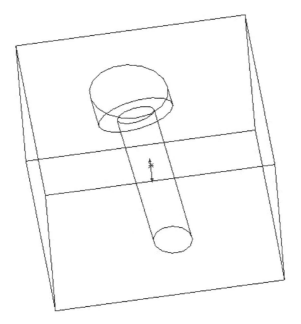

Exercise Complete

Exercise 20: Mirror

Start a new **Part File.** Select the **Extruded Boss/Base** Command and select the Top Plane to sketch on.

Create a sketch that looks like the figure shown below.

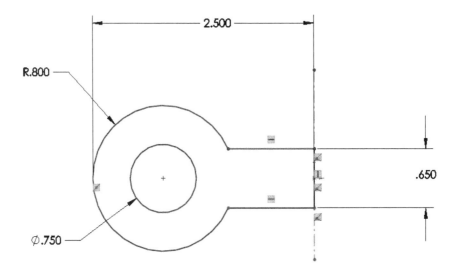

Exit the sketch.

Extrude above the sketch plane a distance of **0.5in** and click **OK** to exit the extrude feature.

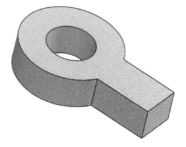

Click the **Mirror** Command.

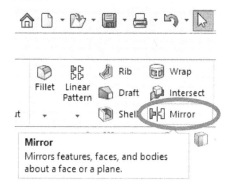

In the **Mirror** Properties Manager, select the right face of the model. The preview should match the figure below. Click accept.

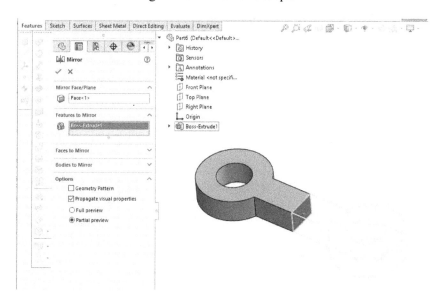

Click the **Extrude Boss/Base** Command and select the Top face of the model.

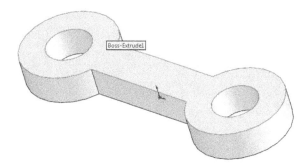

Using the **Circle** Command, sketch the 4 circles shown below. *Note: You can move the mouse over the center of the inner hole, then its edge and SolidWorks automatically snaps and previews the center of the circle. Once that occurs, sketch the circle and follow the steps on the opposite side.*

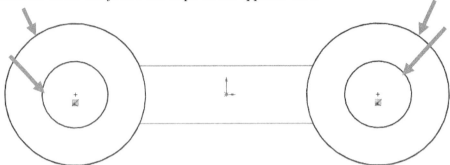

Exit the sketch.

Extrude above the sketch plane a distance of **0.5 in** and click **OK.**

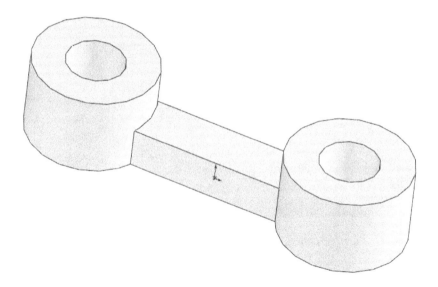

Exercise Complete

Exercise 21: Draft, Fillet and Chamfer

Click the **Extruded Boss/Base** Command button and select the Top Plane. Use the **Ellipse** tool and create the sketch shown below.

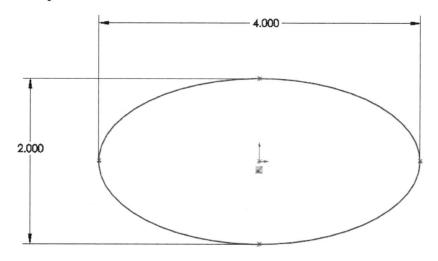

Exit the Sketch.

Extrude above the sketch plane to a distance of **1in**.

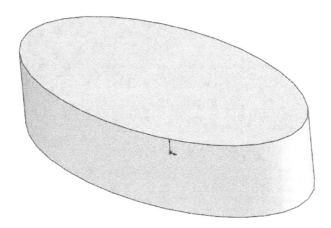

Click on the **Draft** Command.

In the **Draft** Properties Box, select the top face as the Neutral Plane and the elliptical edge as the Draft Face. Enter **15 degrees** for the draft angle.

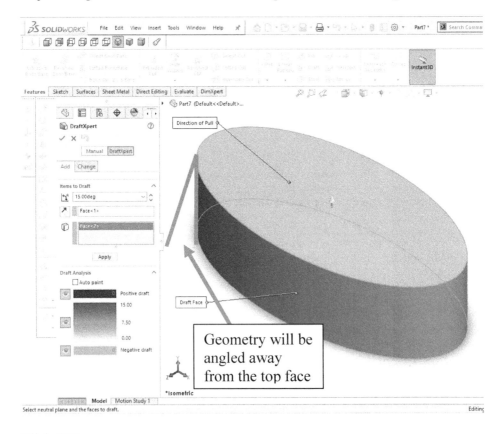

Click **OK**.

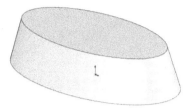

Next click on the **Fillet** Command.

In the **Fillet** Properties box, select either the top face or the top edge. Enter **.25in** for the radius.

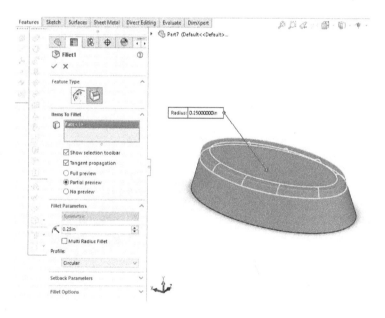

Click **OK.** Your model should resemble the following figure.

125

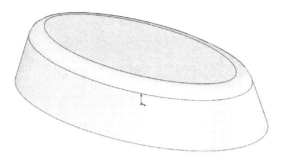

Next, click on the **Fillet** drop down menu and Select **Chamfer.**

In the Chamfer Properties box, select the bottom edge with an Angle Distance of **.5 in** and angle of **45 degrees**.

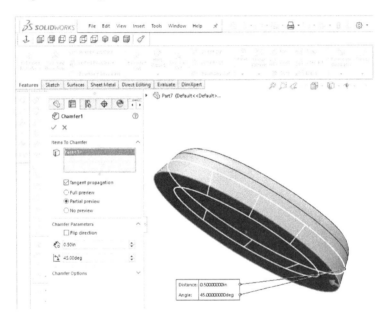

Click **OK**. The part should look like the following figure.

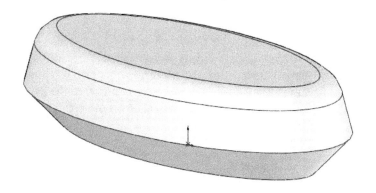

Exercise Complete

Exercise 22: Sweep Along a Path

Many engineered products are the result of taking something with a constant cross section and forming it or bending it into shape. In SolidWorks we can easily accomplish these shapes using the **Sweep** command. To create a sweep, as with most solid features, it is possible to either sketch before the sweep, or sketch within the sweep tool. In this exercise we will sketch before the sweep.

Choose the **Front Plane** to sketch on and draw a square as shown below.

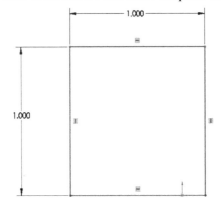

Close Sketch and create a new sketch on the **Right Plane** as shown below.

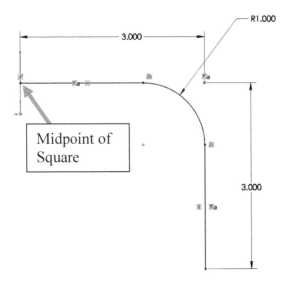

Midpoint of Square

Exit the Sketch.

128

Click on the **Swept Boss/Base** Command.

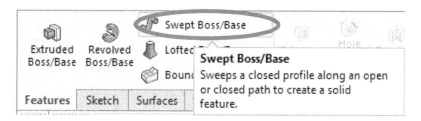

In the Sweep Properties, click on the square as the Profile. Then click on the lines and curve as the Path. The model should resemble the one below.

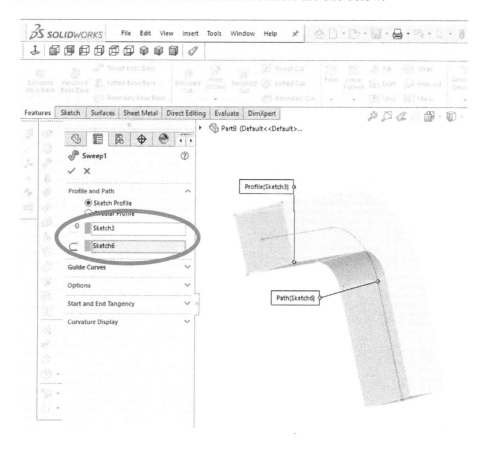

Click **OK** and the part will look like the figure shown below.

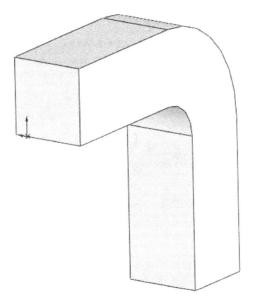

Exercise Complete

Exercise 22-B: Sweep Along a Path

Many sweeps are the result of a section that is driven along a path that is bent in more than one direction. Here is an example of how to use the Sweep command to create such a beast. Begin by creating the path shown on the Front Plane.

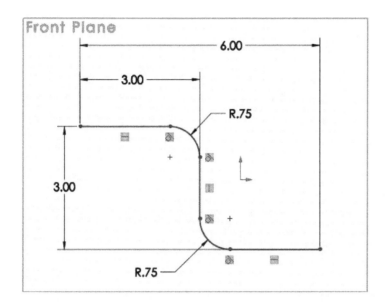

Now create the datum plane shown below. It goes through the point at the end of the sketch and is parallel to the top plane. To do it you must Select **Reference Geometry/ Plane** with in the features menu. Then select the end point and the top plane from the Feature Manager Design Tree.

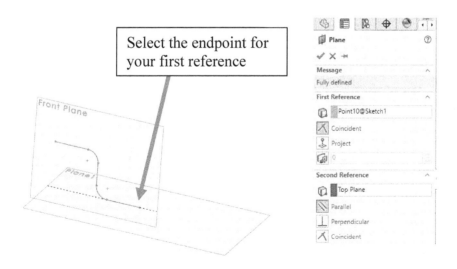

Select the endpoint for your first reference

Next create a sketch that is connected to the previous sketch but lies on the new plane.

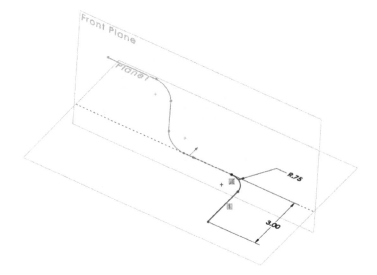

Now create a new sketch on a plane that goes through the start point of the initial sketch as shown below.

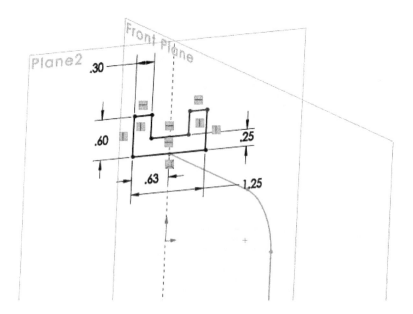

Next select the first two sketches, select the **Curves** command and **Composite Curve.** This will make one curve out of the two separate sketches. Finally, you can use the Sweep command to finish the shape.

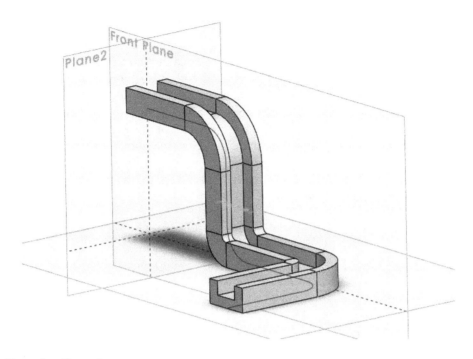

Exercise Complete

Exercise 23: Thin Wall

Many components throughout all industries, a soda bottle or a tube for example, have some sort of hollow geometry associated with them. To create geometry of this nature you can use the **Shell** command. To use the **Shell** command, you first need to create a solid. Then you can apply a **Shell** to it. Usually there is a face where the **Shell** "comes through", like the open side of a water glass. You will be prompted while using the **Shell** command to "select faces to remove".

To begin this exercise, click the **Extruded Boss/Base** button and select the **Top Plane.** Create the sketch below.

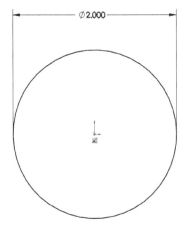

Extrude to a distance of **4 in** as shown below.

Create a **sketch** on the **Front Plane** as shown in the following figure.

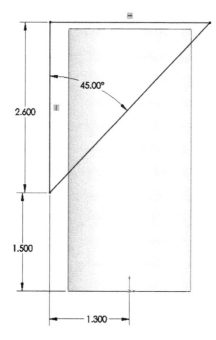

Click the **Extruded Cut** Command. Click on the new sketch and select Mid Plane as the Direction. Select a width that will cut through the entire cylinder and click **OK**.

Rotate the model. It should resemble the figure below.

Now select the **Shell** Command and select the angled face as shown below.

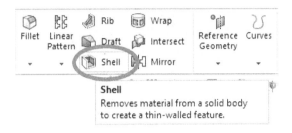

The **Shell** Command is set to shell inwards. Set the Thickness to **0.125 in**.

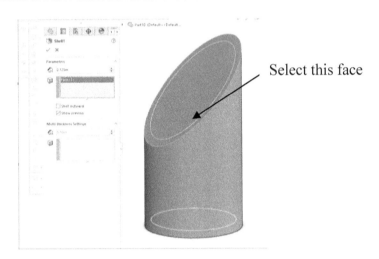

Select this face

Click **OK**. The finished part should look like the following model.

Exercise Complete

Exercise 24: Mounting Bosses

Create the following sketch and extrude by **0.5in**. Then create a shell to a thickness of **0.125 in**.

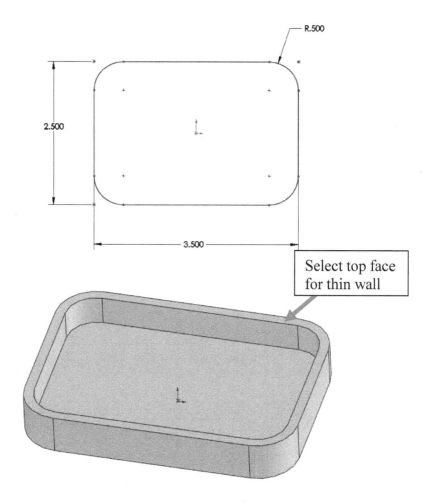

Click on **Insert/Fastening Feature** and select **Mounting Boss.** When the Mounting Boss Property Manager opens, fill in the dimension as shown in the following figure.

137

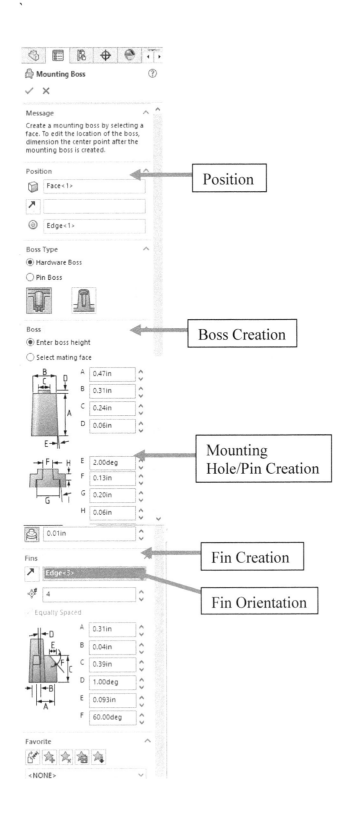

Position

Boss Creation

Mounting Hole/Pin Creation

Fin Creation

Fin Orientation

To choose the location of the boss, select the bottom of the shelled form. The second box is for direction but can be left blank if the inferred direction shown in the preview is acceptable. For the third box, select the curved edge to position the boss along the face you chose.

In the box under Fins, select the edge to the right of the curve to orient the fins.

Enter the values shown in the diagram on the previous page, then click **OK**.

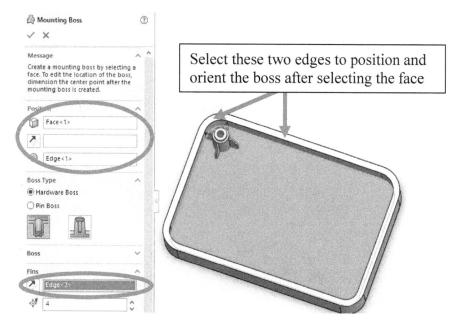

Now you need to use the **Mirror** tool to create the other three bosses. Recall the earlier exercise to mirror across a plane.

139

Mirror again, this time across the right plane, and select the two bosses as "Features to mirror" before clicking **OK**.

Exercise Complete

Exercise 25: Loft and Sketch Pattern

You're now going to receive an introduction to the creative muscles of SolidWorks: Surfacing tools. Being a designer requires more than just being able to create simple geometries. It also calls for the ability to generate complex yet visually stunning designs for use in many fields. Start a new file and create the sketch on the Top Plane as shown below. Then **Exit** the **Sketch** and **Extrude** it to **.125 in**.

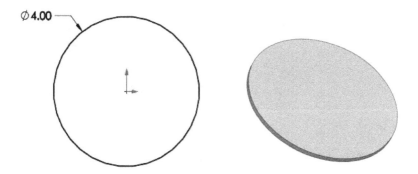

Create another sketch on a new plane parallel to the Top Plane and offset by **1.0in** below it. Draw a concentric circle that has a **3 in** diameter as shown in the following figure.

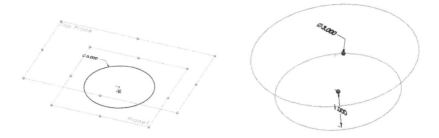

Exit the **Sketch** and create another sketch on second plane parallel to the Top Plane offset by **2.0 in** below it. Draw a concentric circle that has a **1.5 in** diameter as shown in the following figure.

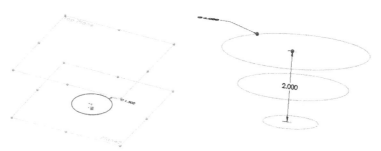

Exit the sketch.

To create a Loft, which is a type of surface, go to **Insert/Surface/Loft**.

In the Loft Property Manager, you need to select the circular profiles. Be sure to create each loft by selecting each profile in succession.

Note: Lofts, like many other surfacing tools, can end up looking different than you expect. At times, they may even look more visually stunning than what you had in mind.

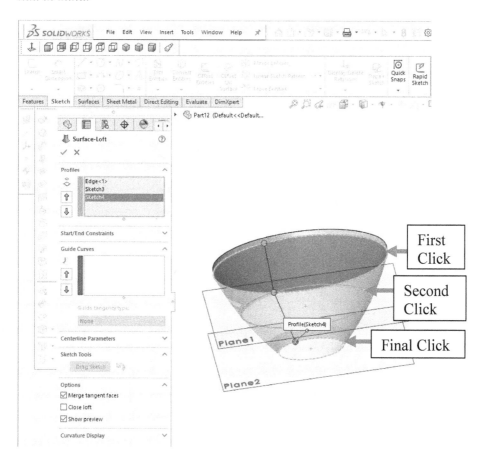

Click **OK**. Your loft should resemble the one below.

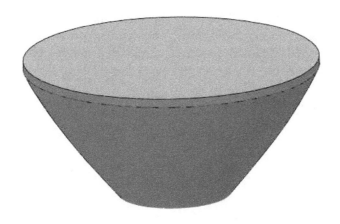

A great Sketch tool to use is the **Linear Pattern** Command. The Linear Pattern Command also encompasses a **Circular Pattern** Command. Start by creating the sketch on the top surface of your model as shown below. *Note: You can create a rectangle by using the Center Rectangle tool in the Rectangle Command. Also, the Display Style here was changed to Hidden Lines Removed for clarity.*

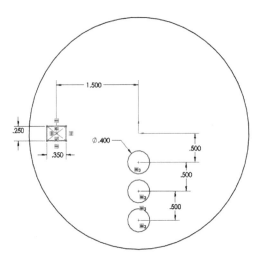

Now, while still in the Sketch Command, select the Linear Sketch Pattern, and in the dropdown menu, select **Circular Sketch Pattern**

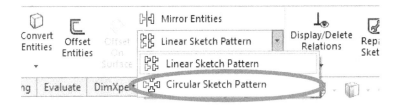

In the **Circular Pattern Property** Manager, select the three circles and the rectangle as the "Entities to Pattern." The number of patterns is 6, with "Equal Spacing" selected. Below the number of patterns, you can change the radius of the pattern. Move it so you notice the point moving as well. Move the point over the origin so everything is centered.

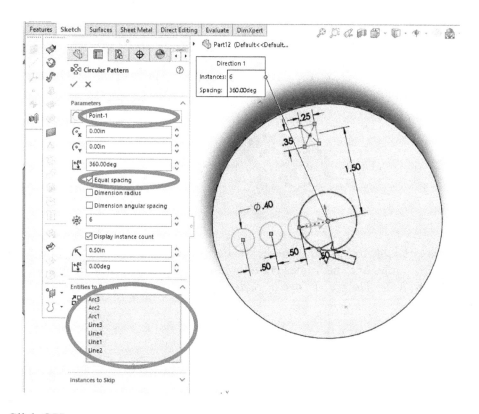

Click **OK**.

Now, go to Extruded Cut, and cut the pattern out with a Direction of Through All. Your model should resemble the one below.

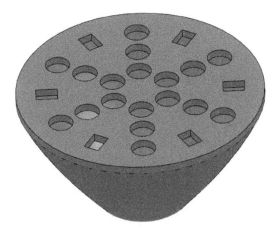

Exercise Complete

Exercise 26: Vent Command

Open a new part and create the Extruded part below. The diameter is **4 in** and the thickness of extrusion is **0.125 in**.

Now, create a Sketch like the one below on the Top face of the part. Add three concentric circles and the 4 lines crossing through the origin all **45 degrees** from each other. *Note: The part's Display Style was again changed for clarity.*

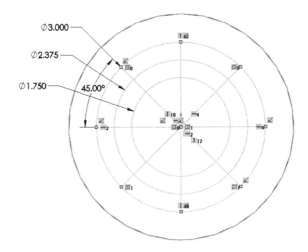

Now, go to **Insert/Fastening Feature/Vent**.

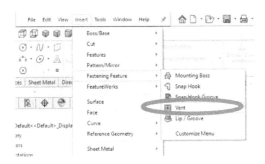

The Vent Property Manager will now appear.

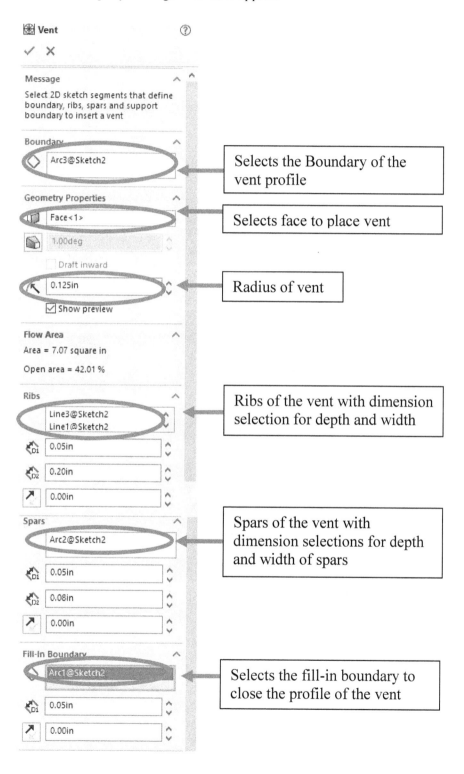

Selects the Boundary of the vent profile

Selects face to place vent

Radius of vent

Ribs of the vent with dimension selection for depth and width

Spars of the vent with dimension selections for depth and width of spars

Selects the fill-in boundary to close the profile of the vent

After you fill in the Vent Property Manager with the indicated segments, your part should resemble the figure below.

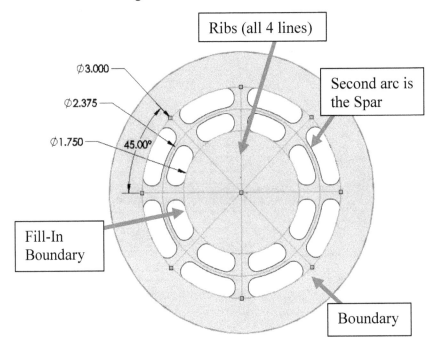

Accept the Vent.

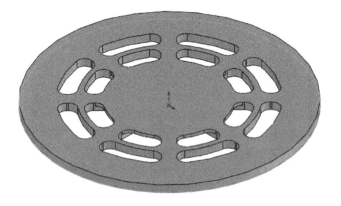

Exercise Complete

Exercise 27: Linear Pattern and Grouping Features

In this exercise we are going to group a number of features and create a pattern in a staggered form. Click on a datum plane and **sketch** a **rectangle** that is **10in x 6.5in**. **Extrude** this by **1.5in** to create a block.

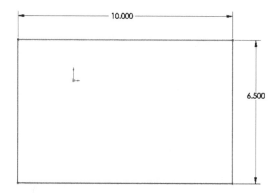

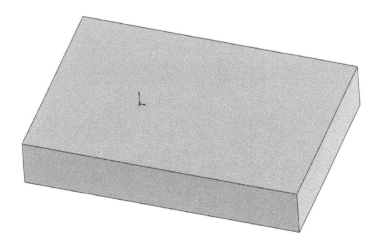

Next, create another sketch on the top face of the block. Select the **Cut** tool. Pick the rectangle from the sketch and cut a distance of **0.5in** into the block that was created, as shown in the following figure.

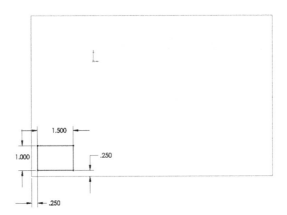

Now create another sketch, a circle that is centered on the inside top face of the rectangular cutout, and **Extrude** it upwards to a length of **1.1 in**. Add **0.15in Fillets** to all the inside edges of the cutout and the top of the cylinder.

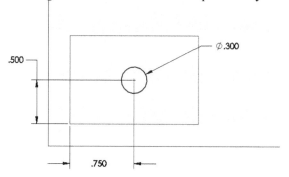

The model should resemble the one below.

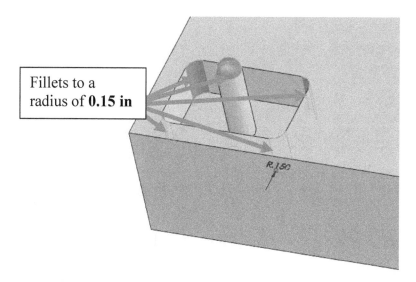

Fillets to a radius of **0.15 in**

In order to create our pattern and make things easier to identify, we want to group the newly created cutout and pin by adding them to a folder. Organizing features in this way is especially useful in a model with many features. Select the three new features and right-click. Go to **Add to New Folder** and name the folder. See the following figure.

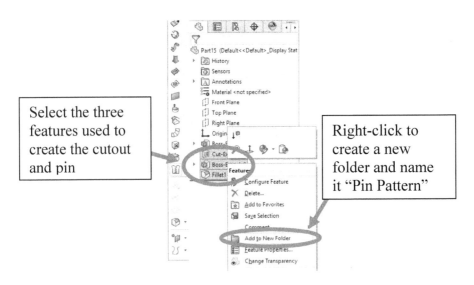

Select the three features used to create the cutout and pin

Right-click to create a new folder and name it "Pin Pattern"

Once, you've created the folder, go the **Linear Pattern** Command Manager and select **Linear Pattern**. Fill in the boxes in the Linear Pattern Property Manager.

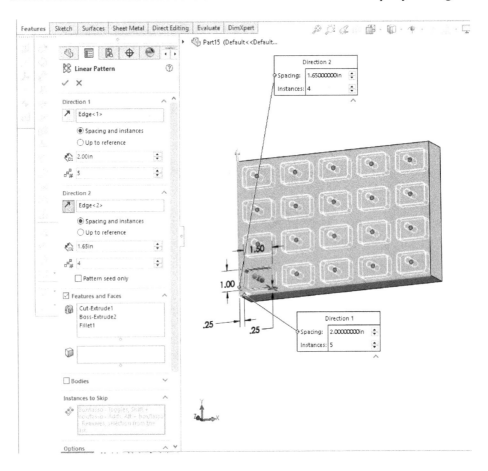

Notice the **Instances to Skip** box? From the Graphics Window you can select which patterns to omit. Once you click in the box, pink dots will appear. Click on the dots of the instances you would like to skip to "turn off" the instance. Once you have selected the dots indicated in the figure below, click **OK**. Your model should resemble the one below.

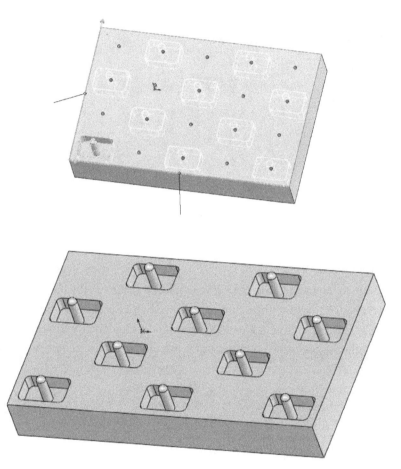

Exercise Complete

Exercise 28: Circular Hole Pattern

Start a new **Part File**. Create the sketch as shown below on the Top Plane and extrude to a depth of **1.25 in** from the Mid Plane.

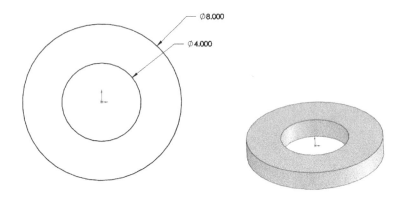

You're going to create a **Circular Pattern** of a hole on the face of the part. Recall Exercise 16? Follow the same steps as in that exercise. If you've sketched the circles from the origin and extruded from the mid-plane, then your point will sit on the origin. If not, dimension the point **.625 in.** from the center of the part.

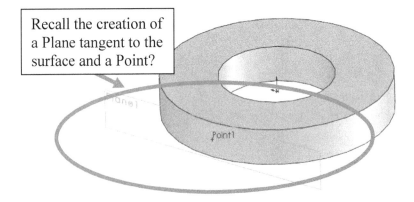

Recall the creation of a Plane tangent to the surface and a Point?

Now, select the **Hole Wizard** and create the hole with the attributes shown below.

Click **OK.**

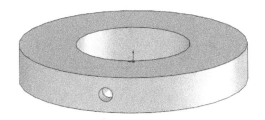

Now, you will use a **Circular Pattern** from the Linear Pattern Command Manager. The pattern will be made from the center of the cylinder. However, as you know by now, you will need a reference feature. Guess which? Hopefully you chose **Axis.** Create an axis reference from the Reference Geometry Command Manager.

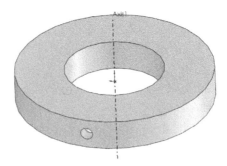

Now go to the **Circular Pattern** feature from the Linear Pattern Command Manager. Add the parameters as shown in the figure below.

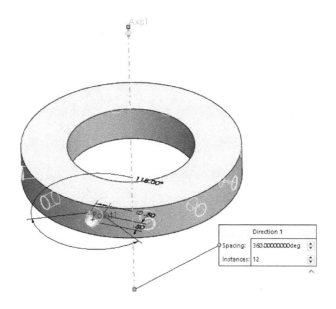

Your model should resemble the one below.

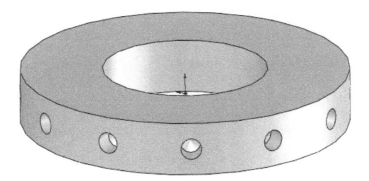

To finish up this model, go ahead and select the **Extruded Boss/Base** Command and sketch a circle on the bottom face of the model with a diameter of **6 in.**

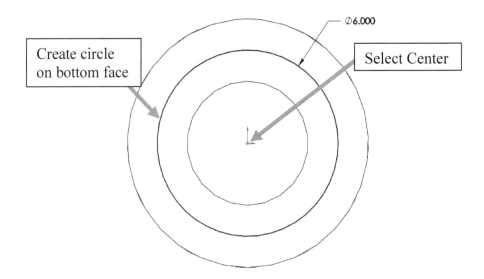

Create circle on bottom face

Select Center

⌀6.000

Accept the sketch and extrude to a depth of **1.5 in.** Your model is now finished and should resemble the one below.

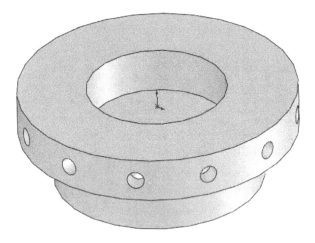

Exercise Complete

Exercise 29: Curved Pattern

Start a new **Part File**. Create the sketch as shown below and extrude to a depth of **0.25 in**.

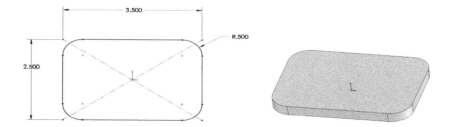

We are going to pattern a hole along a curve. To create the curve let's make use of the already existing geometry and simply offset the edges. *Note: This technique is much quicker than recreating the lines and constraints.*

Create a **Sketch** on the top surface of the solid as shown below by selecting the previous sketch. Go to the Sketch Command Manager, and select **Offset Entities.** Click on the top face of the part, you will notice the sketch is copied and offset. Offset the sketch to a distance of **0.3 in** towards the inside of the part as shown below.

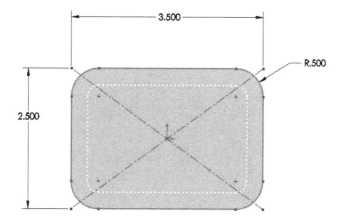

Now, delete the vertical line at the left of the part. Create two separate lines and create an **Equal Relation**.

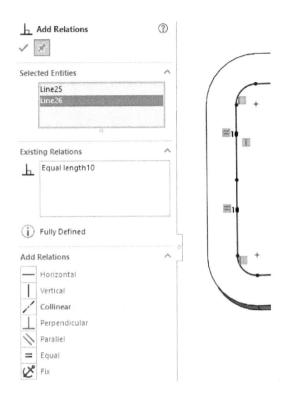

You will now be creating another pattern around the new offset sketch using a **Curve Driven Pattern** from the Linear Pattern Command Manager. First, a feature needs to be created. Use the **Hole Wizard** to create a hole on the new sketch, randomly place it on the face of the part and dimension it so it's on the midpoint of the two equal lines on the left side of the part. Create a **Through All** hole with a diameter of **0.125 in**. as shown below.

Now, select the **Curve Driven Pattern** Command. Select the offset sketch as the Direction. Add **25** for the Number of Instances and check **Equal Spacing**. Now, select the newly created hole as the Feature to Pattern.

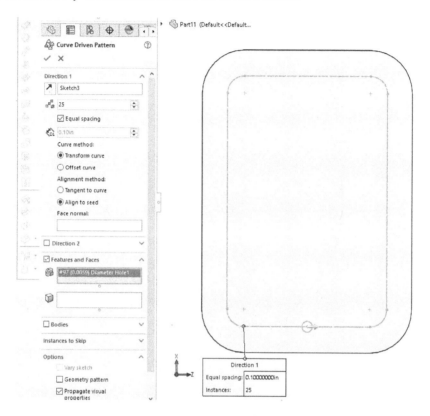

Click **OK**. Your model should resemble the figure below.

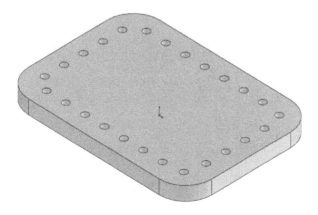

Exercise Complete

Exercise 30: Helical Cut Neural

Create a new **Part File**. Create the sketch on the Top Plane as seen below and extrude to a depth of **3 in.**

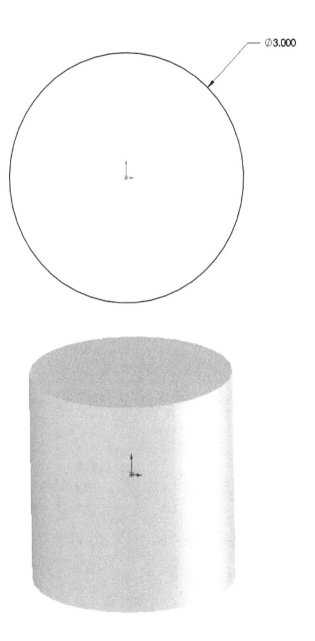

⌀3.000

To create the **Helical Cut**, we need a helix that follows a cross section, along a path that lies on a face. Start by going to the **Curves Command** in the Command Manager and select the **Helix/Spiral Command** from the dropdown menu. Now sketch a circle on the bottom face of the cylinder that snaps to the same diamater as the cylinder. Exit the sketch. When the Helix/Spiral Properties Manager appears, follow the parameters as shown below.

In the Defined By box, select **Pitch and Revolution**	
For the pitch, enter **12 in** and reverse the direction.	

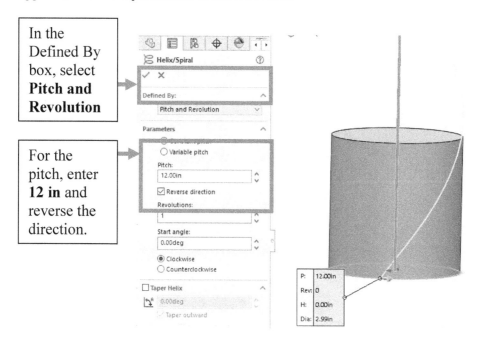

Click **OK**.

Your model should now show the Helix sketch as shown below.

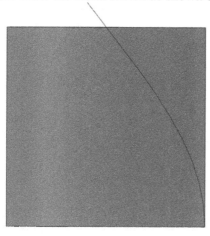

Create the following sketch on the bottom face of the cylinder. Try rotating the cylinder to create a circle at the bottom end of the new Helix curve. *Note: The model has been rotated and shown in Wireframe view for clarity.*

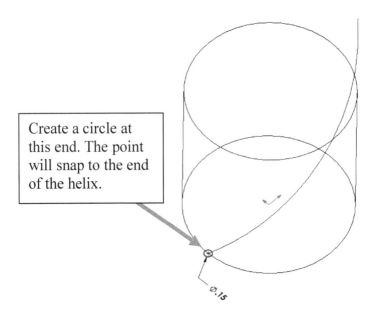

Create a circle at this end. The point will snap to the end of the helix.

∅.15

Now, accept the sketch and exit. Select the **Swept Cut** Command in the Command Manager. The Properties Manager will appear as shown.

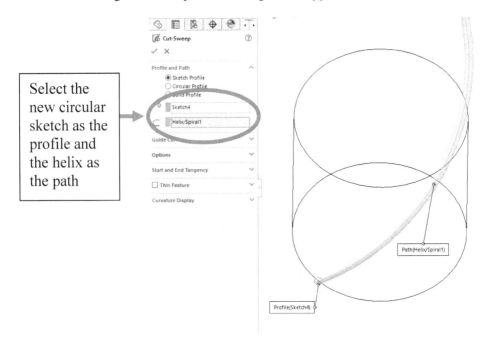

Select the new circular sketch as the profile and the helix as the path

After you click **OK,** your model should resemble the one below.

Click the **Mirror Command.** Mirror the cut across the Front Plane

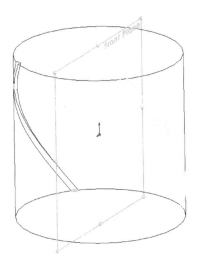

Now, in order to create a Circular Pattern, you need an axis reference as you did in previous exercises. *Note: To have the axis pass through the center of the cylinder, select the Two Planes option and click on the Right and Front Planes to center the axis.*

Once you've created your reference axis, create a **Circular Pattern**. The Circular Pattern Properties Manager appears. Select the axis as the Axis of Revolution. Enter the angle as **360 degrees,** and the number of instances to **45,** with **Equal Spacing** checked. Select the Helical cut and Mirror as the Features to Pattern.

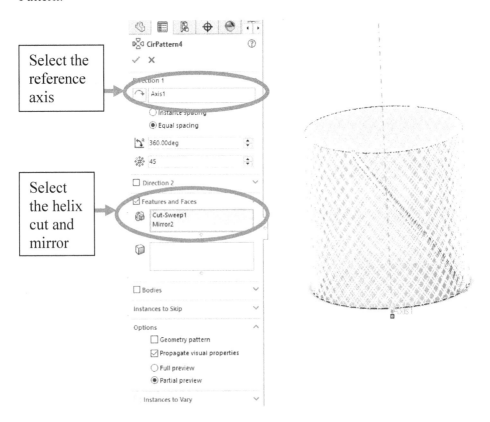

Your model should resemble the figure below.

Exercise Complete

Exercise 31: Intersections and Varying Dimension Patterns

Start a new part and create the extruded part below. The part is **5 in** by **5in** and extruded to a depth of **10 in**.

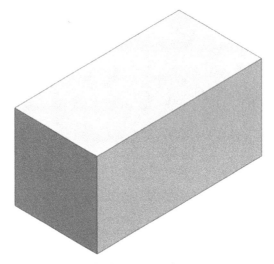

Create a plane diagonally through the part as shown.

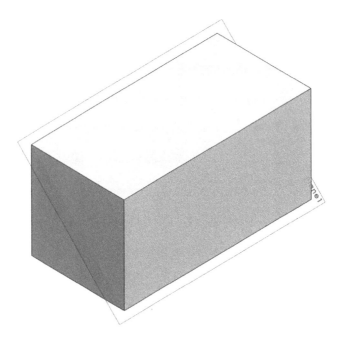

Create the following sketch on the new plane. Center it on the extrude you made earlier. Make sure that it is constrained to the center as well, and not just placed there. *Note: Centering it will be much easier if you adjust your view so that it is normal to the plane.*

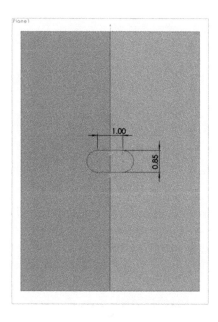

Use an **Extruded Cut** to cut this sketch **5in** in both directions so that it cuts clean through the part. Linear pattern this feature with the inputs shown. Don't click **OK** yet, we're not quite done.

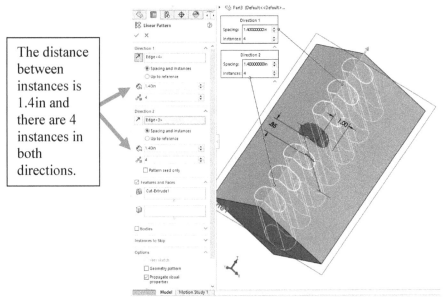

The distance between instances is 1.4in and there are 4 instances in both directions.

This is the fun part! Click "Instances to vary" and then click the **1 in** dimension shown in the image below. *Note: You must select the **1 in** dimension for both directions.* Change the increment value to **1 in** for both direction one and two. The Instances to Vary box should now look like this.

Make sure that "Pattern seed only" is selected before clicking **OK**. If done correctly, your part should now look like this. *Note: If your part doesn't look like*

the one below, it's probably due to constraints placed on the original sketch. Make sure you don't fix any part of the original sketch.

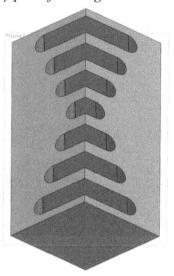

Create the following sketch on the square face of the part. This can be done using lines and a series of concentric arcs. Trim the four line segments denoted with red arrows. *This sketch should be along the same diagonal as the plane you created earlier.*

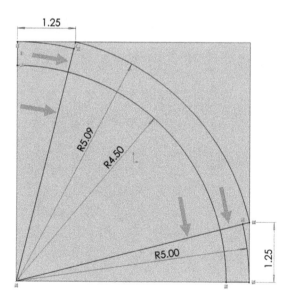

Your final sketch should appear as below.

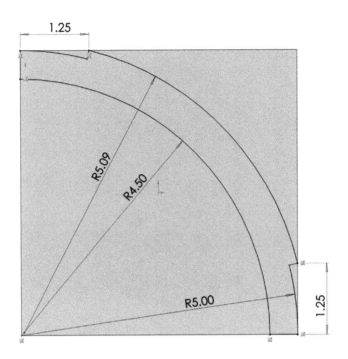

Extrude the sketch you just created **1 in** forward and **11 in** backward. Be sure to uncheck the "Merge Result" box. *By doing this, you end up with two separate entities. This is crucial when using the **Intersect** command.*

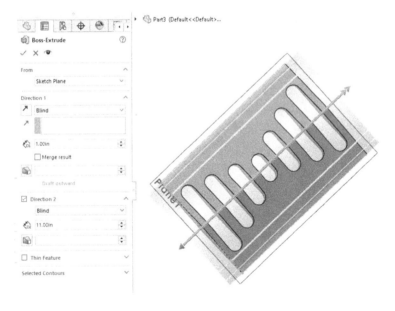

Choose the **Intersect** command located on the "Features" tab. Select the two extrusions as the bodies you wish to intersect and then click "Intersect". Deselect

"Merge Result" and select "Consume Surfaces" instead. Then select every region except where the two bodies intersect. *Note: This tends to be the very last box most, if not all, of the time.* Click **OK**.

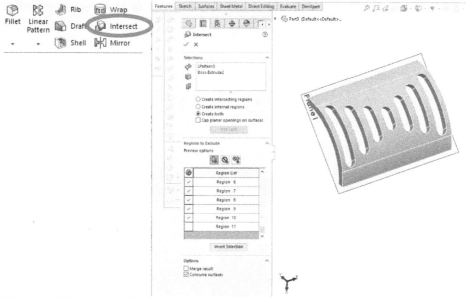

You should end up with the part shown below.

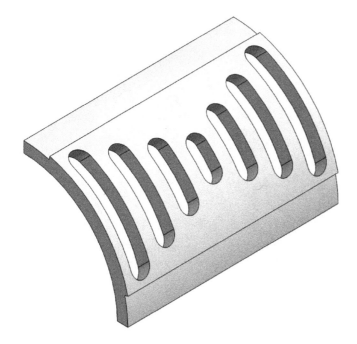

Exercise Complete

Exercise 32: Selective Deletion

Oftentimes, over the span of time a mechanical engineer spends modeling a part, the demands placed on the model change. As a result, so must the model itself. The **Selective Deletion** tool is a modeler's best friend under these circumstances.

Open a new **Part File**. Click the Extrude button and create the **5in x 5in x 5in** cube shown below.

Now create a **2.5in x 2.5in x 2.5in** cube centered on the top of your **5in** cube.

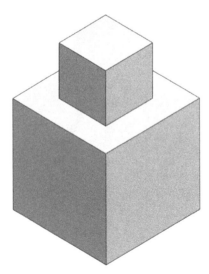

Now create a hole with a 1in diameter on top of the **2.5in** block. Set the depth to "Through All" as shown below. Be sure to place the hole by choosing a surface and then a point rather than using a 3D sketch. We don't want the hole to rely on a sketch as that would make the next part of the exercise more difficult. *Note: the display is set to "Wireframe" for clarity.*

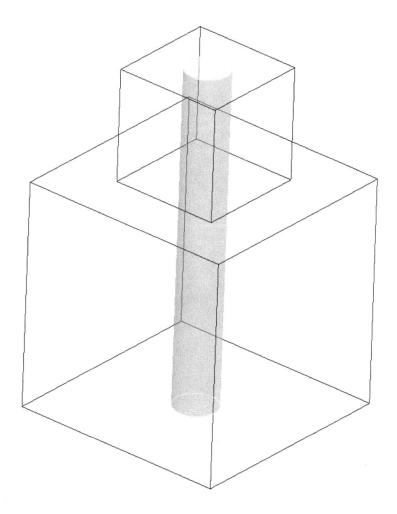

Let's say, for example, that after creating this model, we no longer wanted the **2.5in** cube, but wanted to keep the **5in** cube with the hole through it. Since the hole is a child feature of the **2.5in** cube, normally it would be lost if you deleted the **2.5in** cube. With selective deletion, this can be avoided.

Right click the **2.5in** box and select "Delete".

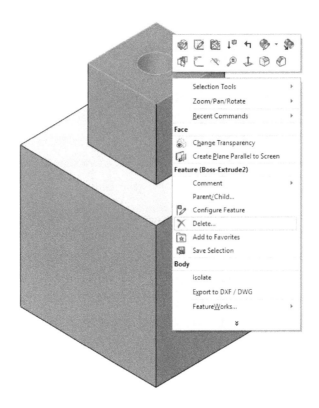

You should get the following window.

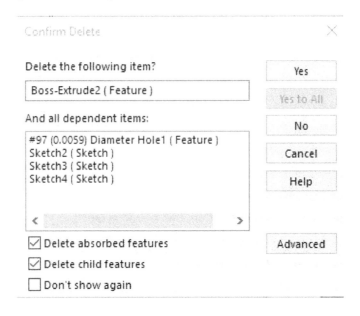

First, click Advanced. Your window should now look like the image below.

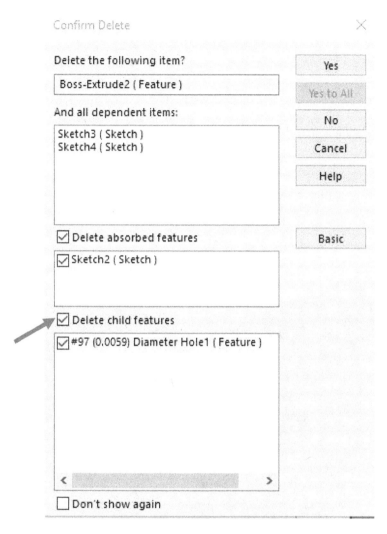

Now uncheck the "Delete child features" box. This will disassociate the hole and the **2.5in** cube, allowing you to delete only the cube. Click **Yes**.

You should now receive the following warning. This is simply to warn you that the hole is no longer associated with any planes or faces.

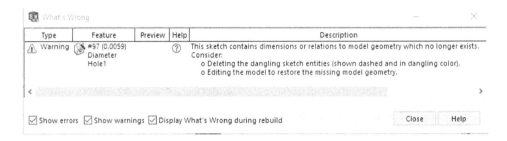

Close this warning and you should have your final model.

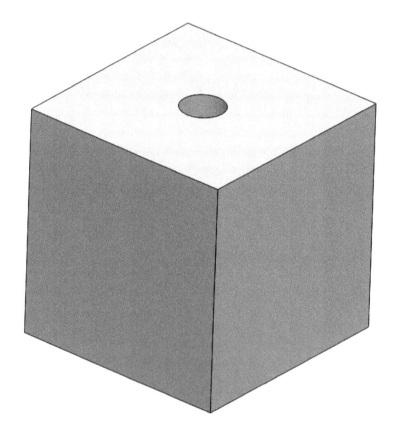

Exercise Complete

Exercise 33: Text tool, Wrapping, Normal Cut

Open a new **Part File**. Click the Extrude button and create the sketch shown below on the Front Plane.

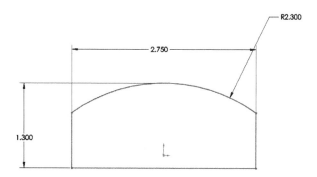

Extrude about the sketch plane a Distance of **5 in.**

Create a plane that is tangent to the curved face.

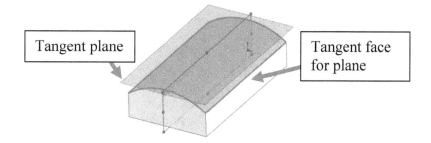

Create a new sketch and center it on the new plane you created as shown below.

In the Features Command Manager, click on the **Wrap** Command. Select the new plane you created. The Sketch Command will appear. In the Sketch Command, click on the **Text** Command.

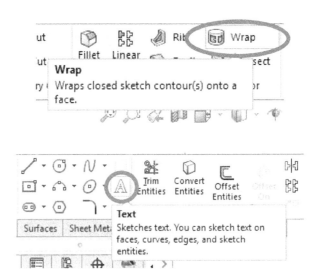

Select the bottom horizontal line of the rectangular sketch you created. Type in any text you wish in the Text Box. Now, locate the **Font** button and click on it. You will have to uncheck "Use document font" to select it. Change the font so that the text fits well within the boundaries of the rectangular sketch.

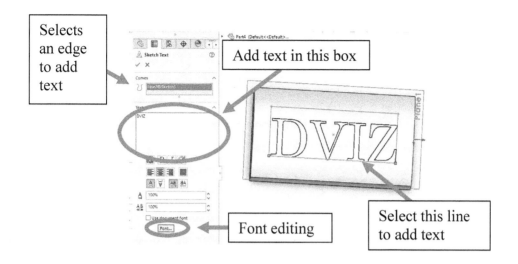

Selects an edge to add text

Add text in this box

Font editing

Select this line to add text

Exit the sketch. In the Wrap Properties Manager, select the curved face as the Face to wrap the sketch. Make sure the Deboss feature is selected in the Wrap Type. Wrap to a depth of **0.25 in**. Click the text as the Source Sketch. Click **OK**.

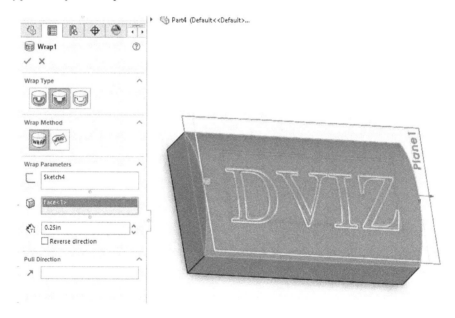

`

Your model should resemble the figure below.

Exercise Complete

Exercise 34: Boundary Surface through 3 sketches

Create a new **Part File**. Create two reference Planes, **2.5 in.** away from and parallel to the Front Plane in both directions.

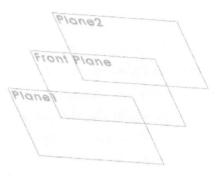

On Plane 1, create a **3 Point Arc** with a radius of **1.5 in.** as shown in the figure below.

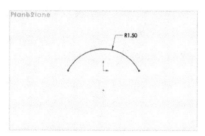

Exit the sketch.

Create a new **Sketch** of an arc with a radius of **3in** on the Front Plane.

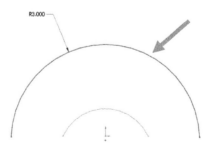

Exit the Sketch.

Create another Sketch of an arc on Plane 2.

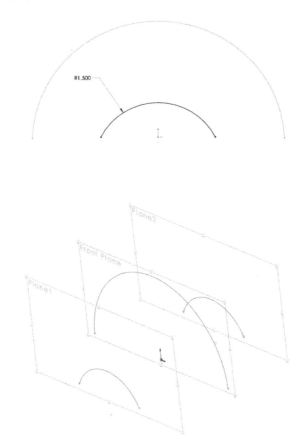

You are now going to delve into more surfacing. Right-click on one of the tabs under the Command Manager. This will allow you to manage the visible tabs. Scroll down and select **Surfaces.** This will add a Surfaces tab. Go into the Surfaces Command Manager and select **Boundary Surface.**

In the Boundary Surface Properties Manager, select the first small arc in the Direction 1 box. Next select the large arc. You should now get the following preview as shown in the figure below. *Note: The preview below has curvature combs shown.*

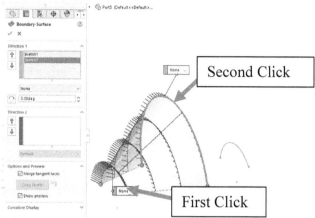

Lastly, select the final arc.

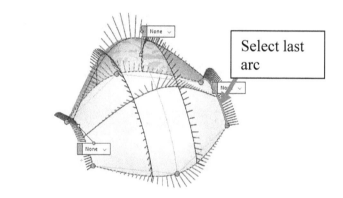

Click **OK**.

Exercise Complete

Exercise 35: Surface with Guide Curves

In a new **Part File** create a **Sketch** on the Front Plane. Sketch a quarter ellipse by trimming three sides as shown in the figure below. Dimensions do not matter.

Now create another quarter ellipse on the Top Plane. Snap the ellipse's end to the end of the previous sketch.

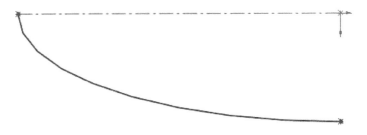

Create a **Sketch** on the Front Plane.

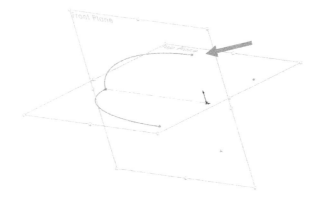

Once again, create another sketch on the Top Plane, but opposite to the quarter ellipse. You could have created half an ellipse instead of two separate sketches, but an explanation of why that will not work will come shortly.

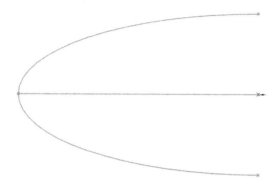

Exit the sketch.

Create another **Sketch** on the Right Plane. Sketch the arc shown in the figure. Snap the top point of the arc to the first ellipse you created.

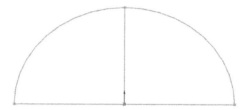

Your 4 sketches should resemble the figure below.

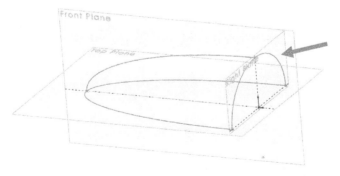

Now, in the Surfaces Command Manager, select Boundary Surface. Select the three ellipses in the order they were sketched in the Direction 1 box.

187

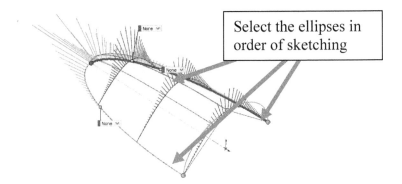

Now, select the arc in the Direction 2 box.

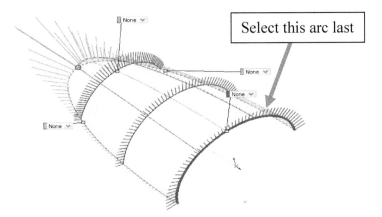

Your model should resemble the figure below.

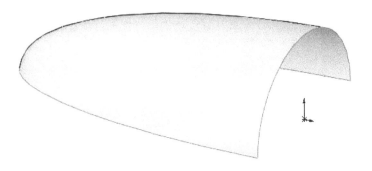

Exercise Complete

Exercise 36: Flatten Surface

This next exercise unfortunately involves features available to only premium users in SolidWorks 2018. If you do not have access to it, feel free to skip this exercise. However, if you can use it, this tool can prove to be a valuable tool to use should you need to define a surface shape which will be bent into a desired shape later in a manufacturing process.

To start, create two sketches: a spline and a curve, that intersect each other as shown below.

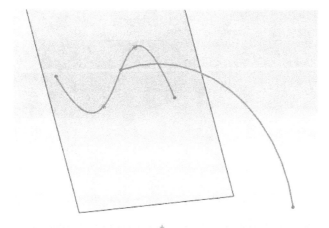

Sweep the two curves to make a surface.

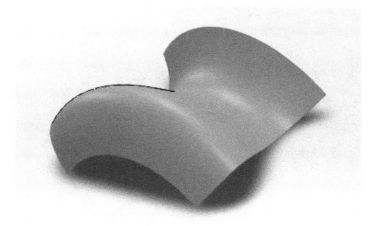

Now, in the surface Command Manager, select the **Surface Flatten** tool. In the menu that comes up, select the surface that you want flattened, and the edge along which you want it flattened. After accepting the flatten, a new surface should appear that is the flattened area of the first surface.

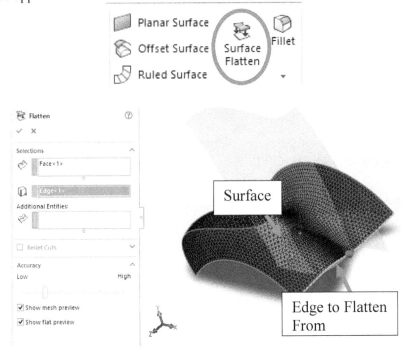

Now hide the initial wavy surface to just view your newly flattened surface.

Exercise Complete

Exercise 37: Converting Surfaces into a Solid

In a new **Part File,** create a Plane parallel to the Front Plane offset to a distance of **5 in**.

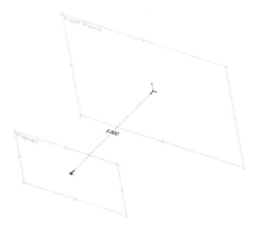

Using the **Circle** tool create a sketch that looks like the following.

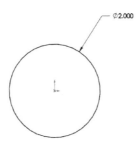

Exit the Sketch.

Sketch an **Ellipse** on the Front Plane that looks like the following figure.

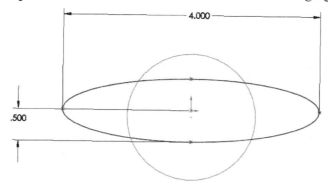

Exit the Sketch.

Under the Surfaces tab click the **Boundary Surface** command in the Surfaces Command Manager. Select the circle first and the ellipse last. You should get a shape similar to the one in the figure below.

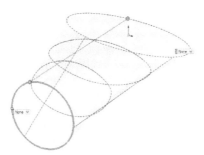

To get a symmetrical shape, you can manipulate the boundary surface with the **Open Contour** tool. *Note: Creating some sketches or points to snap to can help you to create a more symmetric part.*

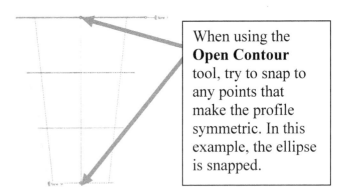

When using the **Open Contour** tool, try to snap to any points that make the profile symmetric. In this example, the ellipse is snapped.

Click **OK**. Your model will look like the following figure.

In the Surfaces Command Manager, locate the **Filled Surface** Command. In the Properties Manager, select the circular edge in the **Patch Boundary** box. This will now fill that edge and create a surface face. Do the same for the elliptical edge.

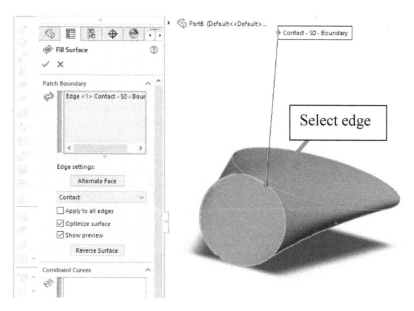

Your model should now resemble the figure below.

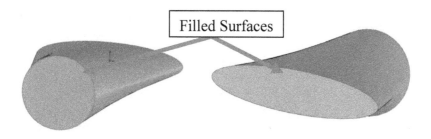

Filled Surfaces

Now, to convert this boundary surface into a solid feature, you need to knit all the features together. In the Surfaces Command Manager, select **Knit Surface.** In the Properties Manager, select all the surfaces in this part in the Selections box. Right below the box, check the "Create solid" box. Accept the changes. Your model should now resemble the figure below.

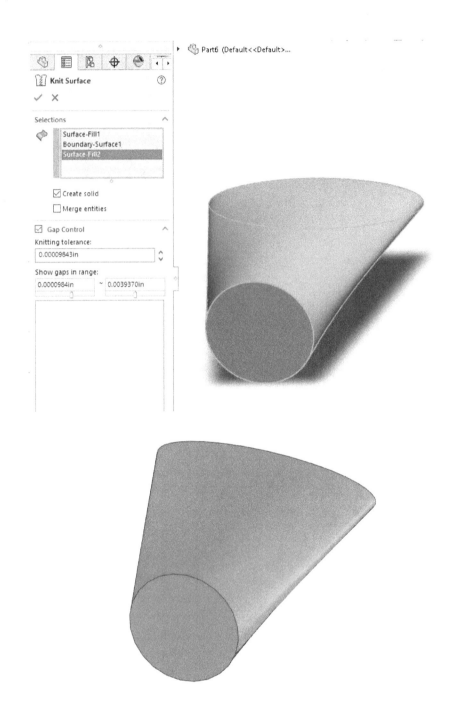

Exercise Complete

Exercise 38: Extruded Surfaces that are Tangentially Connected

In a new **Part File** create a Plane parallel to the Front Plane, offset by **3 in.**

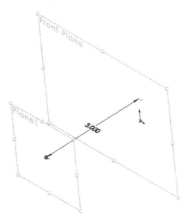

In the Surfaces Command Manager, select **Extruded Surface.** Sketch a Center Rectangle on the new plane.

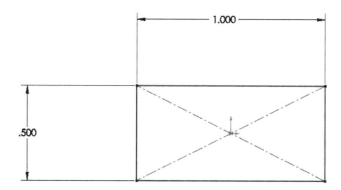

Exit the sketch and extrude the surface to a depth of **1.25 in.** in a direction towards you.

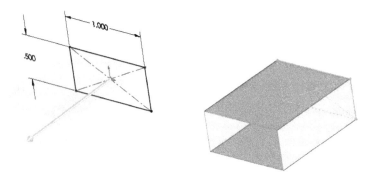

Now, on the Front Plane, select the Extruded Surface Command and sketch another Center Rectangle with the dimensions shown in the figure below. Extrude it to a depth of **3 in**. with a direction away from the previous extrusion.

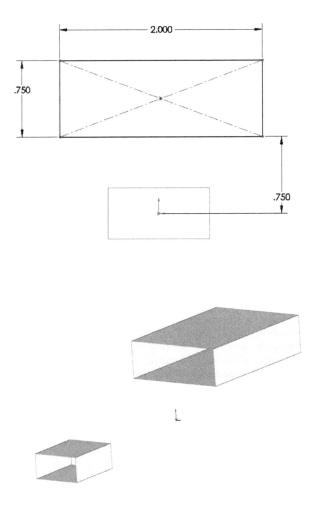

To connect the two rectangular surfaces, you will use the **Lofted Surface** Command. Start by selecting the right edges of each rectangle in the Profiles box. In the Properties Manager window, open the **Start/End Constraints** drop down menu. For the Start and End constraints, select the **Tangency to Face** option with a Start Tangent Length of **1in** and be sure to check the Apply to All boxes.

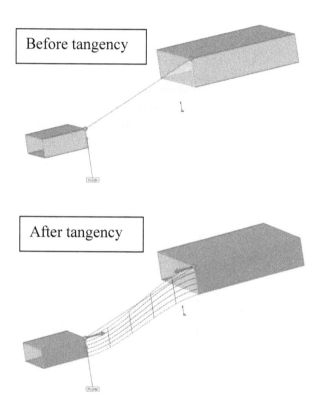

Click **OK**. Now apply another Lofted Surface to the other side.

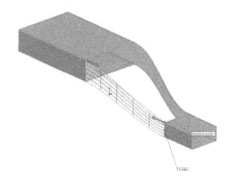

Click **OK**. Now, create another Lofted Surface for the top edges of both rectangles.

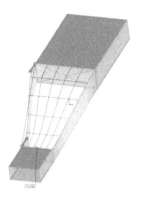

Last, create a Lofted Surface for the bottom two edges.

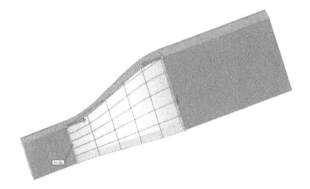

Click **OK**. Your model should resemble the figure below.

Finally, you want to **Thicken** the surfaces. Thickening a surface can be time consuming, especially when there are a number of surfaces. To avoid this, you need to connect the surfaces together. Use the **Knit Surface** Command and select all the Lofted Surfaces and Extrusions from the Design Tree to create a single surface.

In the toolbar, go to **Insert/ Boss/Base/ Thicken**.

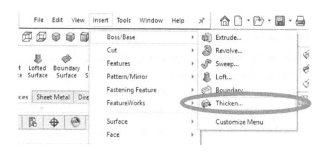

The Thicken Properties Manager now appears. Select the knit surface. Thicken it to **0.100 in**.

Select "Thicken Side 2" to thicken the outside surface

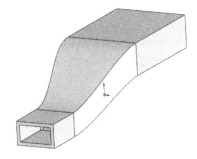

Exercise Complete

Exercise 39: Surfacing, Trim, Sweep, Extend, and Split

In a new **Part File,** sketch the following line on the Front Plane.

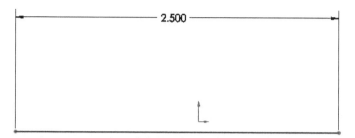

Exit the Sketch

Now create a sketch on the **Right Plane** that looks similar to the following figure. Use the **Spline** Command.

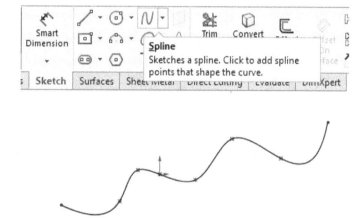

Under the Surfaces Command Manager, click the **Swept Surface** tool in the Surfaces options box.

To Sweep in both directions from the sketch, select Bidirectional in the Profile and Path section.

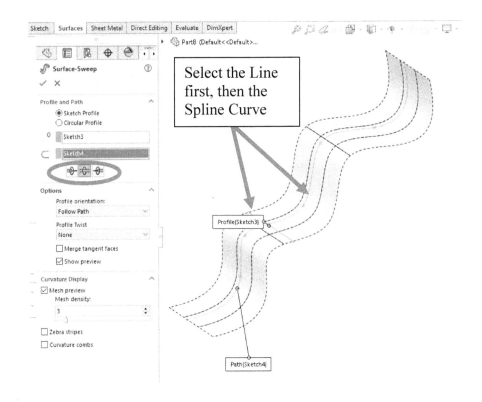

Click **OK.**

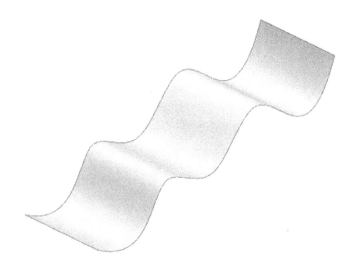

To Split your surface into two separate surfaces, you will be using the **Split Line Command,** which is found in the Features Command, under the **Curves** drop down. Click the **Preview** button then the **Finish** button.

Before you can use the **Split Line** Command, you need to create a Line which is used to split your surface.

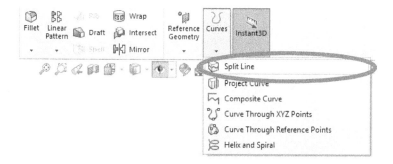

Create a new sketch on the Top Plane. Sketch a line over the surface.

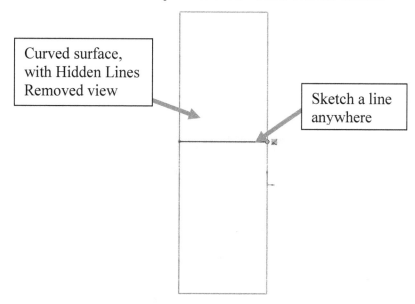

To split the surface, select the new line you just sketched. In the Faces to Split box, choose the Swept surface. Choose the direction. *Note: The direction will depend on where you made your line sketch and whether it is above or below the surface.*

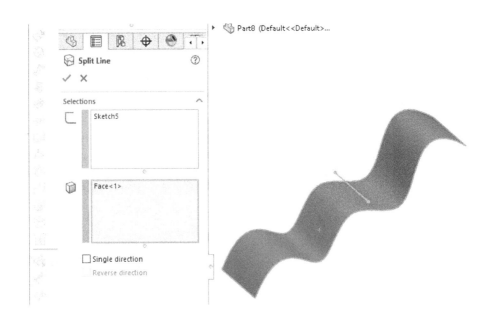

Click **OK**. Now click on either surface. Notice how they are now split!

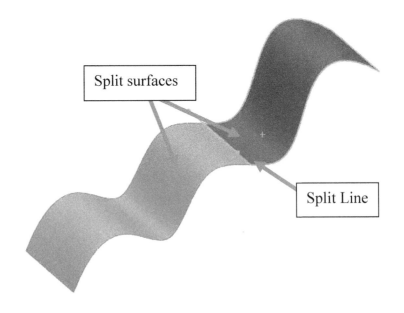

Split surfaces

Split Line

Now, you're going to extend a surface. In the Surfaces Command Manager, click on **Extend Surface.**

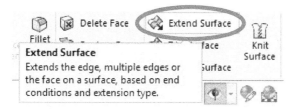

To extend a surface, you can select an edge or face. Choose an edge to extend as seen in the figure below.

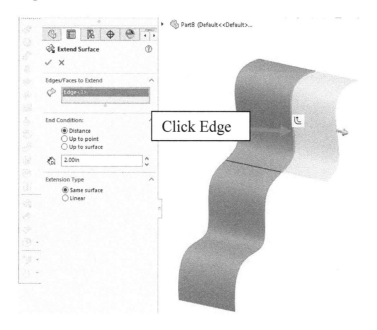

You can change the distance either by moving the arrow in the Graphics Window or setting a distance. Move the cursor to extend the surface.

Accept the changes. Your model should resemble the figure below.

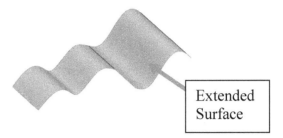

Extended Surface

You can also trim surfaces using a sketch, plane, or surface as the trimming tool. Before you can trim, create a new sketch on the Top Plane similar to the figure below.

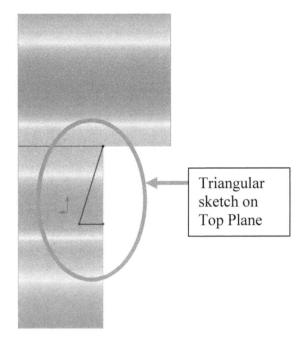

Triangular sketch on Top Plane

Click the **Trim Surface Command** in the Surfaces Command Manager.

The Trim Surface Properties Manager appears. In the Trim Tool box, select the sketch you just created. In the **Sections to Keep** box, click on the outside of the new sketch boundary. The selection for the second box can also be set to **Sections to Remove** if desired.

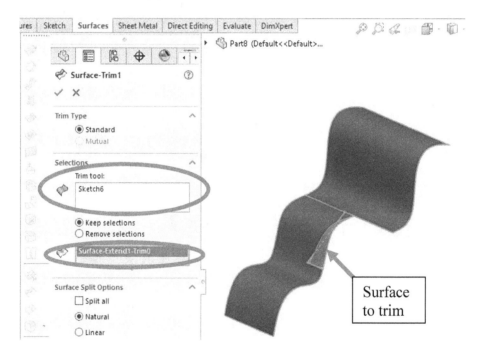

Accept the changes. Your model should now resemble the figure below.

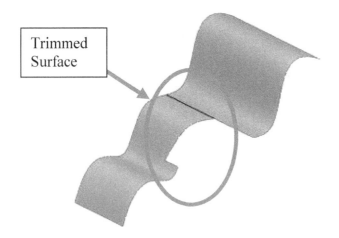

Trimmed
Surface

Now you know some great techniques for creating and editing surfaces.

Exercise Complete

Exercise 40: Offset Surfaces

Start a new **Part File.** Create a sketch similar to the one below. *Note: Recall the Spline Command and Construction Lines.*

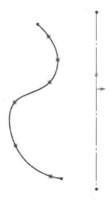

Exit the Sketch.

Under the Surfaces Command Manager, select the **Revolved Surface** Command.

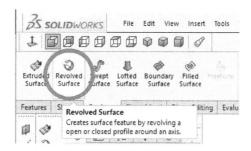

Select the construction line that you created as the Axis of Revolution. Revolve it **360 degrees**.

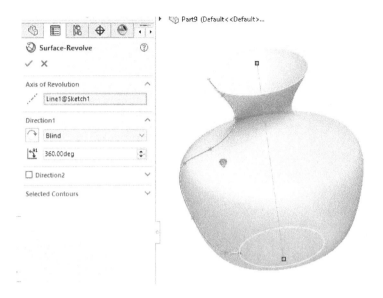

Click **OK**.

Select the **Offset Surface** Command in the Surfaces Command Manager.

In the Offset Surface Properties Manager, select the surface you created in the Parameters box. To offset outwards, click reverse. Select an offset distance of **0.125 in**.

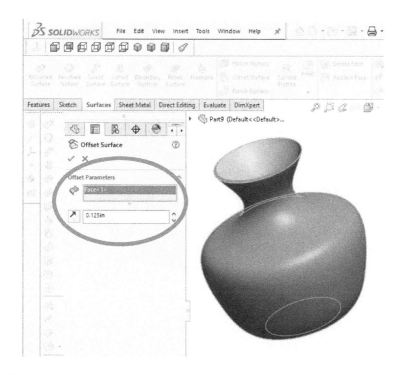

Click **OK**.

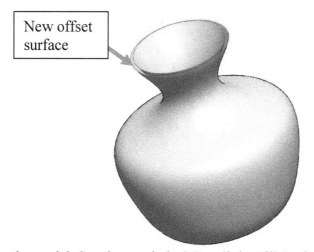

New offset surface

Rotate the model. See the two holes? Recall the Fill Surface Command? To fill the holes, use the Fill Surface Command, select the hole edge and accept. Do the same for the outer hole as well.

211

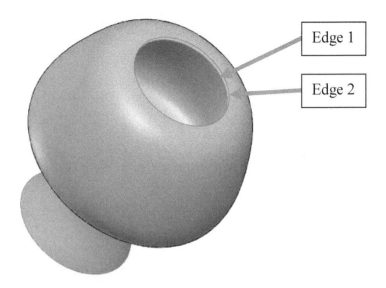

To fill the top two rims, you will need to create another sketch and use the Revolved Surface Command.

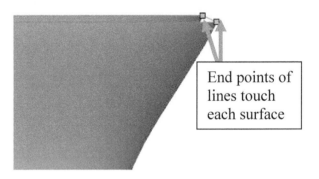

In the Revolved Surface Properties Manager, select the construction line from your first sketch as the Axis of Revolution. **Revolve** with an angle of **360 degrees**.

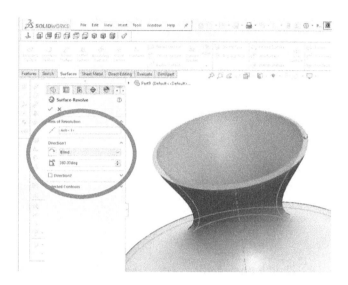

Click **OK**. Finally, use the **Knit** command to create a solid body.

Exercise Complete

Exercise 41: Thickened Cut

Create a New **Part File.** Click the **Extrude** button and select the Top Plane to sketch on.

Create a sketch using the **Ellipse** Command tool that looks like the figure shown below.

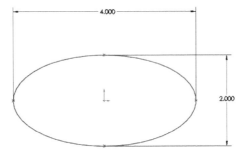

Extrude above the sketch plane a distance of **1in**.

Create a **Sketch** on a plane Parallel to the **Front Plane** that is offset by a distance of **2.00 in**.

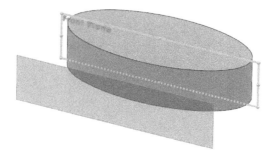

Using the **Spline** sketch tool, sketch a curve on the new plane that looks similar to the following figure. Be creative.

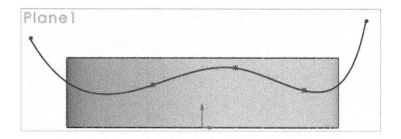

In the Surface Command Manager, select the **Extruded Surface** Command.

In the Properties Manager, select a **Blind** Direction with a depth of **4 in**.

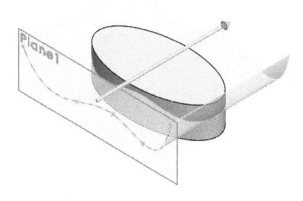

Click **OK**.

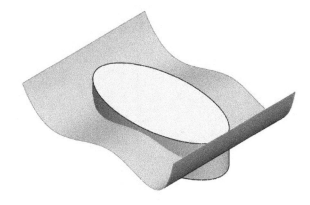

Now, select the **Thickened Cut** Command (**Insert/Cut/Thicken**).

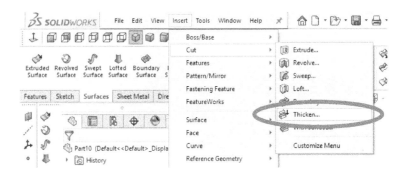

In the Properties Manager, select the Extruded Surface as the Surface to Thicken and thicken the top side to a thickness of **0.10 in**.

Click **OK**.

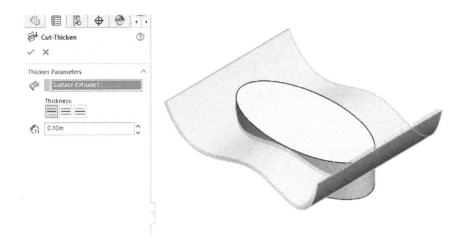

Now, a **Bodies to Keep** window appears. Choose "Selected bodies" and then select the body that will perform the cut. This should be Body 1 in the window. Check the box, then click **OK**.

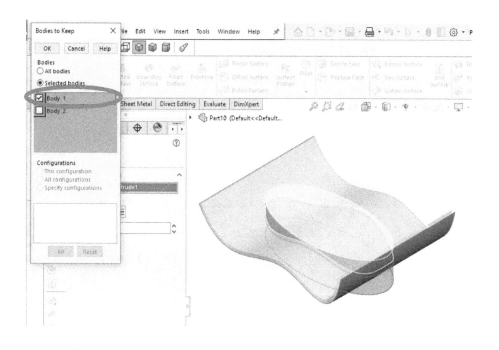

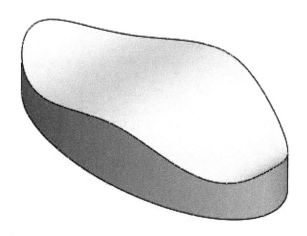

Exercise Complete

Exercise 42: Replace Sketch Entity

Create a new **Part File**. Create the following sketch on the Front plane.

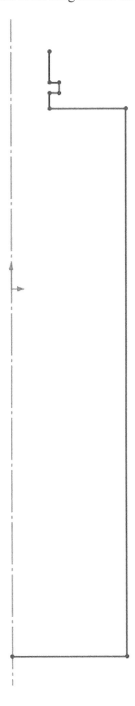

Here is the sketch with only dimensions shown.

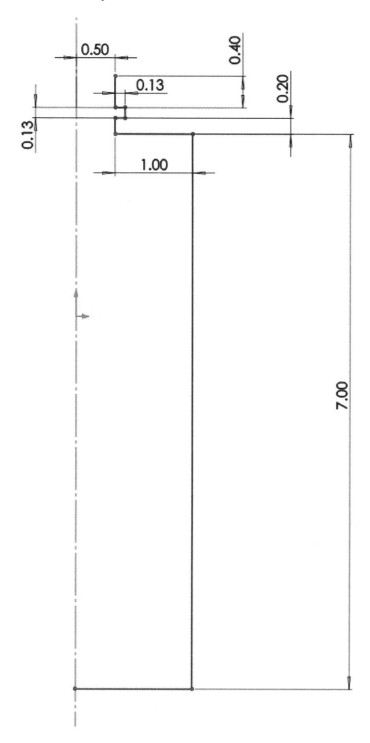

Here is the sketch with only constraints shown.

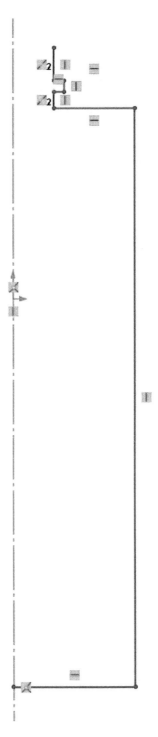

Now click **Revolved Surface** and revolve the sketch around the dashed construction line as shown below.

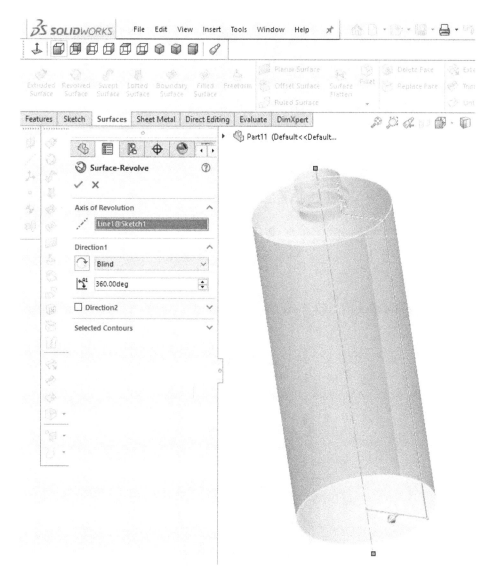

Click **OK**. You should now have the following model.

Use the **Thicken** tool to thicken the model inward **0.1in**. You should now have the following model.

As you can see, this is not a very ergonomic bottle. To fix this, we are going to use the **Replace Sketch Entity** tool. Basically, this tool allows you to swap one sketch entity out for another, all while retaining relationships to features that rely on the sketch.

Find the original sketch in the Feature Manager Design Tree (it will be located under the Surface Revolve) and right click it. Then select "Edit Sketch".

Now click **Style Spline** (located under the original spline tool). Style Spline is a cool spline feature that allows you to create easily dimensioned splines using control points.

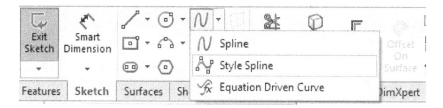

Create a spline similar to the one shown below. The dimensions aren't important, so be creative and shape the bottle to your liking. Just be sure your spline has the same endpoints as the one shown below.

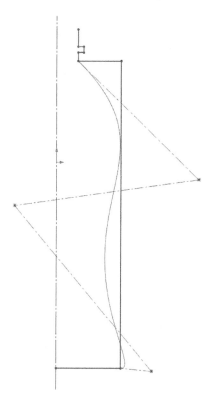

Now right click the top edge of the bottle as shown below and select the **Replace Sketch Entity** icon.

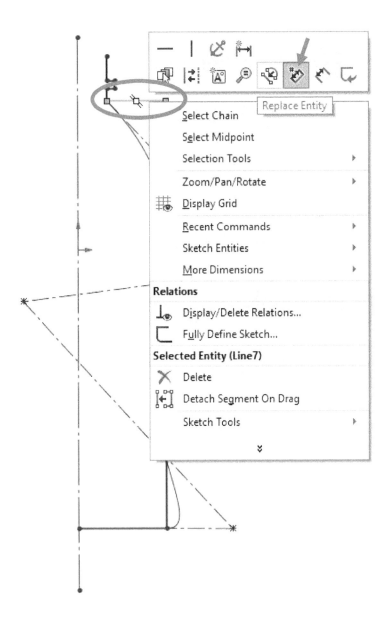

Make sure the "Delete" box is checked, click the spline, then click **OK**.

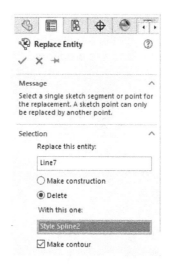

Do the same thing with the side of the bottle. After replacing both of those lines with the spline, you should have the following sketch.

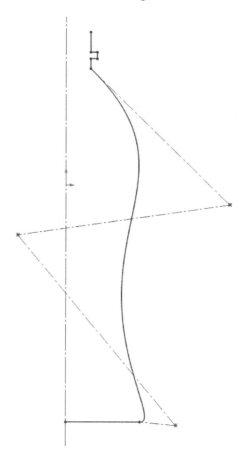

Exit the sketch and your model should automatically update according to your new sketch, leaving you with a far more ergonomic bottle.

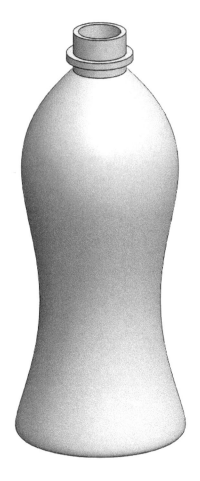

Exercise Complete

Exercise 43: Adding Threads

Create a new **Part File.** While in the Extrude Command, create a **Sketch** that looks like the figure below. Using the **Equal Length** Relation, make all the sides of the hexagon equal in length and make one side horizontal using the **Horizontal/Vertical** Relation.

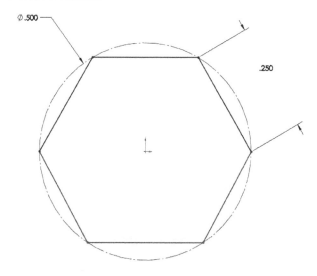

Extrude in front of the sketch plane to a distance of **0.125in**. Add a **Fillet** of **0.025 in** to all edges on the front and back of the hexagon and a Fillet of **0.01in** onto the edges on the sides as shown in the following figure.

Save the part using **Save As** under the name **Bolt.SLDPRT** to use in a later assembly.

Open the **Hole Wizard**. Click on the front face of the hexagonal shape. In the Hole Type box, select **Straight Tap**. The Standard is **ANSI Inch** with a **Bottoming Tapped Hole**. The size is a **1/4-20**. See the figure below to see the rest of the hole specifications.

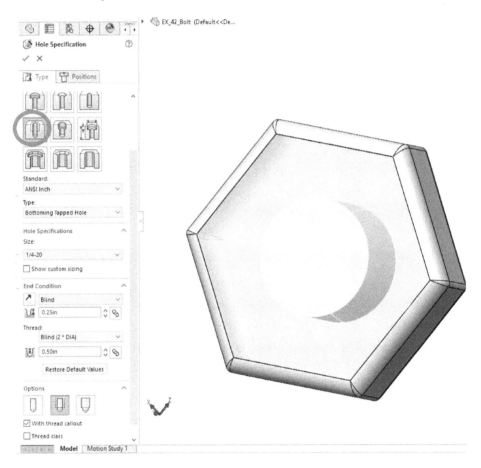

Now choose the hole position. Select the Front face of the model. Recall Exercise 16? Click the position, then move the center point of the hole to the center of the part. Click **OK**.

Notice the dashed circle offset from the hole? That is the Cosmetic Thread, which is shown that way to save time and memory. *Note: Actual thread creation in SolidWorks involves using the **Thread** command in the dropdown under the Hole Wizard. Generating these threads takes up a lot of computer memory which is usually not a good thing. However, if you really want them, it is possible to add them.*

Finally, add a **Fillet** of **0.025 in** to the front of the hole as shown in the following figure.

Using the **Save As** option, save the part again under the name **Nut.SLDPRT**

Open the original part named **Bolt.SLDPRT**

Create a **Sketch** on the back face of the part that looks like the figure below.

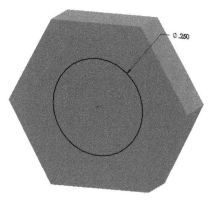

Close the Sketch and extrude a distance of **0.75 in**.

Recall earlier that adding a "real" thread uses up a lot of memory and time. Well, here you will add a Cosmetic Thread by using the **Edit Appearance** Command.

Start by going to the **Cosmetic Thread** Command. Go to **Insert/Annotations/ Cosmetic Thread**.

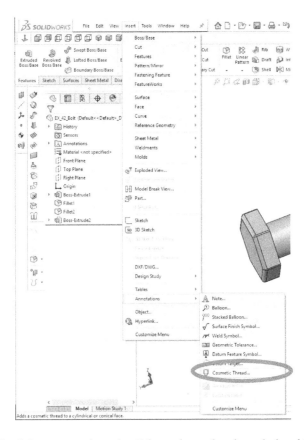

In the Properties Manager, select the Edge where the thread should start. Choose the Edge at the end of the bolt. Use the figure below to complete the parameters.

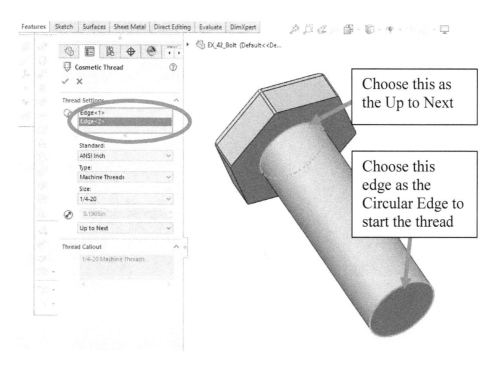

Choose this as the Up to Next

Choose this edge as the Circular Edge to start the thread

Click **OK**. See the dashed circles offset to the inside of the bolt? Those are the cosmetic threads.

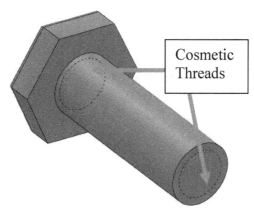

Cosmetic Threads

In the Heads-Up View Toolbar, select **Edit Appearance** to add the visual threads.

Edit Appearance
Edit the appearance of entities in the model.

On the left-hand side, in the Selected Geometry, choose the **Select Faces** icon.
Now select the shank of the bolt. On the right-hand side, in the
Appearances/Scenes dropdown, select the Appearance plus sign. Now, select
the **Metal** tab and choose Steel. Below that, select brushed steel. Double click to
accept the changes. The color of the bolt shank should change.

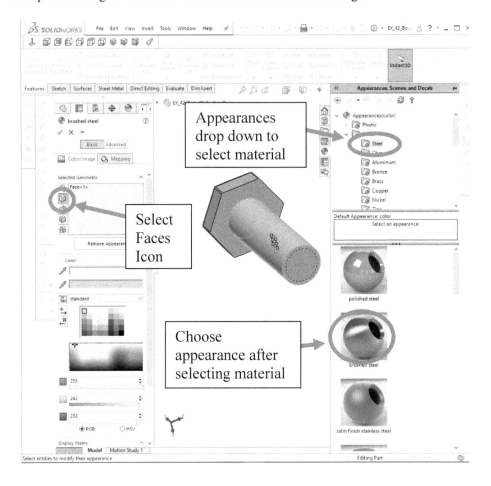

Now, in the **Appearances/Scenes** dropdown, scroll down and open the
Miscellaneous tab. Choose **Pattern**. Below that, scroll down and locate the
Screw Thread pattern. The bolt should now have the appearance of a screw
thread. You can change the size of the plane on the bolt to increase/decrease the
size of the thread. Increase the size and accept the changes. Your model should
resemble the figure below.

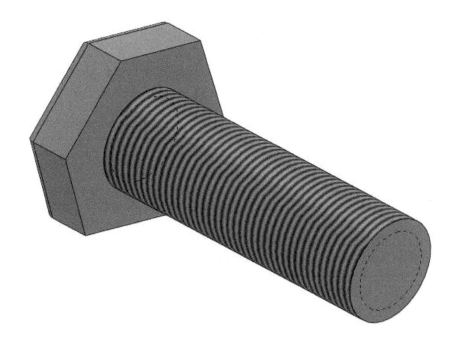

Exercise Complete

Parametric Modeling, Direct Editing

Traditional modeling in SolidWorks, as with many CAD packages, involves the use of parametric features. That is, when you use entities such as extrudes and revolves they are driven by an underlying set of numerical values (parameters) that can be changed at any time. When you change these parameters the rest of the features that are children of the original entity recalculate to produce a new incarnation of the original model. This has been the state of the art since parametric modeling gained major acceptance in the late '80s and early '90s. Recently another technology began to take hold that proved to be a great addition to parametric modeling. In the case of SolidWorks, it's called *Direct Editing*.

Imagine a situation, or perhaps you might recall one, where you needed to make an edit to a parametric model that wasn't anticipated by the original model creation techniques. For example, a model of a speaker housing on an alarm clock has a flat horizontal face on the top that the user is supposed to press to stop it from beeping in the morning. In a desire to improve the experience, the designer decides to tilt the top.

Without the direct editing capability, the job can get complex and lengthy. The designer must go back in the modeling tree to the original revolve for the top, then reorient it and hope that all the little hole features and the subsequent chamfers update. However, using direct editing the designer just highlights all the surfaces to be changed and instructs them to tilt about the axis. The change is explicit in that it partially overwrites the design intent and features that were created before. However, if the hole pattern or any of the other features that preceded the tilt are changed, they will cascade through and update.

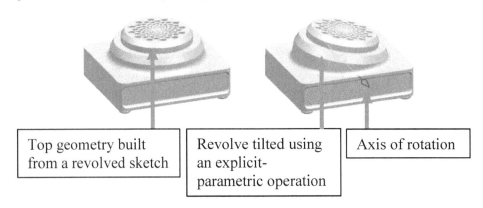

| Top geometry built from a revolved sketch | Revolve tilted using an explicit-parametric operation | Axis of rotation |

Exercise 44: Using Direct Editing

The following figure is of a model created in the traditional sense. It consists of an extrusion, a cut, a fillet, and several ribs and bosses. In this exercise we are going to edit some of the surfaces on this model using the **Direct Editing** Command Features. *Note: You can open this part from the book work files you downloaded or, for fun, you can try modeling something similar yourself.*

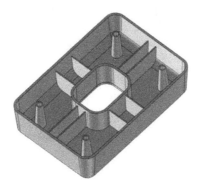

The commands you are going to use are found in the Direct Editing Features.

The first step is to select the **Move Face** Command. Select the top face of the center cutout.

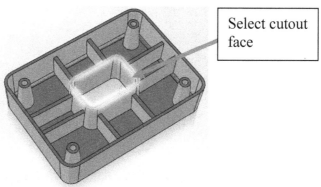

Select cutout face

Next, you will notice the coordinate triad. Select the arrow pointing in the Y-direction. Drag it upwards and you will notice the cutout is now moving as if it were being extruded.

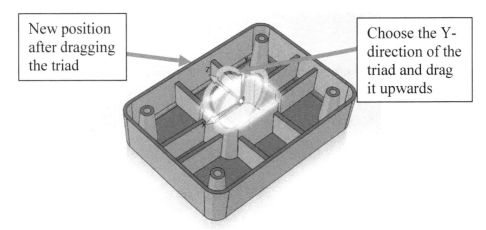

New position after dragging the triad

Choose the Y-direction of the triad and drag it upwards

You can also add a distance in the Move Face Properties Manager. Cancel any possible changes. Now, select the **Move Face** Command again and select the top face of a rib. In the Properties Manager, choose Rotate and in the Parameters section, highlight the first box. You must choose an axis reference to move the face in the direction you seek. Click on the inside edge near the outside face of the center cutout. If you change the angle in the Draft Angle box, you will notice the face of the rib changing.

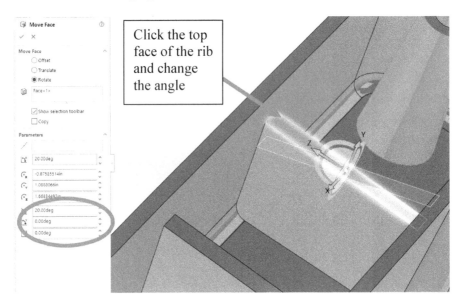

Click the top face of the rib and change the angle

Accept the changes and you will notice how the ribs angle has changed. Not bad!

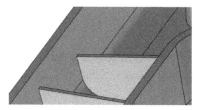

Now let's try to change the thickness of some of the ribs. Choose the Move Face Command again. In the Properties Manager, select **Offset** and choose the face shown in the figure below. Play with the distance parameter. Click **OK**.

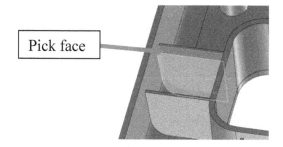

Your rib should resemble the figure below.

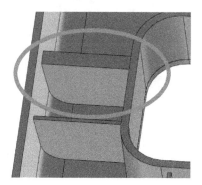

The **Direct Editing** feature is a powerful tool. Play with the other features. Some will be familiar to you and others may not. Direct Editing can be used at almost any time without really affecting the parent/child relation in the traditional modeling sense.

Exercise Complete

Exercise 45: Replace Face

Create a new **Part File**. Create an **Extruded** part that looks like the figure shown below. *Sizes are not important in this exercise, so be creative!*

Create a **Sketch** on the surface shown below.

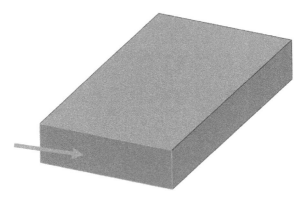

With the **3 Point Arc** tool, draw an arc similar to the one shown below and Exit the sketch.

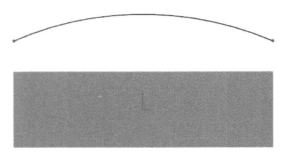

Create another **Sketch** on the face shown below, perpendicular to the last surface you started on.

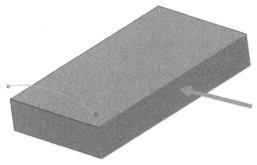

Using the **Spline** Command, draw a curve similar to the figure below.

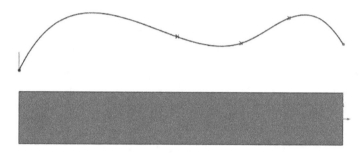

Exit the sketch.

Under the Surfaces tab click the **Swept Surface** Command. Select the arc as the Profile and the Spline as the Path. Click **OK**.

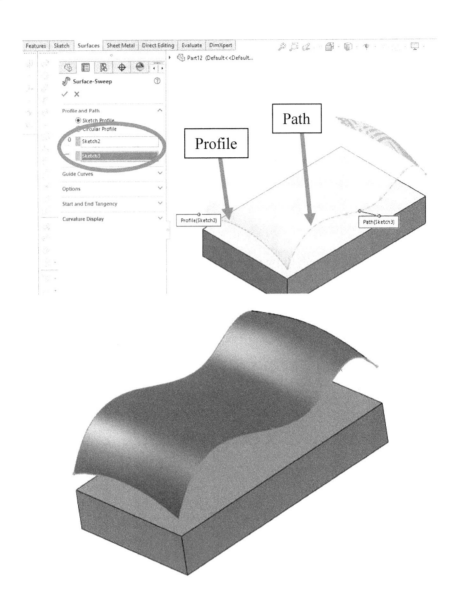

While still in the Surfaces tab, select the **Replace Face** Command.

240

In the Replace Face Properties Manager, select the top face of the part you extruded as the **Target Face(s) for Replacement**, then select the Swept surface as the **Replacement Surface(s).**

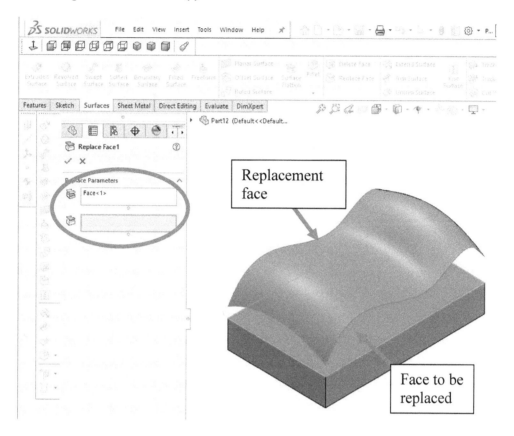

Click **OK.** Your model should resemble the figure below.

Exercise Complete

Exercise 46: Working with Instant3D

Recall the use of Direct Editing from Exercise 44. It allowed the user to modify features (more correctly, faces) in a model. The changes didn't affect the parent/child relationship but still added on new features. SolidWorks has another editing tool that dynamically changes features rather than faces. Instant3D is very powerful and will save you tons of time because it helps you to change features effortlessly. Instant3D is not the same as Direct Editing. Instead, Instant3D is just an elegant way of editing features without going into them in the part tree.

Go ahead and start a new **Part File**. Create the following sketch on the Top Plane and extrude it to **2.5 mm**. *Note: The units are in millimeters. Recall how to change units?*

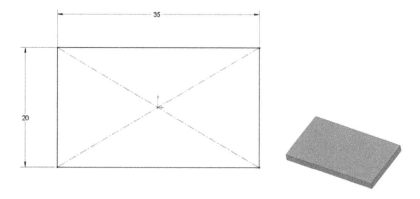

Now draw two small **Rectangles** on the top face of the block. **Extrude** the rectangles **30mm**.

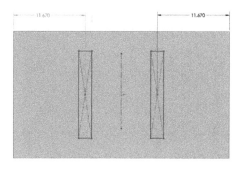 

Now create a circle on the end of the last extrusion. Sketch a circle of **5 mm**. Then use the **Extruded Cut** Command and cut through all.

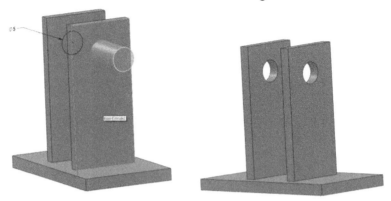

Create another extrude on the bottom face of **25mm** and this time add a **5 degree** draft angle in the **Extrude Boss/Base Properties Manager**.

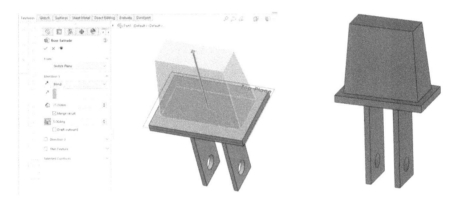

Add a circle with a diameter of **8 mm**, and extrude it to **5 mm**.

Now, add another circle with a diameter of **6 mm**. and extrude it to **30 mm**.

Add Fillets with a radius of **0.50 mm** to the model in the locations shown in the figure below.

Now for the fun part; start editing your geometry using Instant3D. In the Features Command Manager click on **Instant3D.**

Start by clicking on the cylindrical face of the hole you created. Notice the arrow that appears at the center of the circle and the dimension off to the side.

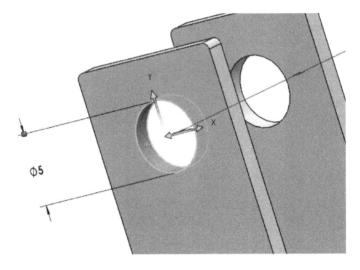

Click and drag on the arrow to manually adjust the dimension or click on the dimension. Instant3D automatically allows the user to change the dimension. Enter **10 mm** then click **OK**. You may have to deselect the feature to be sure it updates in the Graphics Window.

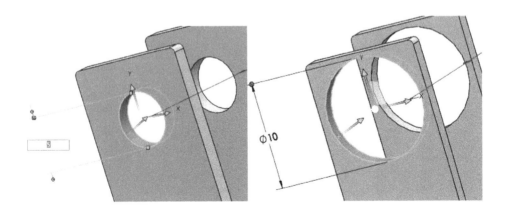

Click on one of the plug fillets. The fillet will highlight and an edge will appear. Left-click and drag down or up to change the radius of the fillet. Instant3D will change the dimension. Since you created the fillets together, changing one will change them all. Try to set the fillet radius to **1.0 mm.**

Note: If you recall, with design intent and the parent/child relationship, whatever feature was created will change, even if it wasn't the feature you intended to change. If you created the fillets on the plug, but also added fillets to the rest of the model at the same time, they will also change in Instant3D.

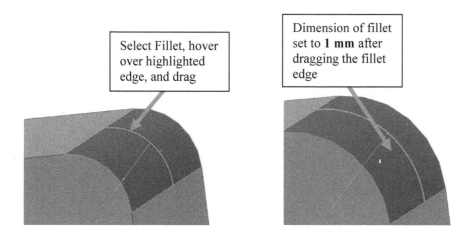

Another nice feature is the ability to edit the dimensions of geometric features by just double-clicking on them in the Graphics Window. With all these tools, your modeling and editing features will be more efficient. Try changing some more features with Instant3D by double-clicking. Enjoy!

Exercise Complete

Exercise 47: Textures, Colors, and Appearance Settings

SolidWorks has some amazing ways to make your model look visually appealing. Adding a nice texture or color can take a model from cool to out of this world. It can also be useful for conveying your message. A model that has texture and color will look significantly more realistic than one without.

To proceed, create a new **Part File** as shown below. You can make a crazy shape like mine, or just something simple.

In the Heads-Up View Toolbar, click on the **Appearances** button.

When you click on the appearances button, two things happen. A color display shows up on the left-hand side of the screen, and a separate menu pops up to the right of the screen.

To change the color of the part, click on a color in the color section in the Properties Manager and apply it.

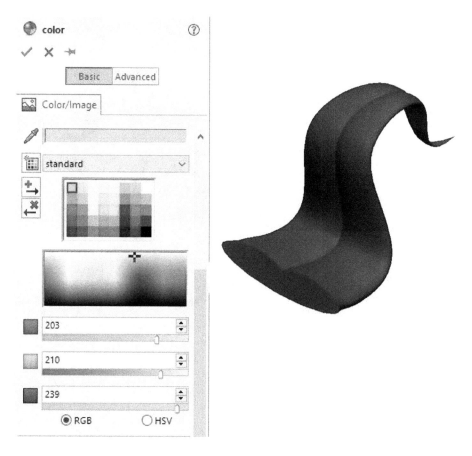

Now that we have added a color, let's change the texture to a pre-programmed texture.

In the menu that pops up to the right, select **Appearances/ Organic/ Miscellaneous.** Scroll down to the images and click on the one labeled **Grass.**

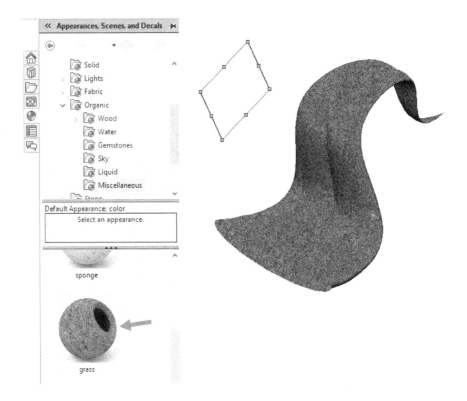

If your grass appears too small, or too large, grab the corner of the pink and blue box that appears within the appearances tool, and drag it out. The larger the box, the more detailed and closer the texture will appear.

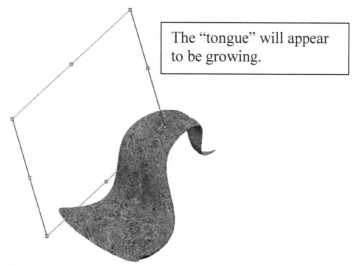

The "tongue" will appear to be growing.

The grass texture is fun, but most likely will not be as useful as some of the others. SolidWorks has a large library of textures like rubbers, metals, plastics, and even skin.

You can also adjust the **Image Quality** of your model to make it look nicer. Notice that the edges of the model below are "choppy" and not very smooth.

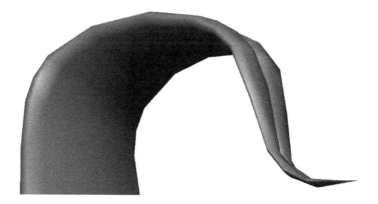

Go to **Tools/Options** and click on the **Document Properties** tab within the window that pops up.

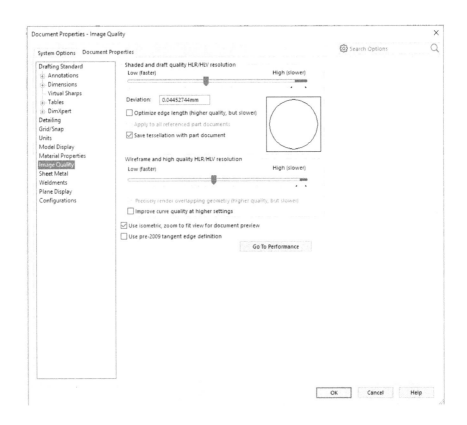

Click **Image Quality** on the left and use the slider to change the image quality from low to high.

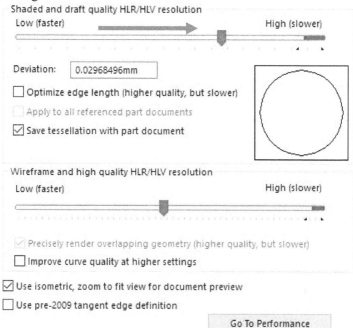

Look what happens to the model when the image quality is set to high.

Note: Notice next to High it says (slower). It may be worth it to work on your model in low quality until you want to show it off

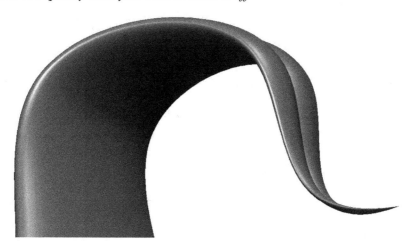

Exercise Complete

Exercise 48: Assembly 1 – Nut and Bolt

Assemblies in SolidWorks can be very straightforward. This exercise will show you how to create a very simple one. The first step is to create an assembly file. An assembly file is very similar to a normal part file. However, instead of creating geometry in the assembly file itself, the designer adds existing part files into the assembly file. The first part added to the assembly will be '**Grounded**' i.e. fixed in space. *Note: it is possible to remove the 'grounded' restriction.* All other parts added to the assembly in this exercise will be positioned using the '**Mate**' Command. The relate tools instruct the parts how to be positioned in relation to the other parts in the assembly. For example, the designer can constrain a face from Part A to be attached to the face of Part B. Once this relationship is created, the two faces will always be attached unless that relationship is removed.

Open a new **Assembly File** located in the New Document tab in the toolbar menu.

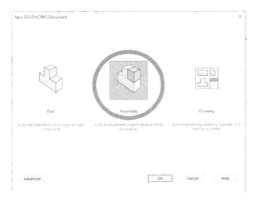

Note: Make sure to check that the units of the new assembly file correspond with the units of the parts to assemble. It is possible to change the units in the same way that they are changed in a basic part file as shown at the beginning of this book.

Once the assembly file is open, parts can be added to the assembly. The first part inserted into the assembly will automatically be positioned on the origin as the Base part when you click **OK**.

To insert components, click on the **Insert Components** Command and select **Browse** to import a file.

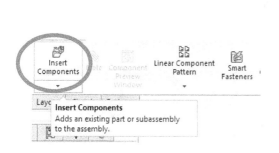

Now, browse to the folder where you saved the **Bolt.SLDPRT** and select Open. Use your mouse and move the part around the Graphics Window. To set the part directly on the origin, move your mouse over the Accept button and click on it. You will notice the bolt has now been set at the origin. Go ahead and browse your folder again and insert the **Nut.SLDPRT**. Move/drag the nut next to the bolt.

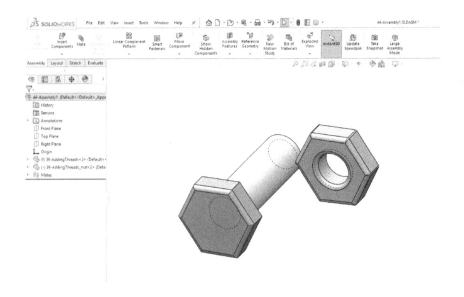

It is possible to move a part once it is in the window just by clicking on a part and dragging it in "space," or by using the **Move Component** Command in the Assembly Command Manager. Try moving the bolt. What happens? Since it was the first part into the assembly, it is grounded as described in the beginning of the exercise.

Now, to insert the nut into the bolt, use the **Mate** Command Manager. Select it from the **Assembly Command Manager.**

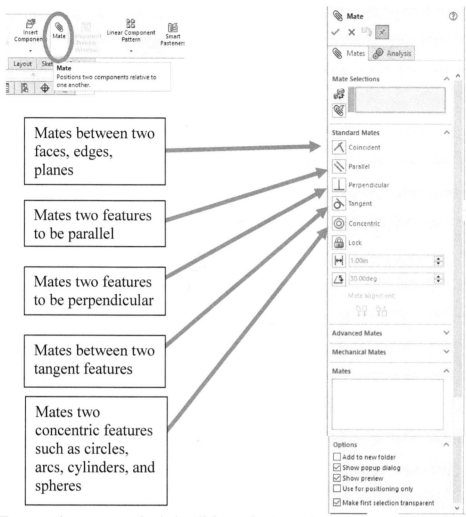

Mates between two faces, edges, planes

Mates two features to be parallel

Mates two features to be perpendicular

Mates between two tangent features

Mates two concentric features such as circles, arcs, cylinders, and spheres

To mate the nut onto the bolt, click on the Mate Command. Now select the **Concentric** mate in the Mate Properties Manager. Click on the shank of the bolt and the inner face of the nut. Once you do that, the nut will insert itself onto the shank of the bolt. The Mate Command window will appear in the Graphics Window. You have the same options as you do in the Properties Manager. Click **OK**. *Note: You can also select circular edges when using the Concentric mate. Try that instead.*

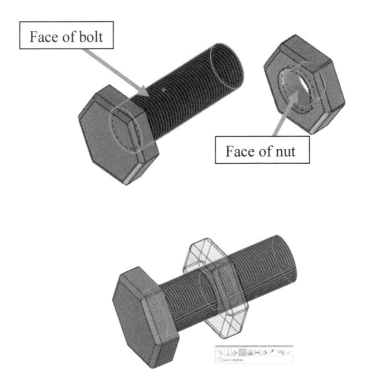

Try moving the nut by dragging it along the axis of the bolt shank. The nut is now constrained and allowed to move in **2 degrees of freedom** (one translation and one rotation).

Once you've accepted this mate, the Mate Properties Manager is still open. Now, select the back face of the head of the bolt and then the face of the nut. SolidWorks automatically selects the **Coincident** mate. Accept this mate.

Click on the front surface of the Nut, and the corresponding surface of the bolt, as shown below.

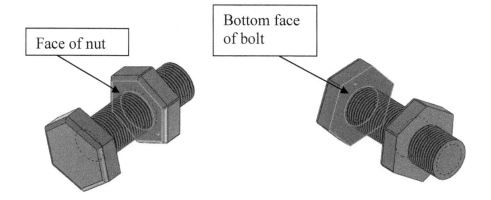

You can also align the nut and bolt so two of the faces are in the same plane.

Your assembly should resemble the figure below.

Exercise Complete

Exercise 49: Assembly 2 - The Lever

Create a solid model that looks like the part shown below. *Note: All dimensions are in inches (in).* Save this model as Lever Base.

Lever Base

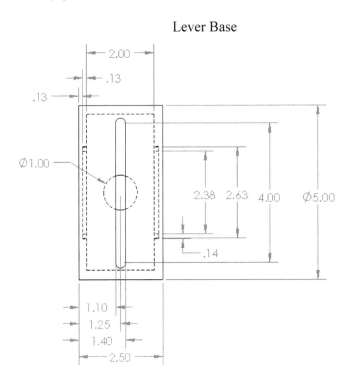

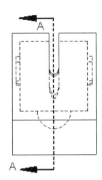

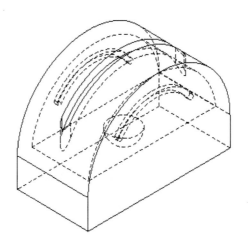

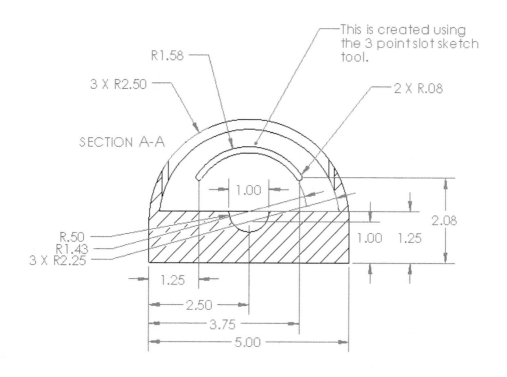

This is created using the 3 point slot sketch tool.

R1.58

3 X R2.50

2 X R.08

SECTION A-A

1.00

2.08

R.50
R1.43
3 X R2.25

1.00   1.25

1.25

2.50

3.75

5.00

Now create this model and save it as Lever Handle.

Lever Handle

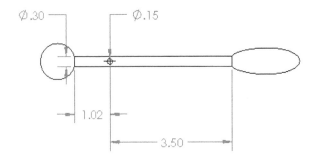

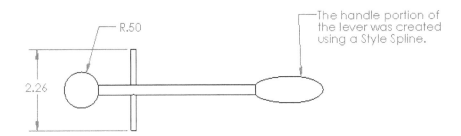

R.50

2.26

The handle portion of the lever was created using a Style Spline.

Once you've created both of the models, open an **Assembly File**. First insert the Lever Base.

Since the Lever Base is inserted first, it will automatically be fixed and everything inserted afterwards will be free floating (unless designated otherwise by the user of course). This is a good thing for us as we want the handle to move but not the base.

Now click **Insert Component** and insert the Lever Handle. You should have the following assembly.

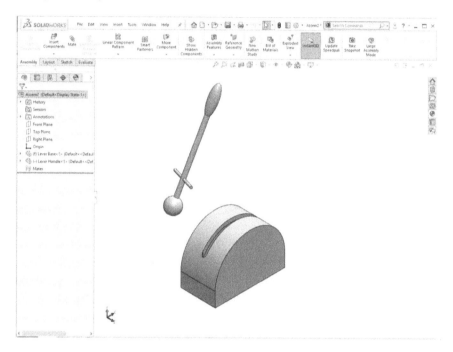

Click the "Display Style" button shown below and change the display style to "Hidden Lines Visible". This will allow us the see the features on the inside of the Lever Base much more easily and will allow us to mate the Lever Handle with said features.

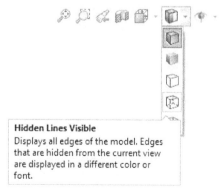

After doing this, your assembly should look like the one shown below.

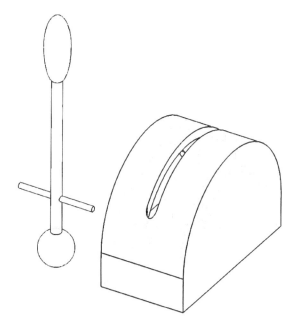

Using the **Mate** tool, mate the sphere at the bottom of the handle with the hemisphere removed from the inside of the base. Use a concentric constraint to do this. *Note: You may have to right-click the hemisphere removed from the base and click "Select other" to select it.*

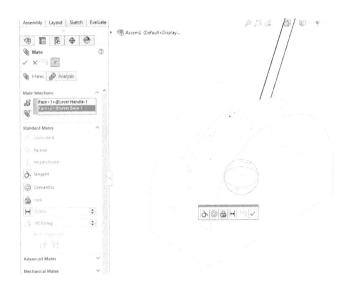

Click **OK** to create this mate. Now select the cylindrical face of one of the small cylinders jutting out from the lever handle and the curved slot in the Lever Base on the corresponding side. Use the **Slot** constraint located under the "Mechanical Mates" tab.

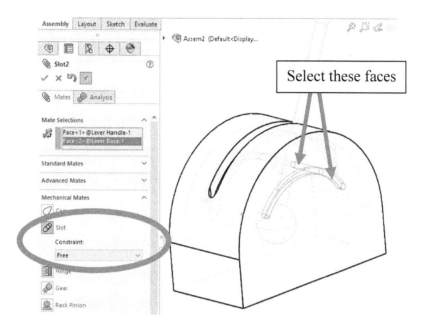

Click **OK** to create this mate and then do the same thing with the cylinder and slot on the other side. Once you've done that, go back to the "Display Style" menu and select "Shaded with Edges". You should now have the model shown below.

You'll notice that you can now freely move the lever from side to side. Give it a try!

Exercise Complete

Exercise 50: Assembly 3

Create a solid model that looks like the part shown below. *Note: All dimensions are in inches (in).*

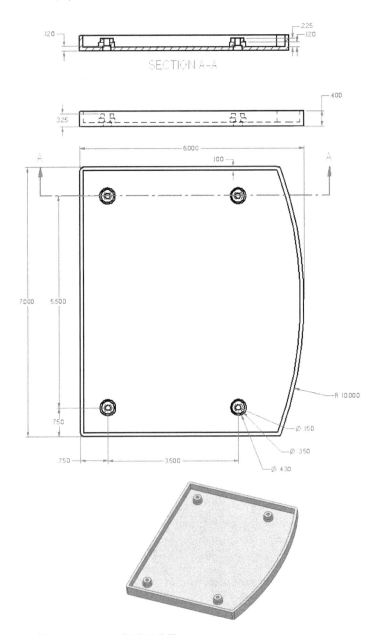

Save this file as **Bottom.SLDPRT**

Open a new part file and create a part that looks like the following figure.

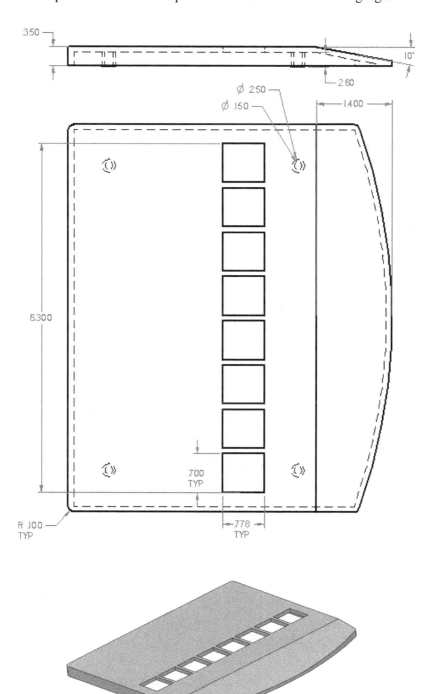

Save file as **Top.SLDPRT**

Open a new **Part File** and create a part that looks like the figure shown below.

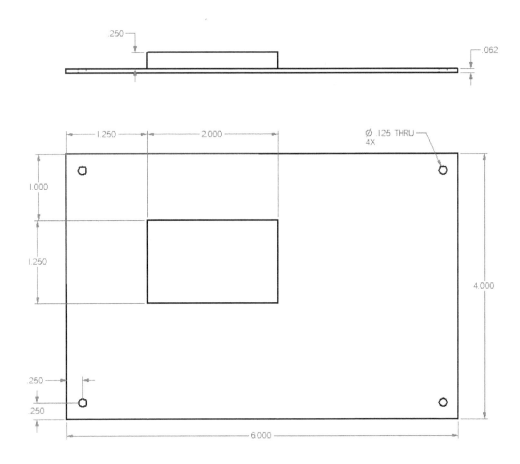

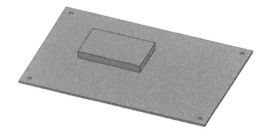

Save file as **PCB.SLDPRT**

Open one more new **Part File**, and create a part that looks like the following figure.

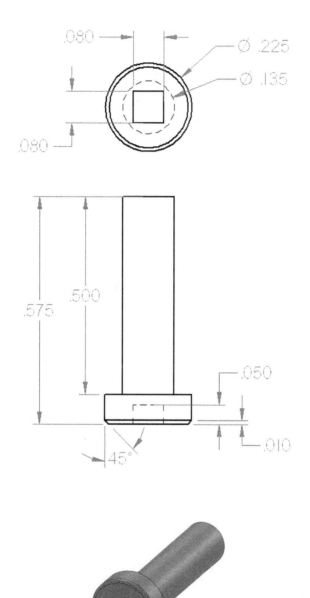

Save the file as **Bolt.SLDPRT**

Create a new **Assembly File.**

*Note: The units of the new **Assembly File** must correspond with the units of the parts that are being assembled. It is possible to change the units as shown at the beginning of this book.*

Once inside the assembly, insert the part saved as **bottom.SLDPRT**. Set it at the origin. Recall Assembly 1. Now insert the four copies of the **bolt.SLDPRT**. *Note: To insert multiple copies of the same or different components, in the Mate Properties Manager, make sure you click on the Push Pin so that it turns blue. This will keep the window open.*

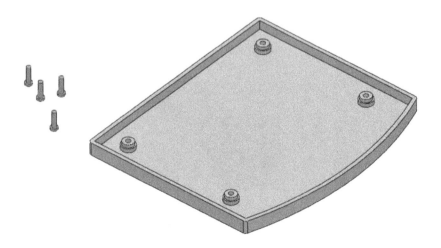

To begin to assemble the parts, click on the Mate Command. Select the shank of the bolt and the cylindrical face of one of the mounting bosses on the tray. SolidWorks automatically selects the Coincident mate. Click **OK**.

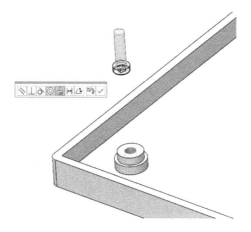

Now select the inner face of the head of the bolt and rotate the assembly to select the inner face of the tray. SolidWorks will automatically select the Coincident mate. *Note: The bottom tray's appearance was set to 'Change Transparency' for clarity by right clicking the part in the Assembly Design Tree.*

Inside face of head of bolt

Inside face of mounting boss on bottom of plate

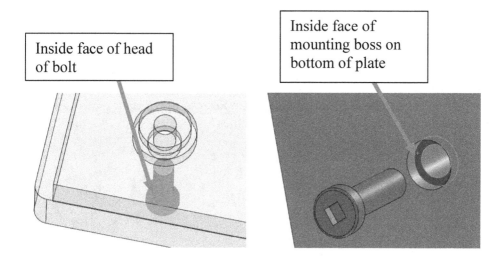

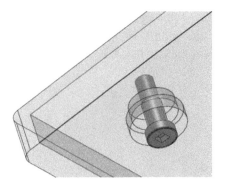 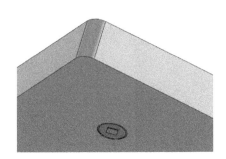

Do this for all of the bolts.

With all the bolts mated to the bottom tray, the assembly should now look like the following figure.

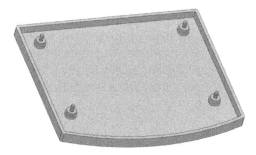

Now insert the part saved as **pcb.SLDPRT**. Mate two of the holes, opposite from each other to their corresponding bolts using the **Concentric** mate. Then select the bottom face of the **pcb** and one of the top faces of the mounting boss. Use the **Coincident** mate to mate the two parts together.

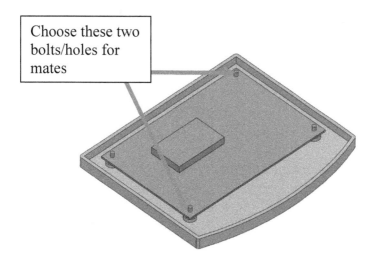

Choose these two bolts/holes for mates

Now insert the part saved as **top.SLDPRT**. **Mate/align** the shank of two bolts with the cylindrical faces of the top tray.

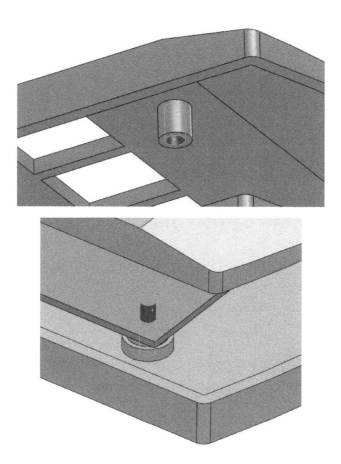

Now mate the top face of the bottom tray to the bottom face of the top tray using the **Coincident** mate.

273

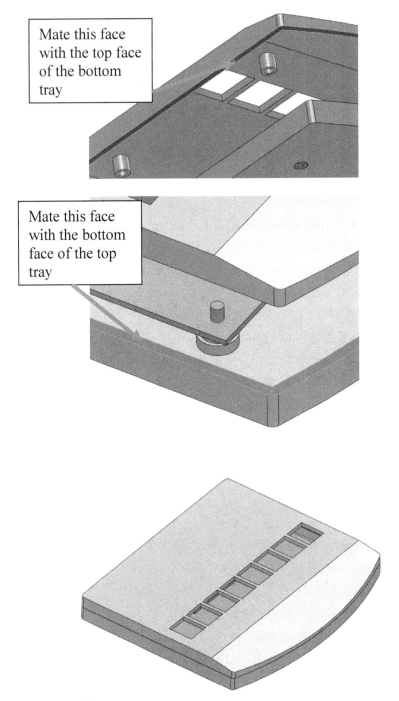

Mate this face with the top face of the bottom tray

Mate this face with the bottom face of the top tray

Exercise Complete

Exercise 51: Assembly 4 - Chain Assemblies

Sometimes during the assembly process, it can be time consuming to manually assemble repetitive instances of the same mating arrangement, and you might feel chained down by the mind-numbing repetition of it all. Luckily, SolidWorks provides us with a Linear Pattern tool in assemblies just for this purpose.

To start, create a **New Part File** and make a single link of chain like the one shown below.

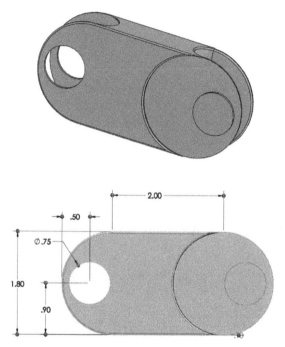

Now that we have our chain link to pattern, we need a path that the chain will follow. To make it, create a **New Part File** and in it add the sketch seen below.

With both the chain link and chain path created, we are now ready to create a new assembly. Select **File/New/Assembly** and place the chain path as the first component. This will be the grounded part in the assembly.

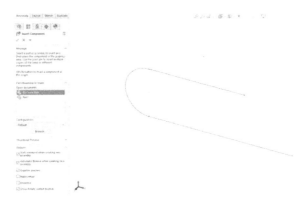

Next, insert one instance of the chain link part. Find the **Linear Component Pattern** Command (near the **Mates** Command) in the Assembly Command Manager. Select **Chain Component Pattern** from the dropdown. When selecting the path, try to select the midpoint of the arc so the entire path is selected. Fill in the following details.

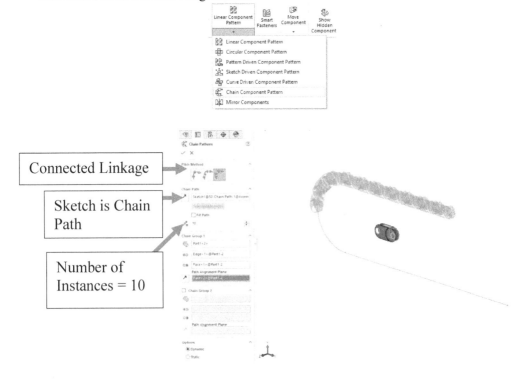

Connected Linkage

Sketch is Chain Path

Number of Instances = 10

Make sure that the entire sketch is included for the applied chain path, and that the arrow indicating the direction of the pattern points into rather than away from the line to ensure that there is enough room for SolidWorks to create all 10 instances of the chain. You can change this direction using the arrows by the Chain Path box.

For Chain Path 1, select the open circular edge as Path Link 1, the thin cylinder edge as Path Link 2, and the inside face of the slot as the Path Alignment Plane.

When you are done, you should have a continuous chain that can move freely along the sketched path. Try dragging it around!

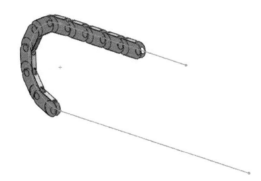

Exercise complete

Exercise 52: Assembly 5 - Pipe

Create a solid model that looks like the part shown below and **Save** it as **Pipe.SLDPRT**

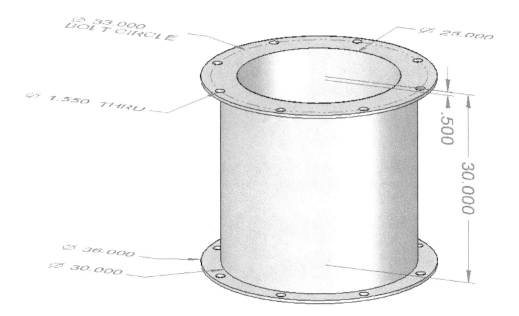

Create another part using the revolve tool that looks like the figure shown below and Save this one as **Bottom.SLDPRT.**

*Note: This part will mate with **PIPE.SLDPRT** so the number of holes, size, and their distance apart are the same.*

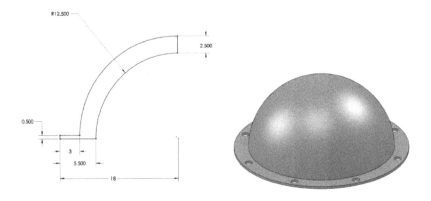

Revolve another part that looks like the figure shown below and Save it as **Top.SLDPRT.** Create the same hole pattern as the last two parts as shown below.

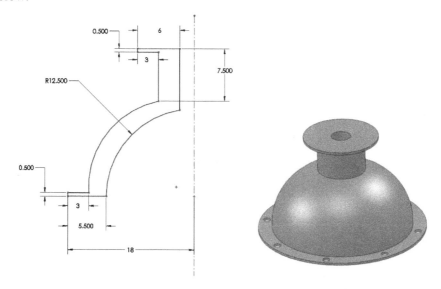

Create a new part that looks like the figure shown below and Save it as **Bolt.SLDPRT**

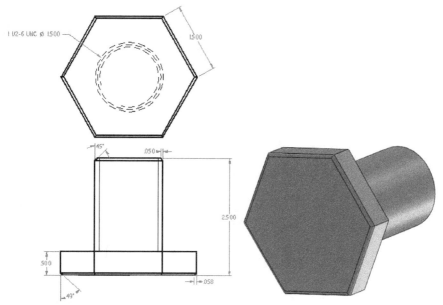

Create a **Nut.SLDPRT** and **Washer.SLDPRT** as separate part files to go with the Bolt. *Note: The Nut has the same dimensions as the head of the bolt.*

279

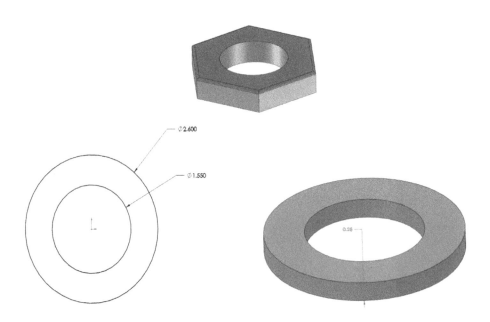

Create a new **Assembly File** and insert the **Pipe.SLDPRT, Bottom.SLDPRT** and **Top.SLDPRT** into the screen. Mate the Top to the Pipe using two of the holes and the **Concentric** Mate. Then mate the faces using the **Coincident** Mate.

Concentric mates with cylindrical faces

Coincident mate with bottom face of the Top part to the top face of the Pipe

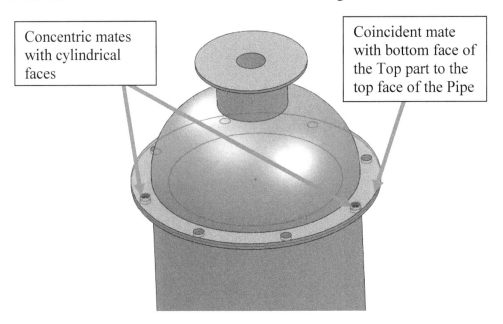

Use the same procedure to mate the **Bottom** part to the other side of the **Pipe.**

Your assembly should resemble the figure below.

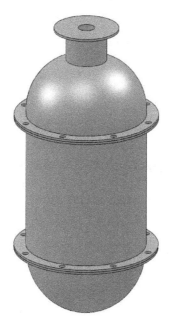

Insert two Bolts, two Washers, and two Nuts into the screen.

Mate one bolt to the Top and Pipe using the **Concentric** mate. Then mate the face of the bolt to the Top part. Then mate the washer and finally the nut.

First, click on the Bolt and the Hole to align them. Then mate the surface of the head of the Bolt to the Top piece.

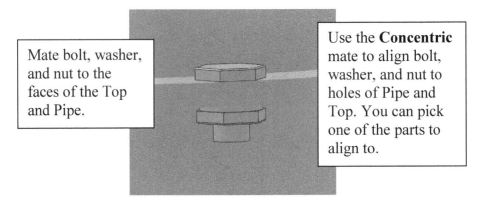

Mate bolt, washer, and nut to the faces of the Top and Pipe.

Use the **Concentric** mate to align bolt, washer, and nut to holes of Pipe and Top. You can pick one of the parts to align to.

Follow the same procedure to assemble the bolt, washer, and nut for the Bottom and Pipe.

Now you want to add the rest of the bolts. The easiest way is to pattern them. Choose the **Linear Component Command** in the **Assembly Features** Command Manager. Use the drop down and select **Circular Pattern.** In the Properties Manager, select the inner cylindrical face of the Top part for the Pattern Axis.

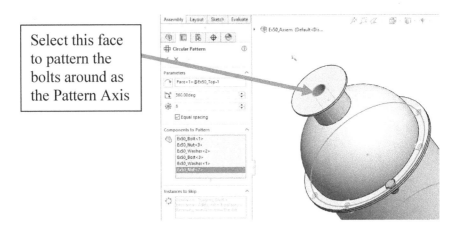

Select this face to pattern the bolts around as the Pattern Axis

Choose an angle of **360 degrees** with equal spacing and a total of 8 bolts. Then select both of the bolts, washers, and nuts from the Top and Bottom parts.

Accept the changes. Your completed assembly should resemble the figure below.

Exercise Complete

Exercise 53: Assembly 6 - "Do Nothing"

Create a solid model that looks like the part shown below and Save it as
Base.SLDPRT

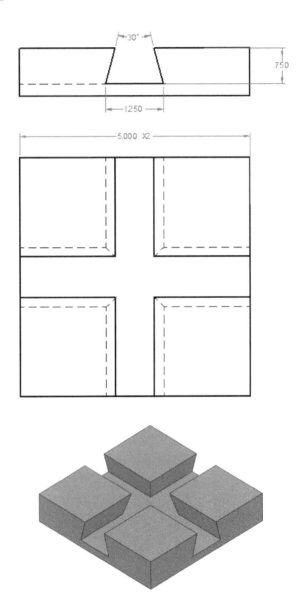

Create another part with a threaded hole in the center that looks like the figure shown below and Save it as **Key.SLDPRT**

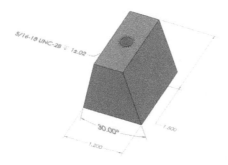

Create another solid model that looks like the figure below and Save it as **Crank.SLDPRT**

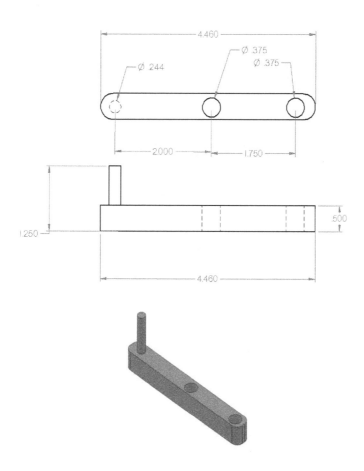

Now enter the following address in your internet browser address bar.

http://www.mcmaster.com/#90298a619/

This address will show a ready-made shoulder bolt that can be purchased from the McMaster-Carr website. *Note: DO NOT purchase this part for this exercise; this is simply to simulate using vendors' components.*

The website will show a bolt drawing that looks like the following figure.

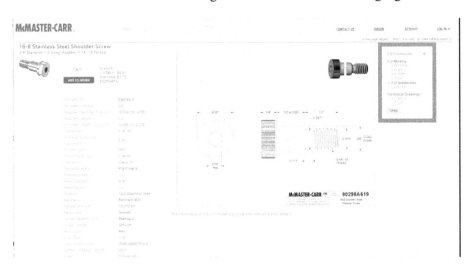

In the top right corner of the page, select the type of file to download from the dropdown menu. In this case, the **3-D SolidWorks** file will work best. Select it and click the **Save** button right below the dropdown.

Save this part as **Shoulderbolt1.SLDPRT.**

Open a new **Assembly File.**

Note: remember to change the units to inches if necessary.

Insert the Base first followed by the Key.

Mate the bottom of the Key with the Base by selecting the inner edge of the cut on the Base with an edge on the Key. Then choose the **Distance** mate and enter **0.025 in**.

In the **Mate** menu on the left type **0.025 in** into the **Placement** box and mate one angled side on the Key with the corresponding side on the Base.

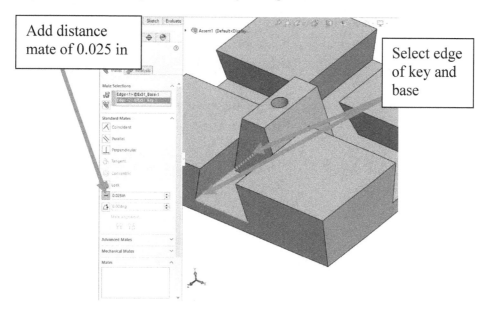

Add distance mate of 0.025 in

Select edge of key and base

Insert another Key and follow the same procedure to mate it to the Base in an adjacent slot.

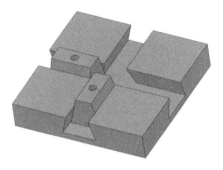

Next, insert the **Crank** into the screen, along with 2 Shoulder bolts.

Mate the bolts to the Crank using the Concentric mate. Then mate the faces using the Coincident mate. Now, using the same mates, attach the bolts and Crank to the two Keys.

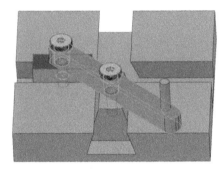

Your completed assembly should resemble the figure below.

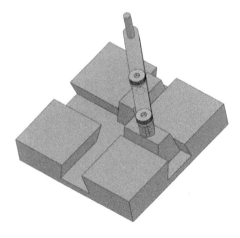

One great feature in SolidWorks (which is also included in the Student Edition) is SolidWorks Motion. This Add-In allows you to simulate real world motion and analyze an assembly when subject to motors, forces, etc.

For this exercise you will be creating a Basic Animation. At the bottom of the Graphics Area, you will notice two tabs: **Model** and **Motion Study 1.** Model is what you are already in. Click on Motion Study 1. You are now in SolidWorks Motion.

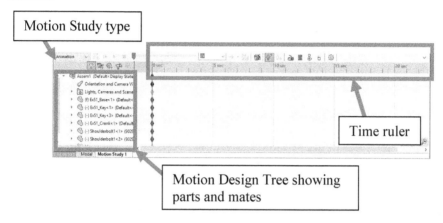

Now select a **Rotary Motor** to add it to the crank.

In the Motor Properties Manager, select Rotary Motor for the Motor Type. Below that, in the Component/Direction box, select the cylindrical face of the crank pin as shown in the following figure.

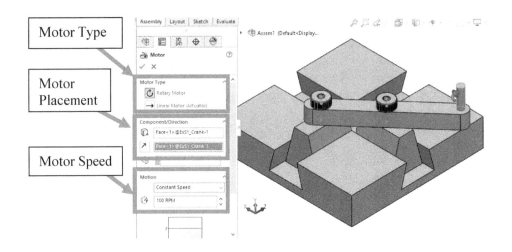

Motor Type

Motor Placement

Motor Speed

In the Motion box, leave the Motor Type at Constant Speed and change the speed to 20 RPM. Click **OK**. In the Motion Study screen, click on **Calculate.** This will run the Motion Study. You should notice your assembly moving. Play with other features, such as changing the length of play. Also try the **Animation Wizard** to create exploded views, collapsed views, and revolved views. *Note: Exploded and Collapsed views will be discussed in more depth in Exercise 62.*

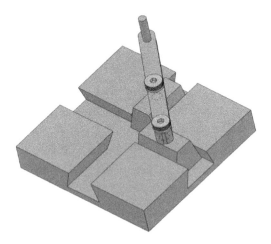

Exercise Complete

Exercise 54: Assembly 7 - Cam tool "Hurdy Gurdy"

Create a solid model that looks like the part shown below and Save it as **Back.SLDPRT.**

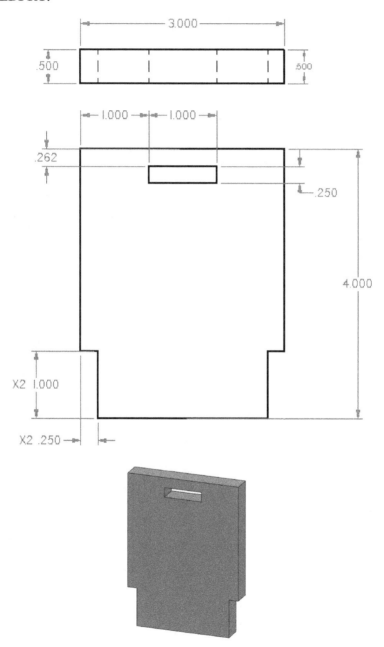

Create a part that looks like the figure shown below and Save it as **Cam Reader.SLDPRT**

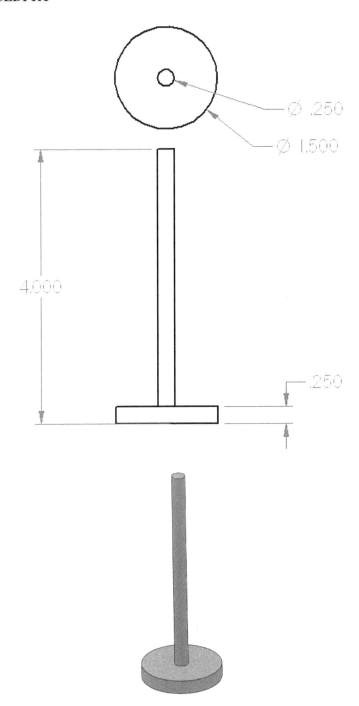

Create a part using a 3-point arc and an ellipse that looks like the figure shown below and save it as **Cam Rod.SLDPRT**

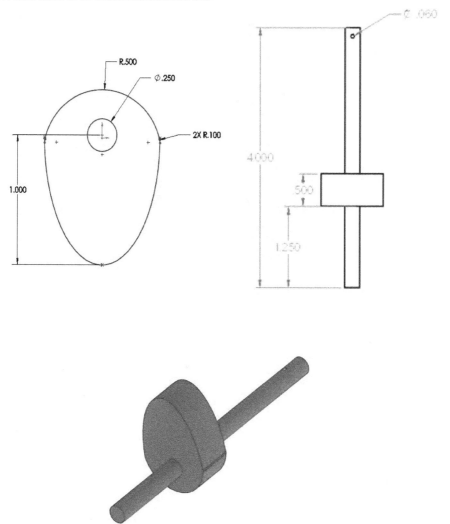

Create another part that looks like the figure shown below and Save it as **Side.SLDPRT**

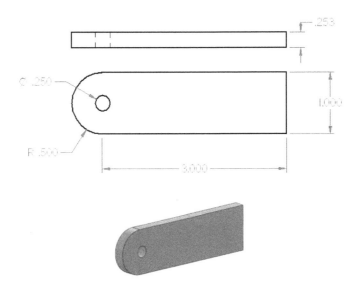

Create another part that looks like the figure shown below and Save it as **Crank.SLDPRT**

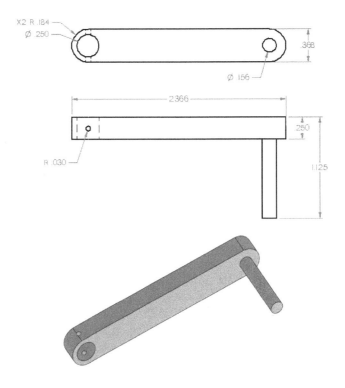

Create another part that looks like the figure shown below (with a swept cross-section diameter of .03) and Save it as **Pin.SLDPRT**

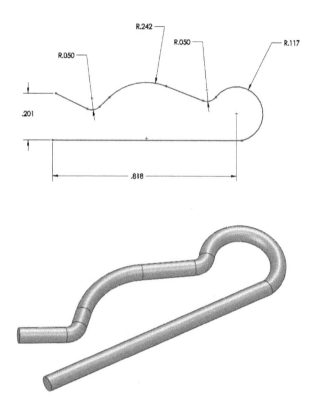

Open a new **Assembly File**.

Note: Remember to change the units to inches if necessary.

First insert the Back from the Parts Library into the screen followed by three Sides.

Position the first Side into the slot of the Back by **Mating** three pairs of faces using the **Coincident** tool. First **Mate** the two sides as shown by Selection 1, then do the same for the pairs of faces shown in Selection 2 and 3.

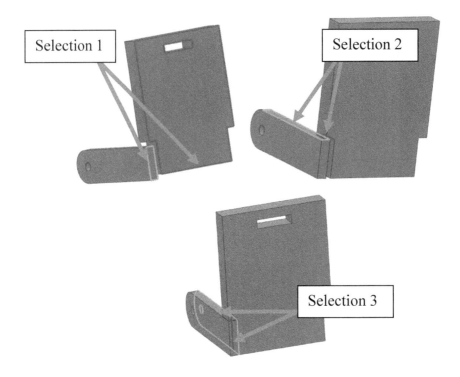

Repeat this process for the second side.

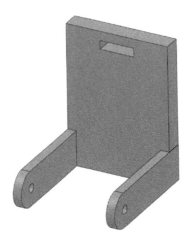

Insert another Side piece into the slot at the top of the Back by using the **Coincident** mate on the sides shown by the three images below.

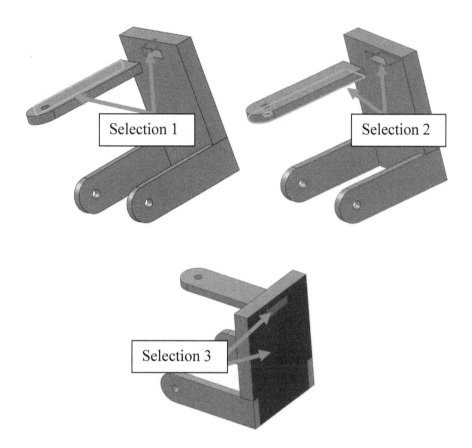

Insert the Cam rod into the assembly and mate it using the **Concentric** mate into the hole of the first Side. Then use the **Coincident** mate to mate the left face of the side to the left face of the rod. Your model should now look like the following figure.

Insert the Cam reader into the assembly. Use the **Concentric** mate for the shaft and the hole of the third Side then use the **Cam Mate** in the **Mechanical Mates** box to relate the cam to the reader.

To create the Cam Mate, select one of the curved faces on the Cam. All other curved faces of the cam should automatically select as well. In the Cam Mate Properties Manager, click on the Cam Follower box, then select the bottom face of the Cam reader.

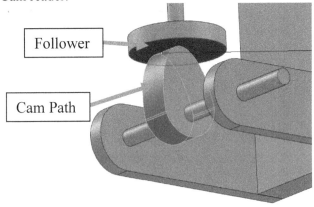

Insert the Crank into the assembly and mate the right side of the cam rod to one of the holes on the crank.

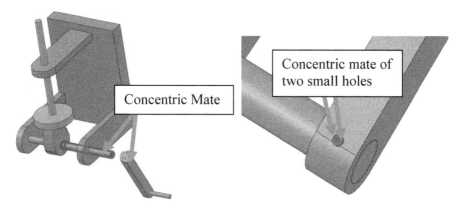

Concentric Mate

Concentric mate of two small holes

You can now insert the **Pin** as well, positioning it using a **Concentric** mate with the small holes.

Open a new **Motion Study** and place a **Rotary Motor** about the Cam rod or crank and set the speed to **20 RPM**. Accept the changes. Use **Calculate** and play the animation to watch the cam move.

Exercise Complete

Exercise 55: Assembly 8 - Top Down Assemblies with an ID Model

There is a great technique, used chiefly by people in the consumer products industry that is extremely useful. Some call it *top down modeling*, and others call it *master modeling* or *template modeling*. This technique allows you to work collaboratively in a way that gets the product on the market faster. The essence of the technique is this; you start with a single model that represents the entire exterior of a product (the industrial design) and use it to drive the shape of the actual components. In other words, the assembly has a main solid model that all the other models refer externally and associatively to.

The reason why the technique saves time and gets you on the market faster is because a number of designers can create sub-components even as the main industrial design model is changing. The part break-up can begin before the industrial design is even complete. The technique allows all sorts of folks in cross-functional groups to review the progress and make suggestions as the subcomponents are being defined.

Top Down Modeling is not quite a panacea because certain changes made to the initial model will not be tolerated by the subcomponents. Also, there are some organizations that are either too big or not sophisticated enough to keep track of the industrial design model and all that it implies. In essence, it is a technique to be used only when there is a real chance of it saving time. Some good examples are handheld meter devices, monitors, and electronic housings of many types. It is not a great technique for creating a motorcycle or a complex piece of machinery.

To practice the technique, first create a new model and save it as "**industrial design.SLDPRT**". The model should look like the one shown below.

A look at the modeling tree reveals that this model is the result of one extrusion with a first and second direction and drafts on both set to **12 degrees.**

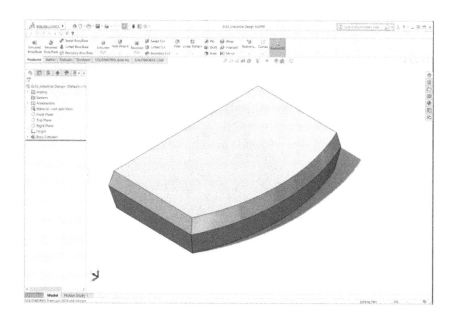

The actual dimensions of the solid are as shown below.

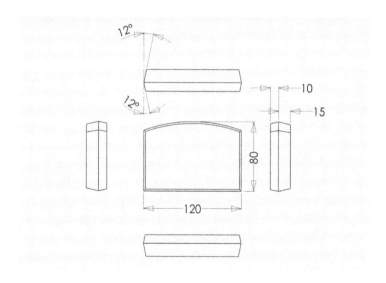

The next step is to create the assembly that will hold the industrial design model and the other pieces of the assembly. Select **File/Make Assembly from Part.** Once you select **OK** you will get the menu below.

Since the industrial design part is selected, you can click **OK** to accept it as the first component of the new assembly.

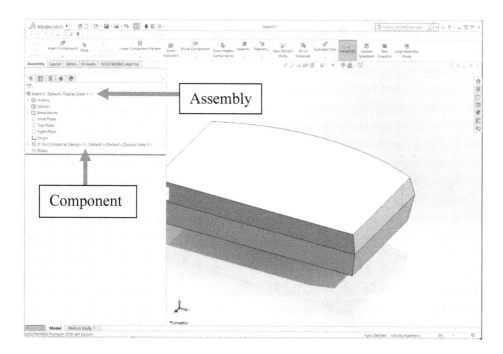

Look closely at the Feature Manager Design Tree and you will see that the component is assembled into the assembly file. The next step is to make a **New Component** that will borrow geometry from the industrial design model.

Select **New Part** from the dropdown under **Insert Components.** Click **OK.** You will now see the new part in the tree. In this example it is **Part4**.

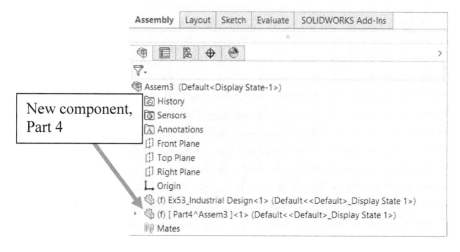

The next thing to do is right-click the new component in the modeling tree then select **Edit Part**.

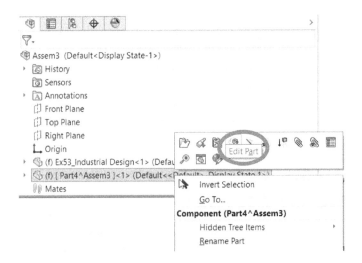

You may also right-click on the part again and use the **Rename** command to name the part **Top Cover**.

The next bit is a cool trick. In the **Surfaces** tab you will find the **Offset Surface** command. Set the offset value to zero and select all the "top" surfaces of the industrial design model. What you are doing in essence is creating associative copies of each surface into the new component.

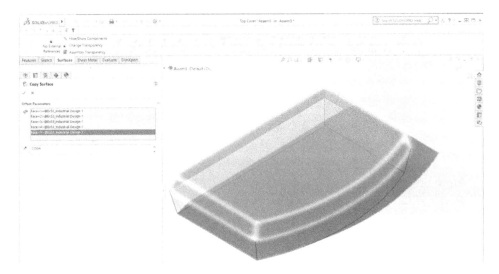

Once you have selected them all, click **OK** to signify that you are done.

Next, right-click on the new component in the model tree window and select **Open Part.**

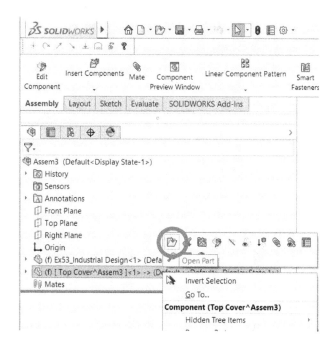

Now the new component will be the displayed part and as you can see. The copied surfaces are the only things in the file.

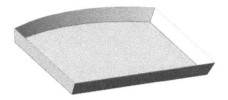

The next thing to do is open the **Surface** tab and find the **Filled Surface** command. This is the command that will enable you to create a surface on the edges of all the surfaces that you have copied from the industrial design model. The result will be a closed set of surfaces but not a solid.

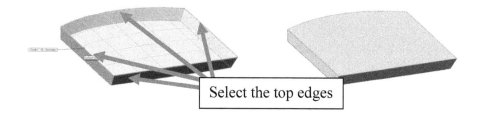

Select the top edges

Once you have the surface created, you can use the **Knit** command with the "**Create Solid**" option checked.

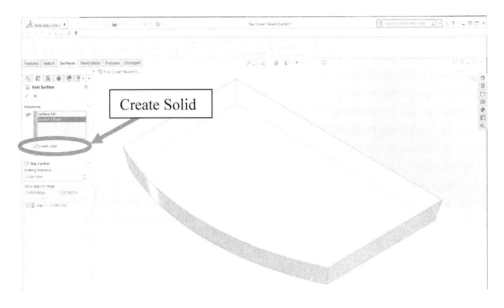

Once you have created a solid, you can add details such as the shell operation or lettering on the top that reads "Top Cover."

Next, use the **Window** command to go back to the assembly and you will see the top cover superimposed on top of the ID model.

In order to do the bottom portion of the assembly, you have to click on the Assembly part file in the modeling tree and choose Edit Assembly. Now the assembly is the active part so when you create a new component it is created in the assembly. The next step is to select **New Part** once again. Rename the part "Bottom Cover." Edit the Bottom Cover by performing the Offset Surfaces and

306

the Filled Surface commands as shown for the Top Cover. Knit it all together, Shell it, and add some text to create the model below.

When you go back to the Assembly the result looks like the figures below. On the left you have the assembly. On the right is the exploded view.

Once you have the components all done it is time to see how cool the technique is. When you change the industrial design model it controls the other models. For example, navigate to the industrial design model and change the depth of the bottom direction to 50. Next go back to the assembly and notice that there is a corresponding change in the **Assembly Part Files**. *Note: You may have to click* **Rebuild** *to update the parts with the change.*

Exercise Complete

Exercise 56: Assembly 9 - Assemblies Using Product Coordinate Systems

There are two main ways an assembly defines the geometric relationships between components: 3D location, and geometric constraint. When components are related by 3D location, which is also known as the product coordinate method, they are positioned relative to a central or global coordinate system that is shared by all the components. It is a lightweight method, but it doesn't automatically adjust the locations of the components when one in the group changes shape. For example, a three-stage rocket has a first stage that is 10 feet long, a center stage that is 5 feet long, and a final stage that is also 10 feet long. If each component is stacked in the right location, one on top of the other, the entire rocket is 25 feet high. With the 3D location method, should the center stage grow to 10 feet, the final stage doesn't necessarily relocate to the correct new height of 30 feet. The stages don't "feel" each other. There will be an overlap between Stage 1 and 2, Stage 2 and 3 or both sets of stages. In this example it is very easy to see, but in more complex assemblies it may not be.

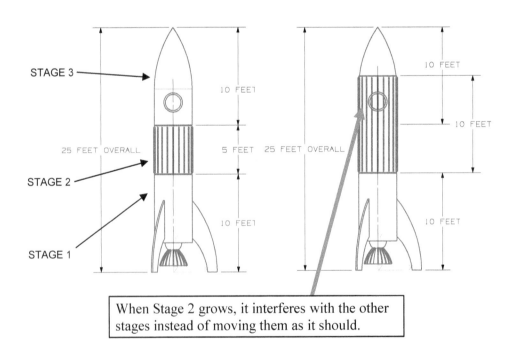

When Stage 2 grows, it interferes with the other stages instead of moving them as it should.

When assemblies are put together using geometric constraints, the surfaces, edges, centerlines, planes, and other 3-D entities are related to each other. For example, the top of Stage 1 of our rocket assembly would have a relationship with the bottom of Stage 2 and the top of Stage 2 would touch the bottom of Stage 3 as shown below.

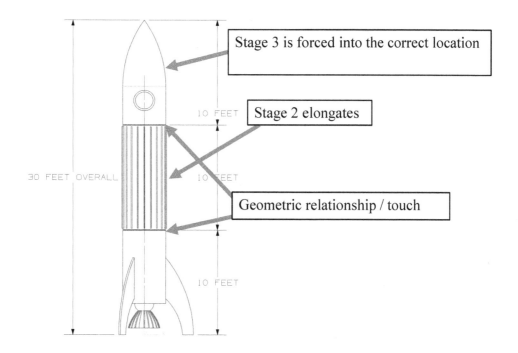

Stage 3 is forced into the correct location

Stage 2 elongates

Geometric relationship / touch

At first glance it would seem that using the "constraints" method is the way to go, but there are many other considerations. Using constraints can get very difficult when you are working on an assembly with many components. When many different groups of people are working with a large assembly, it adds on another level of complexity that makes the global coordinate or 3D location method much easier. Each contributor knows where their component has to end up in 3D space which enables a lot of work to be done without the overhead of having all the other components loaded.

Exercise Complete

Exercise 57: Assembly 10 - Assembly Level Features

In many situations, the best modeling that you can do is modeling that emulates the actual manufacturing process. For example, when a product is put together by welding two plates to each other and a hole is then drilled through both of them, the hole only exists in the welded assembly. The individual components should not show the hole. This scenario can be modeled in SolidWorks using the **Assembly Features** command. Let's try an example. In a component that you name and save as **Plate.sldprt** create a solid block that is **120mm** by **90mm** by **12mm** as shown below.

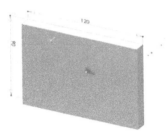

Next, create an assembly with a **60mm** overlap as shown below. You will need a **Coincident** constraint where the two plates touch, another **Coincident** constraint where they align at the top and a **Distance** constraint between the end surfaces shown below.

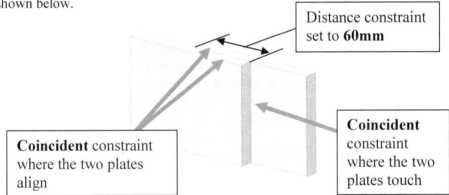

Distance constraint set to **60mm**

Coincident constraint where the two plates touch

Coincident constraint where the two plates align

Once you have created the assembly you can now apply a weld to the edges. Choose **Insert/Assembly Feature/Weld Bead** and select the faces of the plates as shown.

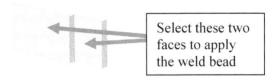

Select these two faces to apply the weld bead

Input a radius of **10mm** for the bead.

Note: You may have to enable "Weld Bead" in the "View" menu to see the weld.

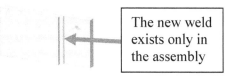

The new weld exists only in the assembly

The next operation is to drill a hole through both plates. Choose **Insert/Assembly Feature/Hole/Hole Wizard** and select the model where shown.

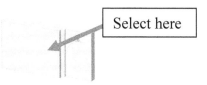

Select here

Input the following specifications:

Hole type = **Counter Bore**
Standard = **Ansi Metric**
Type = **Hex**
Hole Specification = **M16**
Fit = **Normal**
Show Custom Sizing = **Checked On**
Hole Size = **17.5**
Counter Bore Diameter = **30.71**
Counter Bore Depth = **5**
End Condition = **Through All**
Feature Scope = **All Components**

Next click on the **Positions** tab and use the sketch the dimensions shown below.

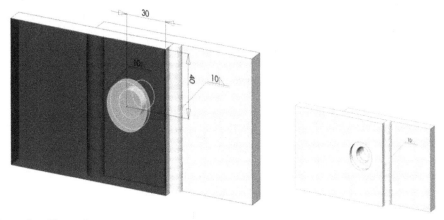

Exercise Complete

Exercise 58: Structural Members

The **Structural Members** tool, located in **Weldments**, is awesome! It allows you to drive different profiles along curves that you have made in the blink of an eye. This can be extremely useful for geometry such as chassis.

To begin, create the curves shown below. *Note: You can use 3D Sketching or sketch on different planes.*

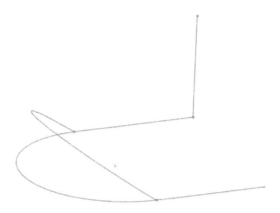

Exit the Sketch.

Click on **Insert/Weldments/Structural Member.** In this menu, you can do quite a bit.

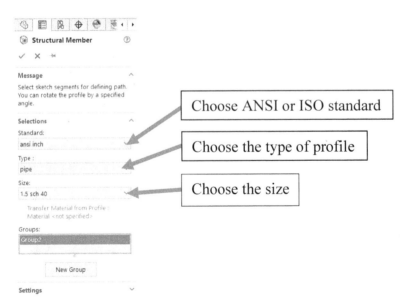

Choose ANSI or ISO standard

Choose the type of profile

Choose the size

In this exercise, specify **ANSI** standard with a **pipe** profile and a size of **1.5 sch 40**.

*Note: If you would like a different size profile than the ones listed, go through the entire process, and after you have accepted the members, you can edit the profile sketch located under the **Structural Members** icon in your part design tree.*

Click on the curves shown below.

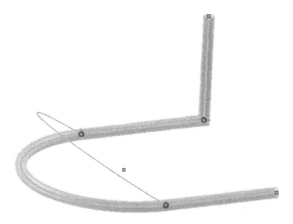

Notice how nicely the corner is mitered together automatically? There are also other corner options located in the **Settings** tab.

Now, click on the **New Group** button and select the other curved piece as shown below.

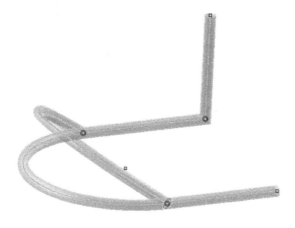

Click **OK**.

Again, the pipes are automatically mitered together neatly.

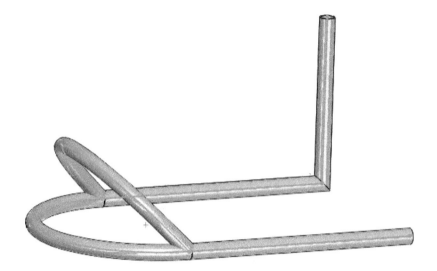

Exercise Complete

Exercise 59: DimXpert, Annotations and Introduction to Drafting

Create a **Sketch** that looks like the figure shown below and **Extrude** it symmetrically about the mid plane to a distance of **6.25 in**.

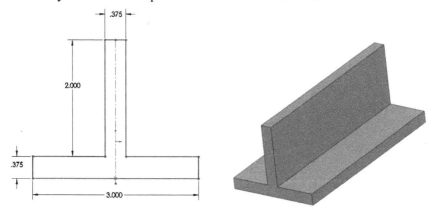

Under the Property Manager, select the DimXpert Manager. You can also set it as a tab in the Command Manager.

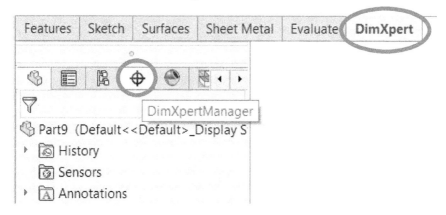

In the **DimXpert Command Manager,** select the **Auto Dimension Scheme** Command.

The DimXpert Property Manager appears.

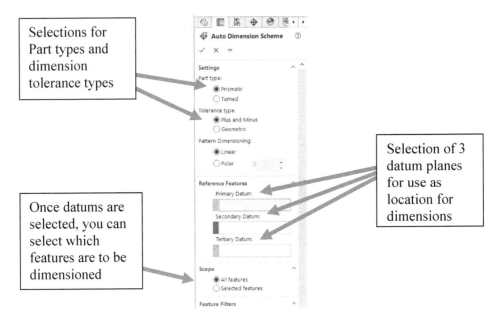

Selections for Part types and dimension tolerance types

Selection of 3 datum planes for use as location for dimensions

Once datums are selected, you can select which features are to be dimensioned

Start by selecting three planes as shown below.

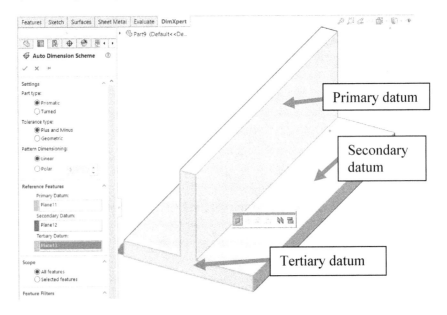

Primary datum

Secondary datum

Tertiary datum

In the **Scope**, select **All Features**. Then select the **Check All Filters** button. Click **OK**.

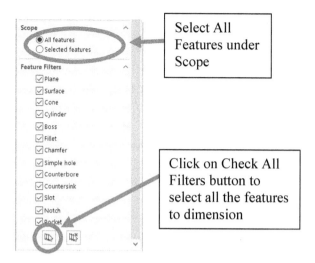

SolidWorks will calculate the dimensions and placements. Your model should resemble the figure below.

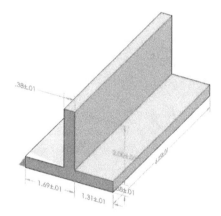

Choose the Front Plane to view the dimensions. Rearrange them for clarity.

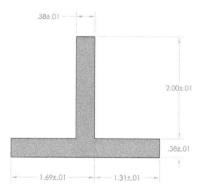

Do the same for the Right Plane. *Note: In this exercise, there are no dimensions in the Top Plane.*

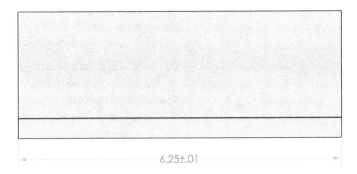

6.25±.01

Let's add some **Annotations**. Go to **Insert/Annotations/Weld Symbol**.

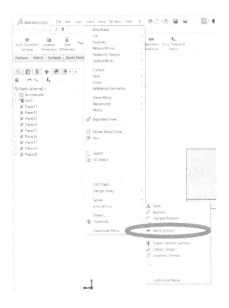

The **Weld Symbol Properties** window appears.

Start by selecting the type of weld symbol. To do so, select the **Weld Symbol** tab. The **Symbols** window opens. Click on the **Fillet** icon. The weld symbol will now appear attached to your cursor in the graphics window.

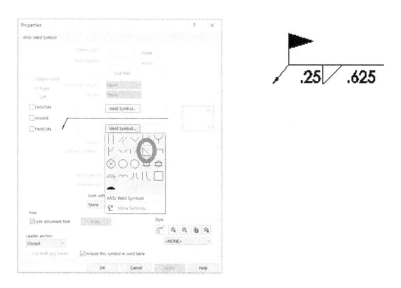

Continue to fill in the selections in the Properties window as shown below.

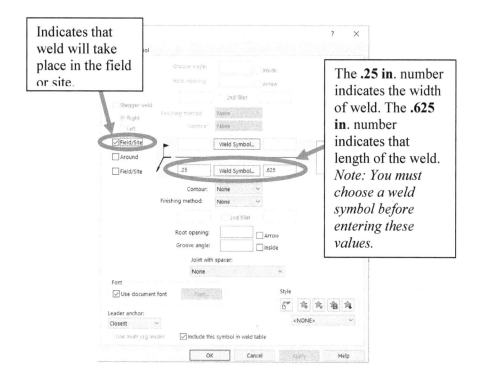

Indicates that weld will take place in the field or site.

The **.25 in**. number indicates the width of weld. The **.625 in**. number indicates that length of the weld. *Note: You must choose a weld symbol before entering these values.*

Now move your cursor over to the model and place the weld symbol on an edge. Let the edge snap and place it on the face of the model. Click **OK** to close the Weld Symbol window.

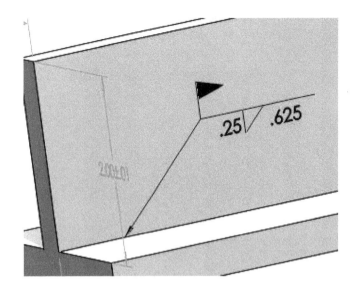

Now let's specify the **Surface Finish** of a side.

Click **Insert/Annotations/Surface Finish Symbol**. When the Surface Finish Properties Manager appears, enter the information as seen in the figure below.

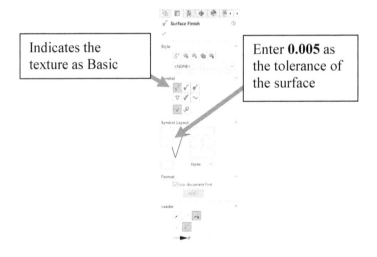

Indicates the texture as Basic

Enter **0.005** as the tolerance of the surface

Notice your cursor is now the texture symbol. Place it on the opposite side from where you placed the weld symbol. Click **OK.**

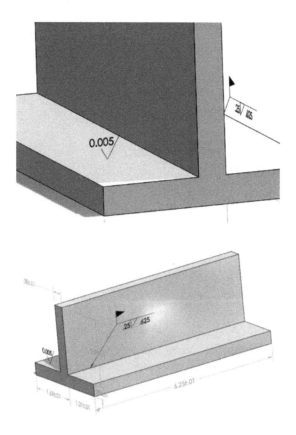

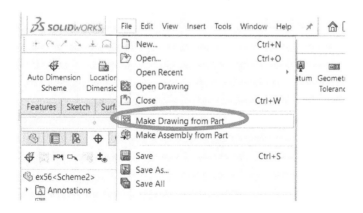

You'll now be introduced to drawings in SolidWorks. This is just a quick guide on how to add a dimensioned part with annotations into a drawing with three basic views (Front, Right, and Top). The following three exercises will provide a more in-depth overview of drafting.

While in the part, go to **File/Make Drawing from Part.**

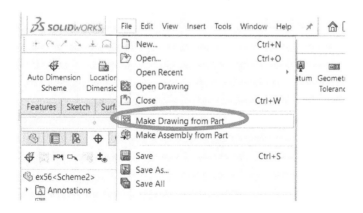

The **Sheet Format/Size** window appears. Select a **C (ANSI) Landscape** as the sheet size. Click **OK**.

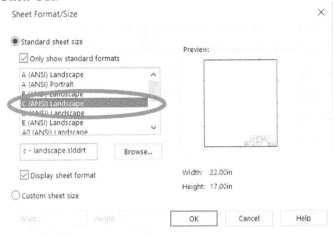

You are now in a drawing file. Your window should resemble the figure below. *Note: Make sure to check that the units are set to English units.*

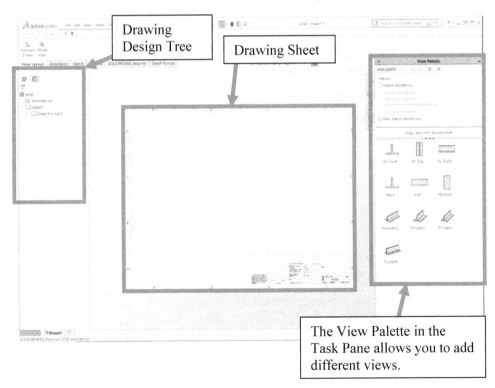

In the Task Pane to the right, the **View Palette** appears. Before you do anything there, notice the design tree on the left is now in the drawing format. Go to Sheet1, right-click, and select Properties.

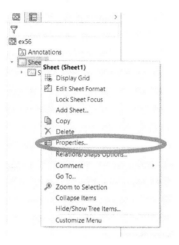

The Sheet Properties window appears. Set the scale to **2:1.5** and the **Type of Projection** as **Third Angle**. Click **Apply Changes**.

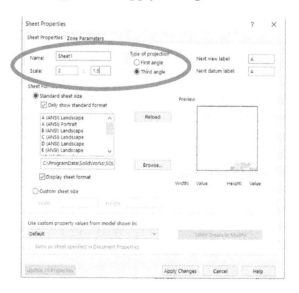

Open the View Palette in the Task Pane. Near the top, in the Options area, click on **Import Annotations,** and make sure **Design Annotations, DimXpert Annotations,** and **Include items from hidden features** are checked. Click the **Refresh** button and drag a Front view onto the sheet.

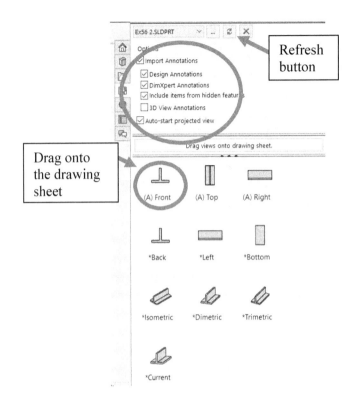

Position the Front drawing view to the far left of the sheet. Position the dimensions and delete redundant ones.

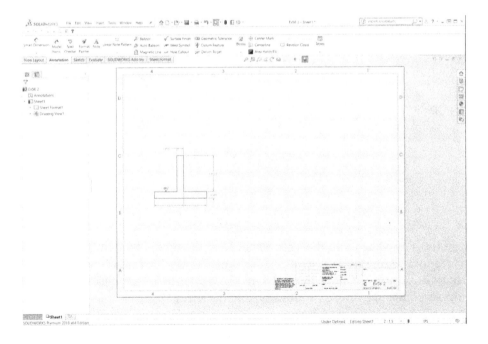

Now, go back into the View Palette manager and drag a Right view onto the sheet.

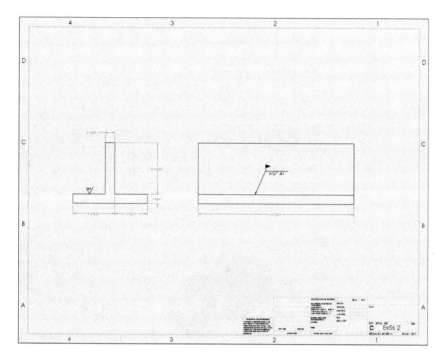

Exercise Complete

Exercise 60: Drafting 1

Create a solid model that looks like the figure below and **Save** it as **Drafting Part.SLDPRT.** *Note: Create the sketch on the Top Plane.*

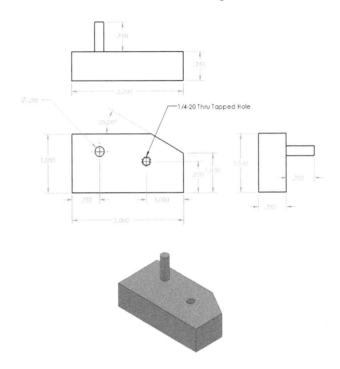

Select **File/New.** In the New SolidWorks Document Window, click **Drawing** then **OK**. You can also go to **File/Make Drawing from Part** while in the **Part File**.

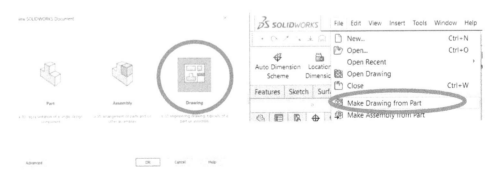

The **Sheet Format/Size** window appears. Select **B (ANSI) Landscape** and click **OK**.

The drawing sheet will now appear in the Graphics Window.

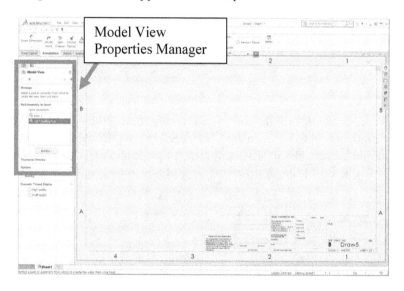

If the part you just created is still open, it will appear in the Model View Properties Manager. In the manager, double click on the part. You are now able to insert it as a model view, usually choosing to insert the part in an Isometric View. The Model View option appears when you first create the drawing. If you are not in the **View Layout Manager,** select it. Click on **Standard 3 View** to insert your part by double-clicking on it in the Properties Manager.

You now have the standard Front, Top, and Right views of your model.

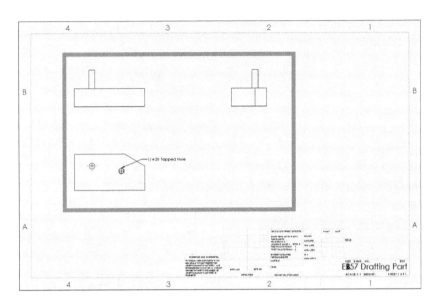

Go ahead and right-click on the top two views and delete them. Now, in the View Layout Command Manager, select **Projected View.** Click on the remaining view, drag the cursor downwards, and click to place the view. Now do the same thing again, but this time drag to the left of the remaining view. Accept the changes.

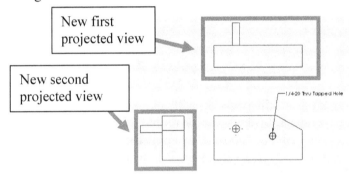

Now drag both the views to opposite sides of their initial placement.

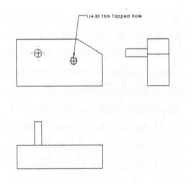

328

Insert one more projected view. This time, drag your cursor to the top right of the base view. You will get an **Isometric View**. Position it in the top right corner of the drawing.

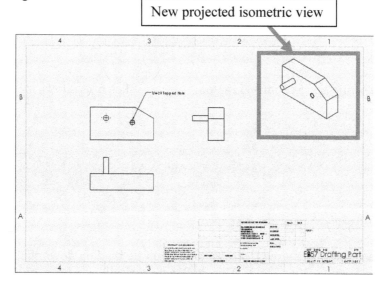

New projected isometric view

To change the scale of the views, select the base view. In the Drawing View Properties Manager, scroll down to **Scale.** You have the option to change the scale to a preselected type or your own. The default for this drawing is set at 1:1.

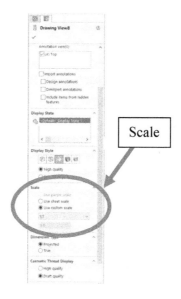

Scale

To sect the view, use the **Section View** tool from the View Layout Command Manager. Within this tool, there are a variety of section types. In this exercise, you have a hole and a cylinder that are offset, so it works well to use the Aligned Section View.

Before selecting the **Section View** tool, create a sketch as shown in the figure below.

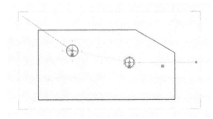

Now, select the 3 lines used to create the sketch by holding down the **Shift** key. Select the **Section View** tool. This will automatically create a cross-hatched Aligned Section View. Position it above the base drawing as shown in the figure below.

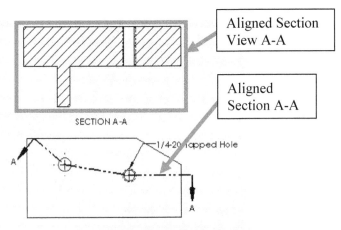

To create a close-up view, or detailed view of a feature, use the **Detail View** in the View Layout Command Manager.

The Detail View will prompt you to create a circle of the area you wish to 'enlarge.' Choose the cylinder. Snap the midpoint of the top of the cylinder and create the circle. Now position the detailed view at an angle to the left of the view.

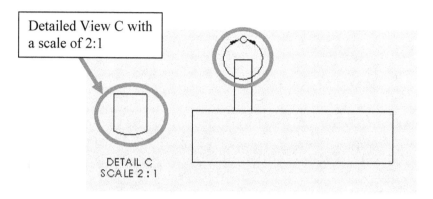

Detailed View C with a scale of 2:1

DETAIL C
SCALE 2 : 1

Now click on the new detailed view. You can change the type of the detail. In the Properties Manager, in the **Detailed** Circle box, under **Style,** select **Connected.**

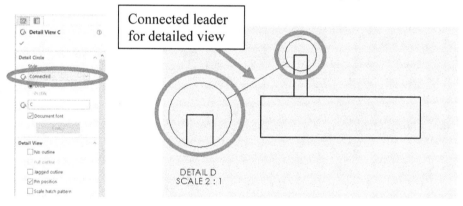

Connected leader for detailed view

DETAIL D
SCALE 2 : 1

Now, create a centerline for the hole in Section A-A, the bottom view, and the right view. In the Annotation Command Manager**,** select the **Centerline** Command. Now click the edges of the hole and accept. *Note: In order to see the holes in the bottom and right views, it is necessary to change the view style. To do so, click on each view and, from the Properties Manager under **Display Style,** select **Hidden Lines Visible**.*

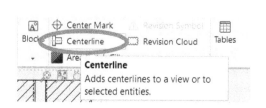

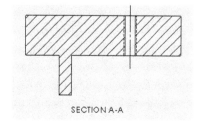

SECTION A-A

Finally, go ahead and dimension the drawing using **Smart Dimension** in the Annotation Command Manager.

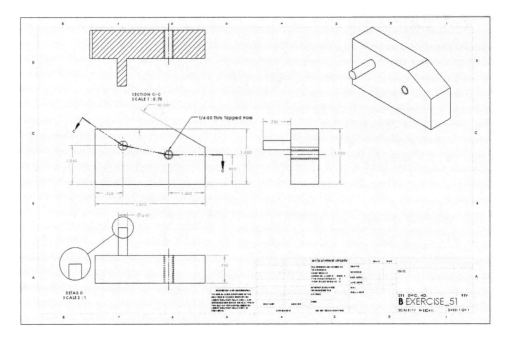

Exercise Complete

Exercise 61: Drafting 2 - Broken View

Create a solid model that looks like the part below.

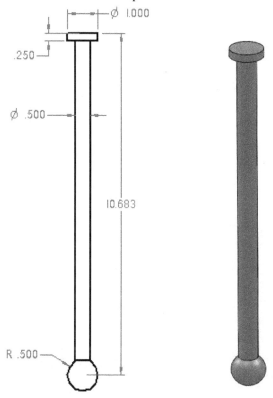

With the part open, go to **File/New**, and create a new drawing. Select an A size format *(A (ANSI) Landscape)* drawing.

Double-click in the Model View Properties Manager and position the part in the drawing. Then go to the View Layout Command Manager and select **Break View.**

In the Broken View Properties Manager, a prompt appears.

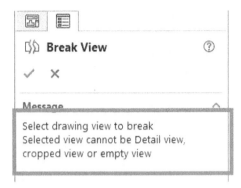

Click on the part you inserted into the drawing.

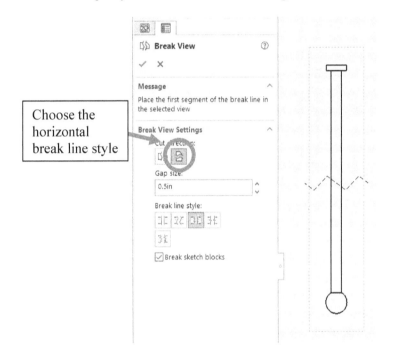

Choose the horizontal break line style

Your cursor now will change to a broken horizontal line. Move your cursor over the center of the part and click to position it. A second line appears. Position it right below the previous line. Your part has now been broken. Change the gap size to **0.20 in** and the Break Line Style to **Curve Cut.** Click **OK**. *Note: If you want to shorten the length of the part with the Break Line Command, drag the horizontal lines farther apart.*

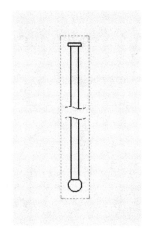

Create a Top view of the cylinder with **Hidden Lines Visible**. Now dimension your drawing.

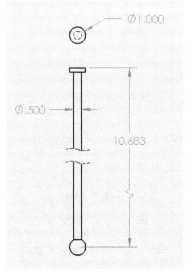

Exercise Complete

Exercise 62: Drafting 3 - Assemblies

Create a solid model of each of the parts below.

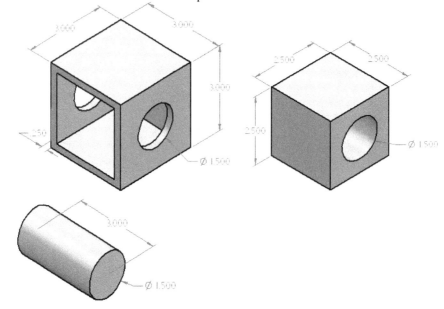

Create a new **Assembly File** and assemble the parts like the figure below.

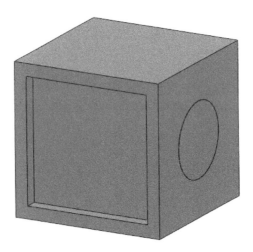

In the Assembly Command Manager, select **Exploded View.**

Click on the right face of the pin. The triad appears. Click on the arrow that moves the pin to the right (X-direction). Drag the pin out and position it to a location you like.

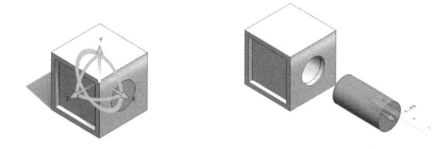

Do the same thing for the inner block and move it out in the Z-direction.

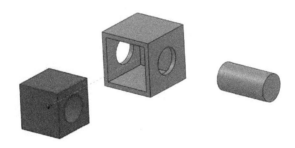

Accept the changes in the Explode Properties Manager. *Note: You can collapse the exploded view by right-clicking the assembly in the Design Tree and choosing* **Collapse.**

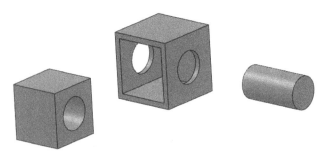

Create a new **Drawing File** with the format set to *B (ANSI) Landscape*. Place an Isometric Exploded view of the assembly. Then, from the Annotation Command Manager, select **Table.** In the dropdown, select **Bill of Materials.**

A prompt appears asking you to select the drawing. Select the assembly. In the Bill of Materials Properties Manager, the default selection is to Create a new table. Click **OK** then choose a location on the drawing to position the table.

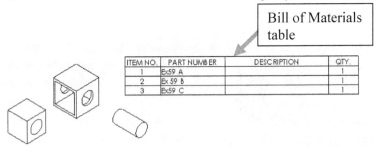

Bill of Materials table

ITEM NO.	PART NUMBER	DESCRIPTION	QTY.
1	Ex59 A		1
2	Ex 59 B		1
3	Ex59 C		1

To add a title to your drawing, go to the Feature Design Tree, right-click on **Sheet Format,** and select **Edit Sheet Format.** Double-click the box that contains **Title** and type in your desired title. At this time, you can also change the font and sizing. Click **OK** and return to **Edit Sheet.**

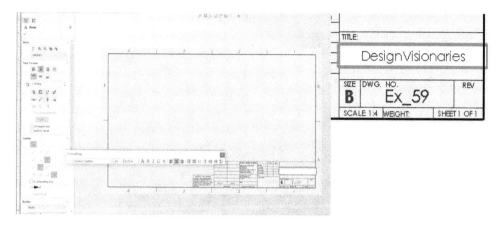

Your drawing should now resemble the figure below.

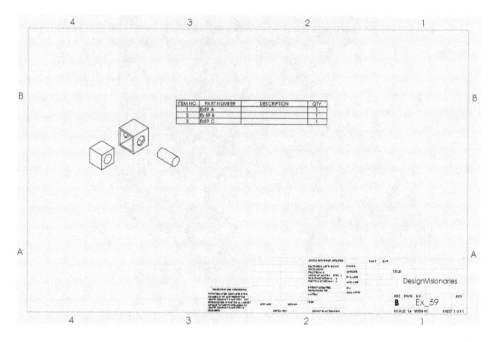

Exercise Complete

Exercise 63: Pack and Go

Once you are done creating all your models, assemblies, drawings, simulations, and more, it may feel like you're ready to send them off to your customer or manufacturer. However, it is sometimes quite a task to put together a nice package of everything you need. If you find yourself lost in a mess of files, **Pack and Go** is your friend.

Open your **Assembly File** from Exercise 54. If you haven't done that exercise yet, download the assembly from our website at *www.designviz.com/goodies*.

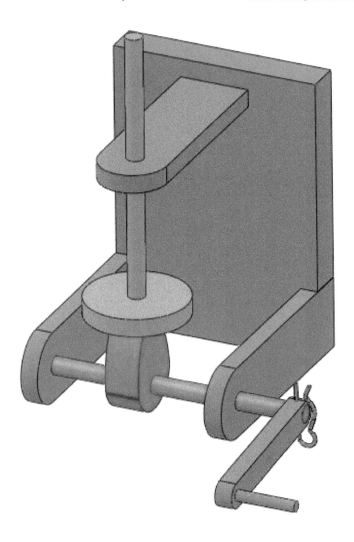

Within the Assembly, go to **File/Pack and Go.** The **Pack and Go** Wizard will appear.

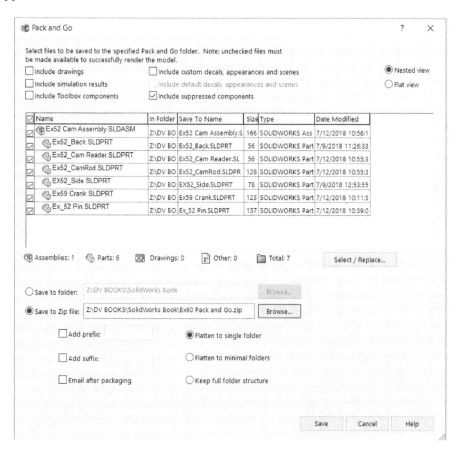

At the top of the window, you have the option to include drawings, simulations, decals etc. *Note: Also try this exercise with an assembly loaded full of drawings, simulation results, decals, and parts to see the full range of possibilities.*

This tool will automatically include all part files associated with the assembly, including the assembly file. If you would only like to bring part of the assembly along, simply uncheck the boxes next to the parts you don't want.

Next, you get to decide whether you want to save your new files to a folder or to a zip file. Choose **Save to Zip File** and browse to the location you would like to place the zip file. *Note: You can add a prefix or a suffix to each file in the package to make it easy for you to specify the difference between files in the future.*

After you click **Save**, your files are copied to the location you specified.

Exercise 64: Sheet Metal 1 - The Basics

The sheet metal commands in SolidWorks are geared toward enabling you to create good sheet metal geometry that can be un-bent into a flat pattern. The advantage of using the sheet metal commands is that they automatically take care of things like uniform wall thickness, bend radius, and calculation of the deformation. The biggest justification for using the full library of Sheet Metal commands is that the commands enable you to quickly create appropriate geometry that would be difficult to do using the other modeling tools. When you create a sheet metal bracket and subsequently un-bend it, it's a great way to validate that your part is actually manufacturable.

For example, the bracket shown below was built using a few of the sheet metal commands. Once done, the design could be flattened to make the flat pattern necessary for the manufacturing stage.

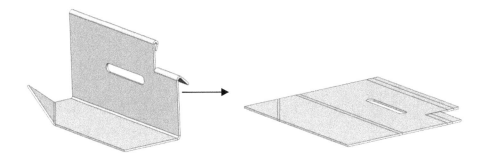

There are three basic methods in SolidWorks that you can use to produce good sheet metal parts. The first method is as follows:

1. Create a **Base Flange.** This is a flat extruded model that is "smart." It has the extra knowledge in the database to allow it to be flattened later. You must check the defaults such as the material thickness and the default bend radius.
2. Add on all the cool features, such as **Edge Flanges**, **Jogs**, **Bends** etc.
3. Use the **Unfold** command to ensure that what you are creating can be unfolded.
4. **Fold** it back when you're done.

The second method is to produce a sold model that represents the sheet metal piece that you desire, and then use the **Convert** command.

The third method is to create a solid that represents the flat pattern using the **Base Flange** command, then use the **Bend** command to create the sheet metal shape.

For example, you can begin by selecting **Insert/Sheet Metal/Base Flange** or by selecting the **Base Flange** from the **Sheet Metal** Tab Command Manager. Remember that you can add or remove the visible tabs by right-clicking an existing tab.

Using this command is very similar to creating an extrusion. You sketch a profile on the datum plane of your choosing and, upon exiting the sketch, SolidWorks applies the default thickness.

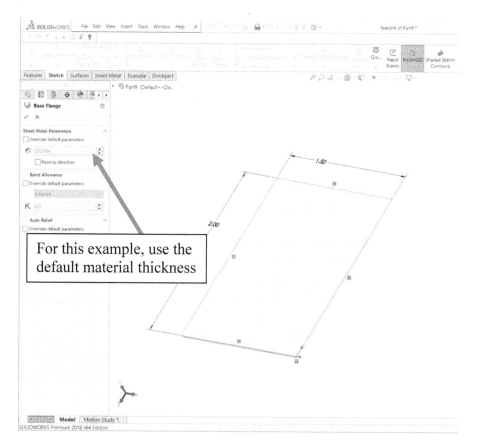

For this example, use the default material thickness

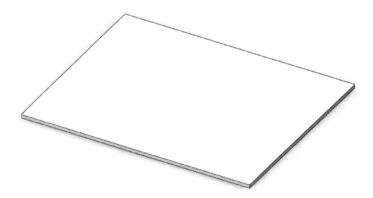

Once you have created the **Base Flange**, look at the Design Tree. You'll notice a new folder called Sheet-Metal. This folder contains many of the properties that can be set for the sheet metal features of your part.

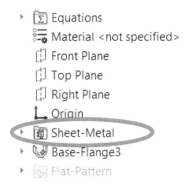

Go ahead and right-click on the **Base Flange** to select Edit Feature. You'll notice that the sections for Sheet Metal Gauges, Bend Allowance, and Auto Relief have disappeared. To edit these properties now, you must right-click the Sheet-Metal folder and select Edit Feature. To edit properties of specific features, click the dropdown by the folder and select the feature you want to edit.

The next part of the exercise is to add two flanges to the base flange that you have created. To do so, select the **Edge Flange** command from the Sheet Metal Command Manager. Select the bottom edge of the short side of the base flange.

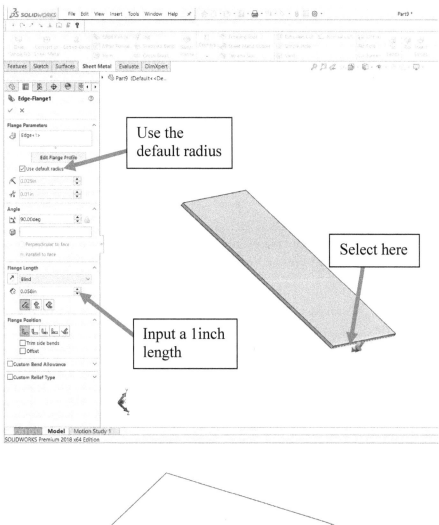

Use the default radius

Select here

Input a 1inch length

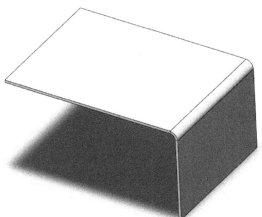

When using the **Edge Flange** command, it is sometimes important to edit the width and shape of the flange. To do this you can use the **Edit Flange Profile** command. To continue with the exercise, select **Edge Flange** then select the edge that is shown in the diagram below.

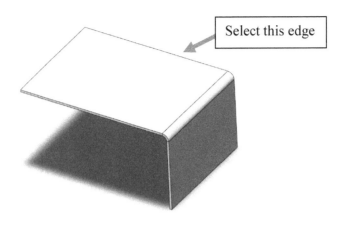

Select this edge

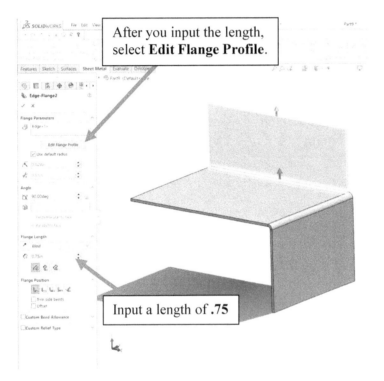

After you input the length, select **Edit Flange Profile**.

Input a length of **.75**

The profile appears and you can edit it using various methods such as putting in different lines, arcs, dimensions, and trims. In this example, create the entities shown in the following diagram, then use trim and dimensions to create the new shape.

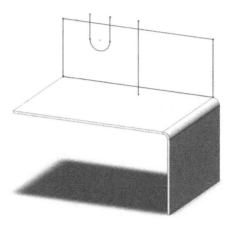

The new profile defines the new shape of the flange. Dimension it as shown.

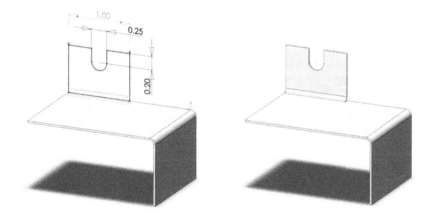

The **Edge Flange** command is also able to create geometry on rounded edges. To try it out, use the existing geometry and make an extruded cut as shown below.

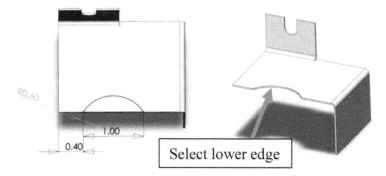

Select lower edge

Next, select **Edge Flange** and select the lower edge of the cut out. Input a flange length of **0.3**.

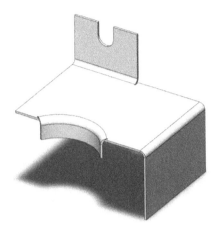

The **Base Flange** command can also be used with a circular sketch to produce a circular flange. To try it out, create a new **Part file** with nothing in it but a sketch with a single arc.

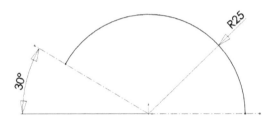

Now select the **Base Flange** command and use a direction value of **1.5**. Use the default thickness.

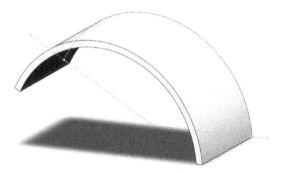

Exercise Complete

348

Exercise 65: Sheet Metal 2 - The Hem and Miter Flange Tools

Now that you have created a simple sheet metal model, let's do something a little more complex. In a new **Part File**, choose the **Base Flange** command and make the following sketch.

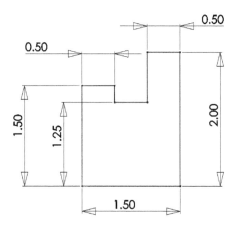

Once the sketch is done, switch the **Use Gauge Table** button to on and use **Gauge 16** for the sheet metal thickness. *Note: If the 'Sheet Metal Gauges' section does not appear in the Properties Manager, create the part then edit the gauge from the Sheet-Metal folder in the Design Tree.*

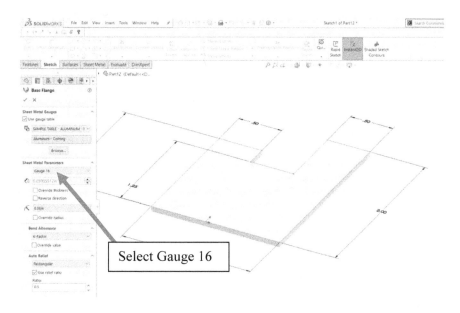

Select Gauge 16

Next add on a hem. Select the **Hem** tool from the Sheet Metal Command Manager.

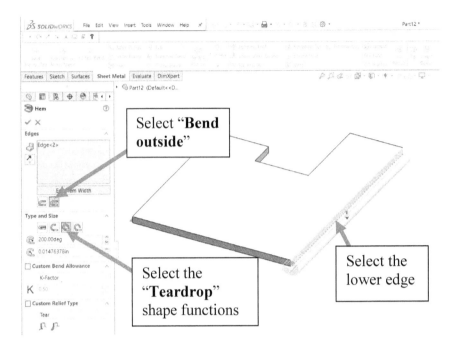

Select "**Bend outside**"

Select the "**Teardrop**" shape functions

Select the lower edge

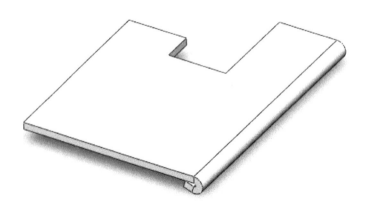

The next type of sheet metal feature that we will add is the **Miter Flange.** The Miter Flange is extremely useful because it allows you to sketch out the path of the flange with as many bends as you want. The geometry is then created along that path.

Select the **Miter Flange** tool and select the edge of the existing geometry. A plane will be created that you may sketch on.

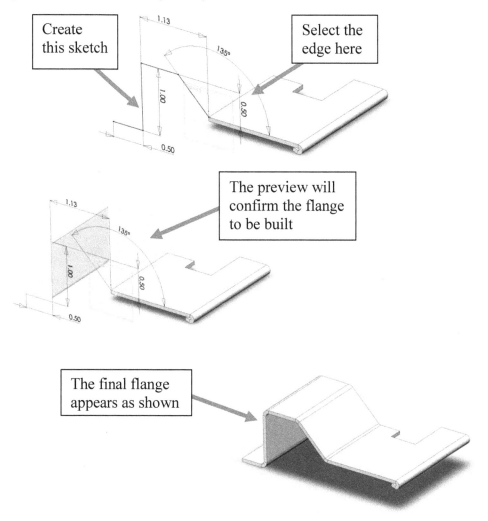

Exercise Complete

Exercise 66: Sheet Metal 3 - The Jog Tool

The **Jog** feature allows you to take existing geometry and add in a section as if you need it to go up and over something or down and under something. This is accomplished by creating a sketch that must be one single line entity. The sketch serves as the start point for the jog. You then give it a **jog offset** which determines how high or low it will go.

To proceed with this exercise, begin by creating a base flange of the dimensions shown. Accept the default thickness.

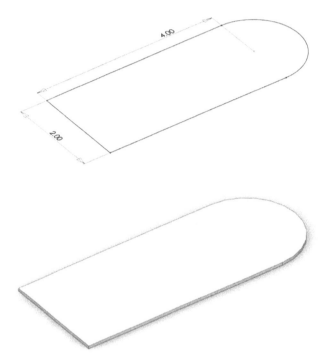

Next, select the **Jog** command from the Sheet Metal Command Manager. Select the top face of the existing geometry and create the single line sketch shown below.

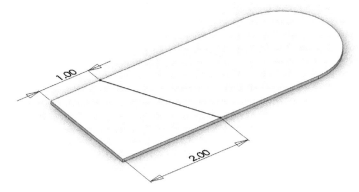

Once you have created the sketch, you must select the side of the flange that will stay stationary. Then, enter **1 in** for the Jog Offset.

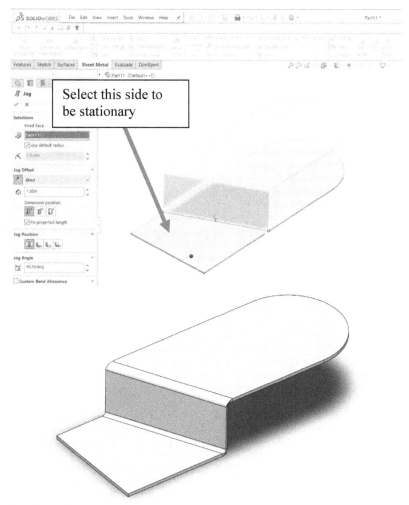

Select this side to be stationary

Exercise Complete

Exercise 67: Sheet Metal 4 - Lofted-Bend

There are two kinds of lofts when using sheet metal: formed lofts and bent lofts. Both have their advantages and disadvantages. Bent lofts are comprised of a series of faces with angular bends between them. They are useful when you need to accommodate sharp angles. However, bent lofts can get messy if you try to use them on a curved sketch. That's where formed lofts come in handy. Formed lofts are smooth surfaces, resulting in a cleaner look, but they cannot be used on sketches with sharp angles.

To illustrate these lofts, we'll create two lofted sheet metal parts. Open a new **Part File** and create the following sketch on the front plane.

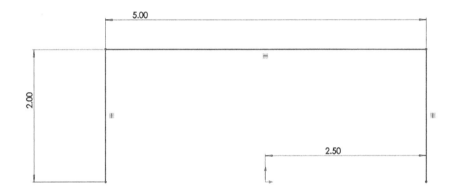

Now create a plane parallel to the Front Plane and offset by **5in**.

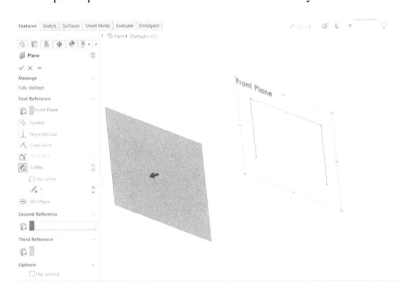

Create the following sketch on the new plane. *Note: The half-circle shares endpoints with the first sketch and the top of the first sketch is tangent to the half-circle.*

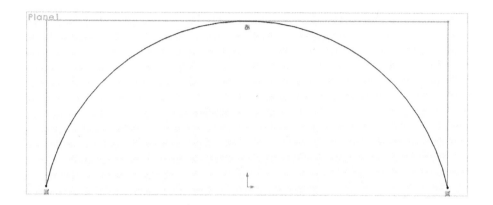

Once you have that sketched, click the **Lofted-Bend** command.

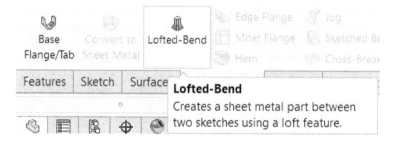

Since one of the sketches has sharp angles, we would be better off using a bent loft. Make sure that the "Bent" bubble is filled in and then select both of the sketches. You'll notice that you can change the "Facet Value", or the number of bends. Change this to 5 and change the sheet metal parameters to match the ones shown in the following picture.

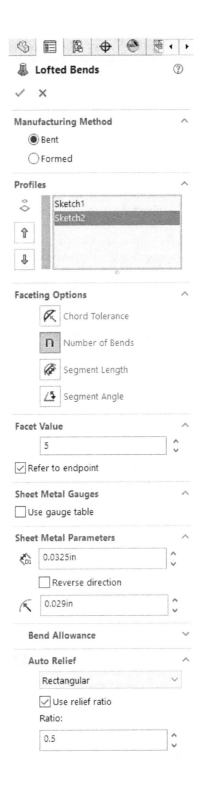

Once you have filed in this information, click **OK**. You should now have the following model.

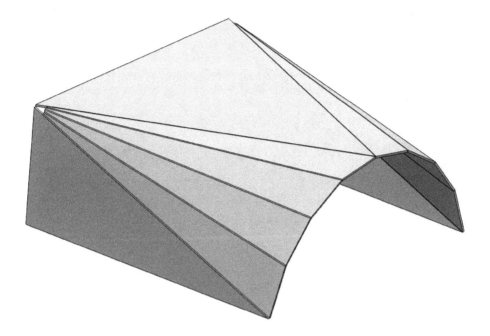

Undo the loft you just did. You should have only your original two sketches. Edit the first sketch to include the fillets shown below.

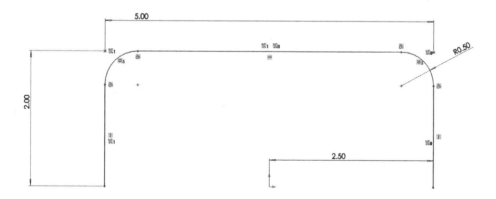

Now that you no longer have sharp edges, a formed loft may be the better choice. In a real-life scenario it will all depend on what your given project calls for, but for the purposes of this example let's say that a formed loft will work fine. Click **Lofted-Bend** again, but this time select the "Formed" bubble. After doing so, select both sketches again.

Click **OK**. You should now have the model shown below.

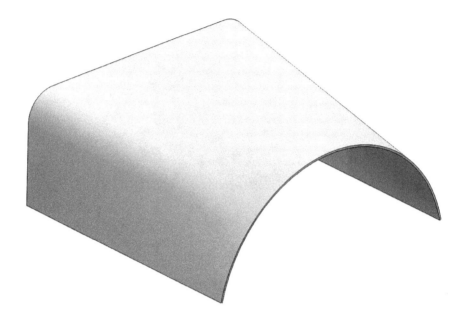

Exercise Complete

Exercise 68: Sheet Metal 5 - Gussets

Gussets are added to a sheet metal part to increase the strength and rigidity of a bend in the metal. Thanks to the **Sheet Metal Gusset** command, creating these structural supports is quite easy.

Open a new **Part File** and create the **10in x 10in** Base Flange shown below.

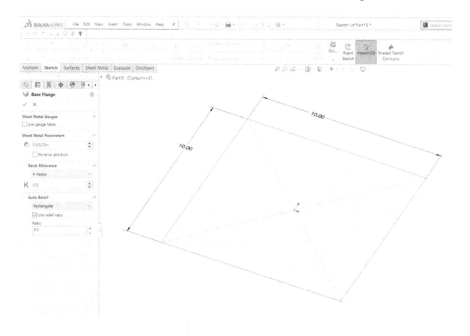

Create a **10in x 10in** Edge Flange along one of the edges of the Base Flange you just created. You should have the model shown below.

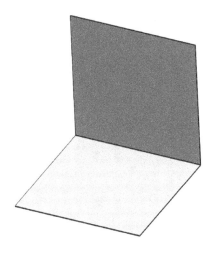

Now click **Sheet Metal Gusset**.

Create a gusset using the information shown in the image below.

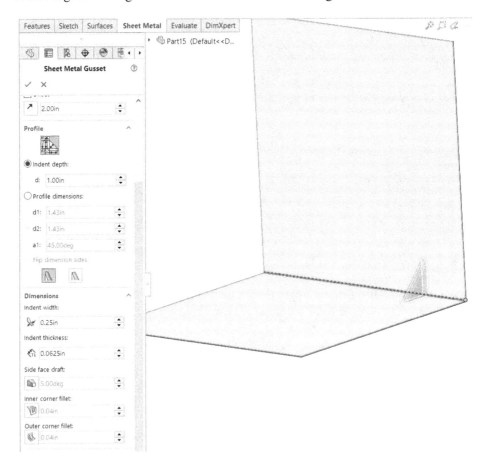

Click **OK**. You should have the following model.

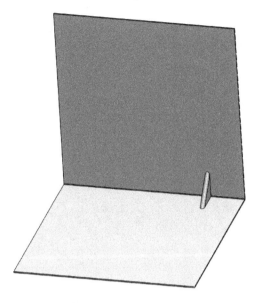

Now use the **Linear Pattern** feature to pattern the gusset along the bend. Use the information shown in the image below to do so.

Below is a visual representation of the linear pattern feature for clarification.

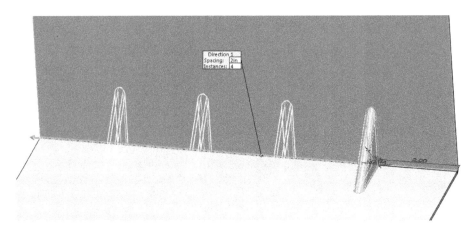

Click **OK** and you will have the model shown below.

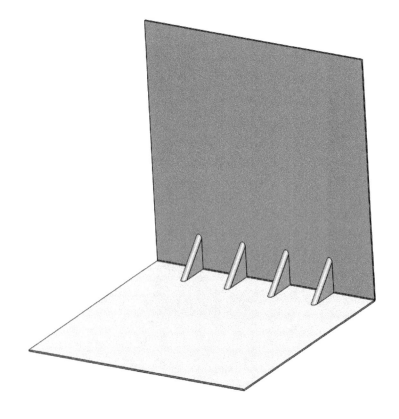

Exercise Complete

Exercise 69: Sheet Metal 6 - Sketched Bend

The **Sketched Bend** tool in the Sheet Metal menu is extremely powerful for creating bends that are at strange angles and in irregular locations. To demonstrate this gem, let's make a tire spike.

Create a new **Part File** and add in a **Base Flange** centered on the origin with the dimensions shown below.

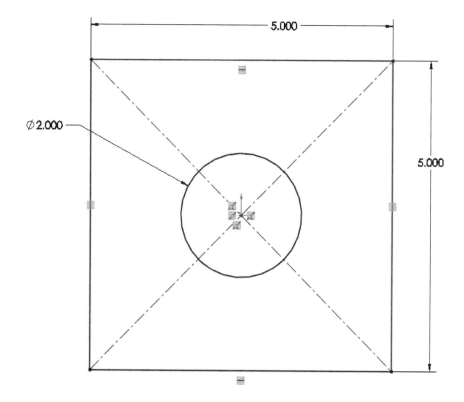

Exit the Sketch.

Accept the automatic thickness and click **OK**.

Click the **Sketched Bend** tool in the Sheet Metal Command Manager or navigate to **Insert/Sheet Metal/Sketched Bend**. Select the top face of the base flange to sketch on.

Sketch a line in the top left corner of the flange as shown below. Then, use the **Circular Sketch Pattern** tool (found in the dropdown of Linear Sketch Pattern) and select the sketched line to create a line at each corner.

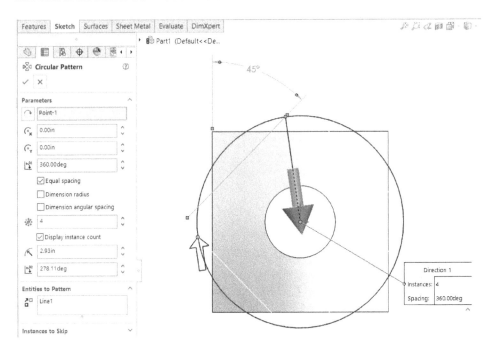

These lines represent where you would like the flange to bend.

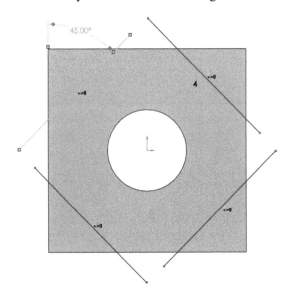

Exit the Sketch.

Click on the face that you sketched on to specify that you want the corners to bend up (normal to the face).

Select the **Bend position** to be on the inside of the sketched line.

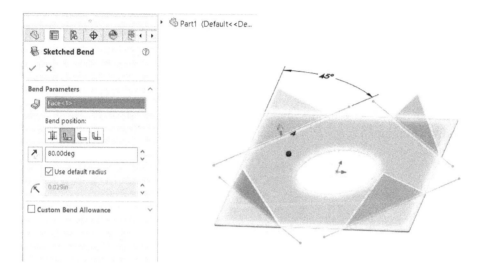

Change the angle of the bend to be **80 degrees.** Click **OK**.

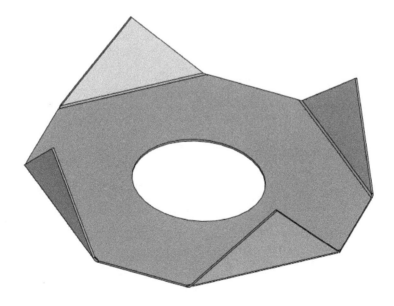

Exercise Complete

Exercise 70: Sheet Metal 7 - The Forming Tool

The **Form Tool Feature** command is an amazing command because it allows you to use pre-defined geometry to affect a sheet metal body. There are a number of standard forming tools that come with SolidWorks. They can be found in the **Design Library**. In order to use these tools, you can first create a sheet metal body. Then, you go into the **Design Library** and select the Forming Tools directory. There you will see more choices, such as embosses, extruded flanges, and louvers.

In order to proceed with the exercise, begin by creating a **12** by **8 inch**, aluminum, **Gauge 16** piece of sheet metal.

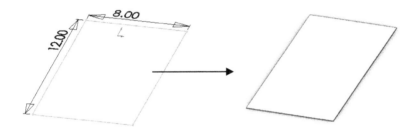

Next, select the **Design Library** section, the **Forming tools** folder, the **Louvers** folder, and finally the **Louver** icon.

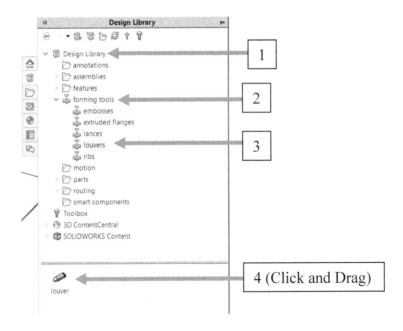

Click and drag the **Louver** icon over to the approximate place on the sheet metal plate where you want to place it. Take note of the instructions that appear to the left, which instruct you on how to orient the feature and select different faces.

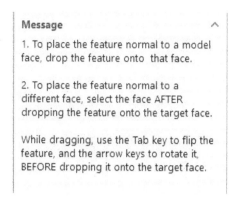

The corresponding forming tool sketch will become available for you to position.

Note: If you can't get this to work, try right-clicking the folder from which you are trying to import a part and designating it a form tool folder.

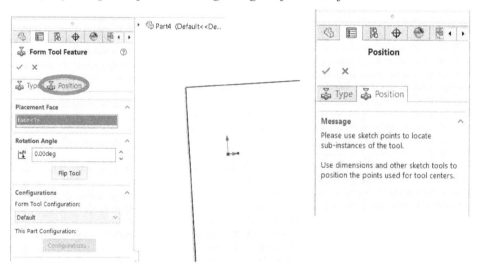

Next, create positioning dimensions and click on **Finish.**

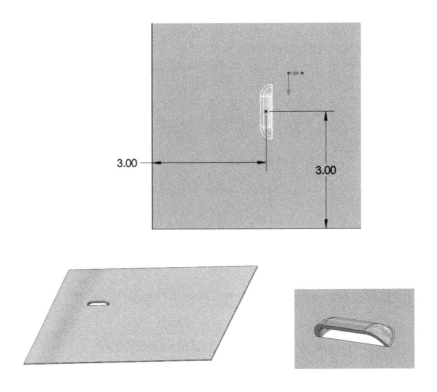

Now try adding a **Rectangular Extruded Flange.**

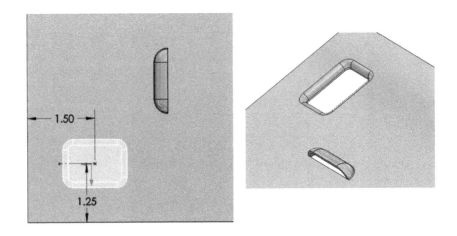

The **Form tool** command also allows you to create your own sheet metal features. It's very powerful and very easy. The basic steps are as follows:

1. Create a solid that will be used as a forming tool
2. Specify what will be its **Stopping Face** (the face where the tool will attach).
3. Identify "**Faces to Remove**" which are the faces that will be cut through the sheet metal when you're done.
4. Save the new forming tool model to the **Design Library**. It will become available to you indefinitely. Note that you must close the file before you use it.

As an example, begin by creating a model like the one shown below.

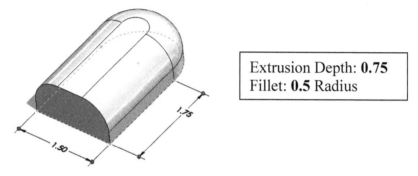

Extrusion Depth: **0.75**
Fillet: **0.5** Radius

Next, select the **Forming Tool** from the Sheet Metal Command Manager. Select the bottom face as the **Stopping Face** and choose the end face as the **Face to Remove**.

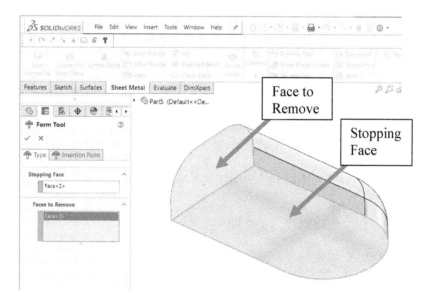

When you're done selecting the surfaces, click **OK** and the model will appear as shown below.

The next step is to place the model in the Design Library. First save the file using **File/Save** and name it **Forming Tool.SLDPRT**.

Next select the **Design Library** icon. This will open the **Design Library Menu**. You may create a new folder for the new forming tool. Here we added a new folder called "cool things I made". Once you have created a new folder, you can click on **Add to Library**.

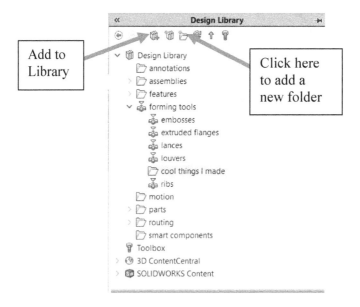

When you click on the **Add to Library** tool you will get a menu that you can add the model to.

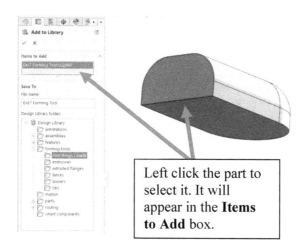

Left click the part to select it. It will appear in the **Items to Add** box.

Click **OK,** and the model is saved into the "cool things I made" folder. Close the forming tool part file.

Finally, click the Window tab and go back to the flat plate model with the other features on it. Now drag your forming tool onto the part as you did previously.

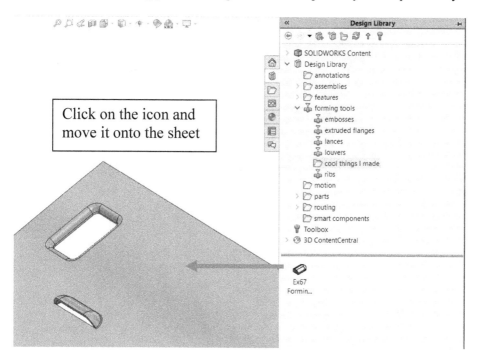

Click on the icon and move it onto the sheet

Once you have moved the forming tool onto the sheet, you can position it as shown below.

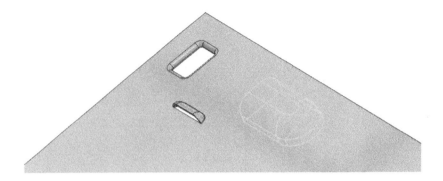

Finally select **Finish**.

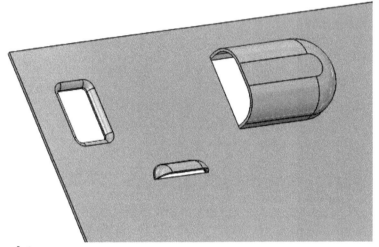

Exercise Complete

Exercise 71: Sheet Metal 8 - Convert to Sheet Metal

The **Converted** tool allows you to create sheet metal objects very quickly by creating regular solid models, shelling them out and converting all the surfaces to sheet metal bends.

To practice this technique, create an **Extruded** block that is **4** by **2** by **5 inches**.

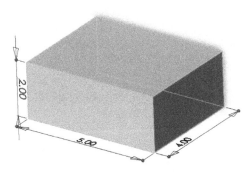

Using the **Shell** command, give the entire solid a **.125** wall thickness. Do not select any of the surfaces, so that the block is hollowed out but closed.

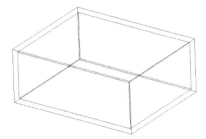

Create an **Extruded Cut** through the top face offset **1 inch** from each edge of the top face.

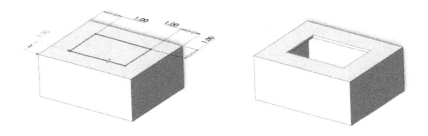

Next, create separate sketches to indicate where each of the **Rips** will be.

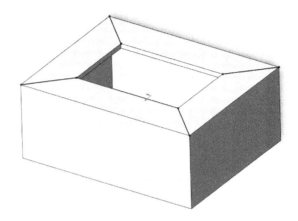

Once you have created the sketches, you can select the **Convert to Sheet Metal** tool from the Sheet Metal Command Manager.

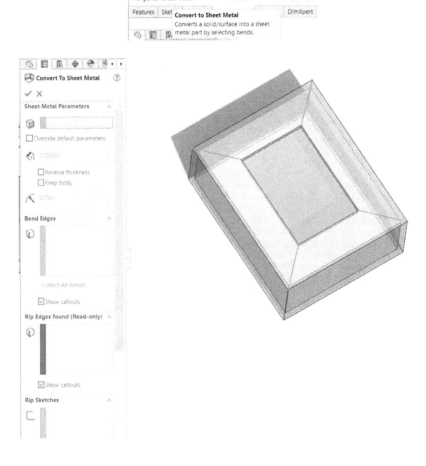

The first selection you need to make is the bottom face. After that, select the bottom four edges and top four edges as the "Bend Edges." The "Rip Edges" will be selected automatically. Finally, select the "Rip Sketches" box and choose the four sketches you created on top.

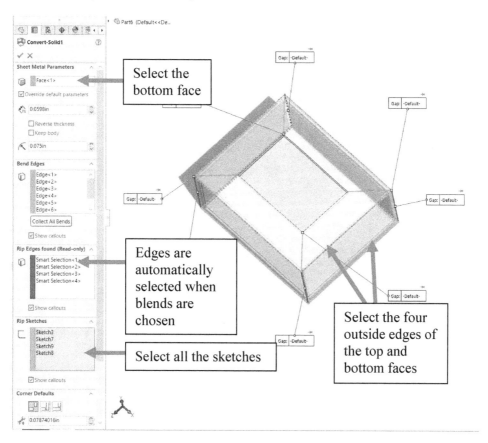

The result is shown below.

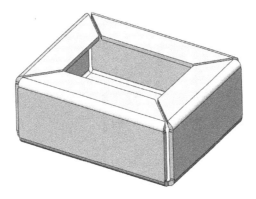

Exercise Complete

Exercise 72: Sheet Metal 9 - Unfold and Fold

In many cases the sheet metal models that you create will have cutouts in them that are best created in the flat state before they are bent up. Contours like grooves and holes sometimes run through bent sections. In cases like these, the best way to proceed is to create your sheet metal item, then unfold it, put in the cutouts, and fold it again.

To practice this technique, create the geometry shown below.

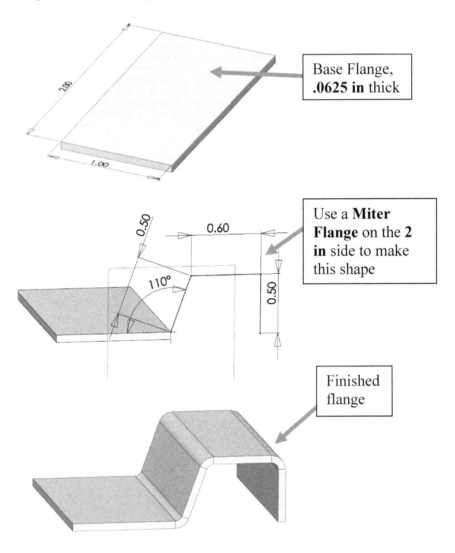

Base Flange, **.0625 in** thick

Use a **Miter Flange** on the **2 in** side to make this shape

Finished flange

Next use the **Unfold** command from the Sheet Metal Command Manager to flatten out the entire thing.

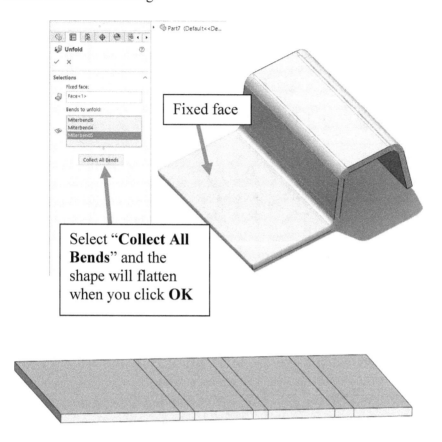

Once you have the shape flattened, use the standard **Extruded Cut** to cut a slot through it.

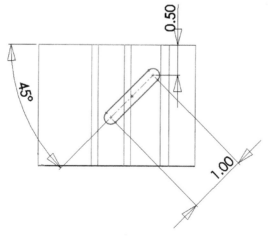

Finally use the **Fold** tool to fold the part again.

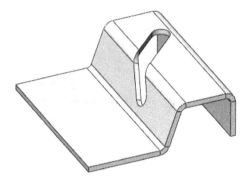

Exercise Complete

Advanced Surfacing and Shape Modeling in SolidWorks

Now that you are familiar with the basic modeling techniques available in SolidWorks 2018, we hope you enjoy this next journey into far more advanced (and, some would say, difficult) modeling. We believe that engineering and design is most exciting when we get to use it in an extremely creative way. There's nothing like the feeling of solving some difficult problem or creating something that never existed before. The tutorials that follow contain many of the esoteric skills required to create the advanced surfaces that go along with consumer products as well as aerospace and medical devices. These exercises will take you to the limit of SolidWorks' capability.

Exercise 73: Projected Curve

This exercise introduces you to some advanced features in SolidWorks. The **Project Curve** Command is a great tool to use to project sketched curves onto a model face to create a 3D curve.

Start by creating the block shown in the figure below. Dimensions are not important here.

Now create a spline on the top face of the block and another spline on the front face.

Now, select the Curves Command Manager in the Features Command Manager. Scroll down and click on **Project Curve.**

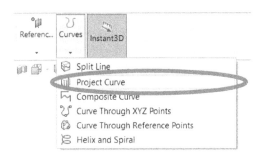

In the Projected Curve Properties Manager, select **Sketch on Sketch** as the projection type. Then, click on the box below and select the two curves you created earlier.

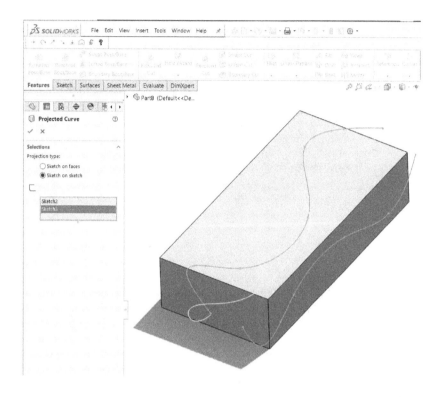

Accept the changes. You will now see the projected 3D curve created from the two 2D sketches. Your model should resemble the figure below. *Note: The block was created to showcase the curve, but this example can be done without using faces.*

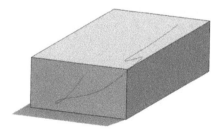

Exercise Complete

Exercise 74: Curve on Surface

To take the **Project Curve** command a bit further, you can project curves onto a surface face, then use them as a trim tool.

To begin, create three sketches as seen in the figure below. Dimensions aren't important, just create three parallel planes, offset from each other, and an open sketch on each of the three planes.

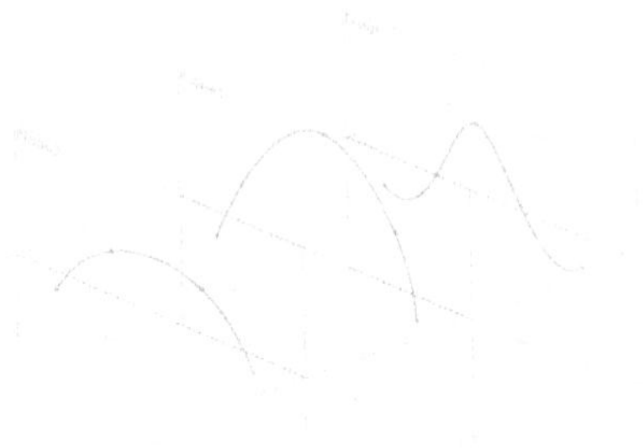

Now create the closed profile on the top plane as shown below

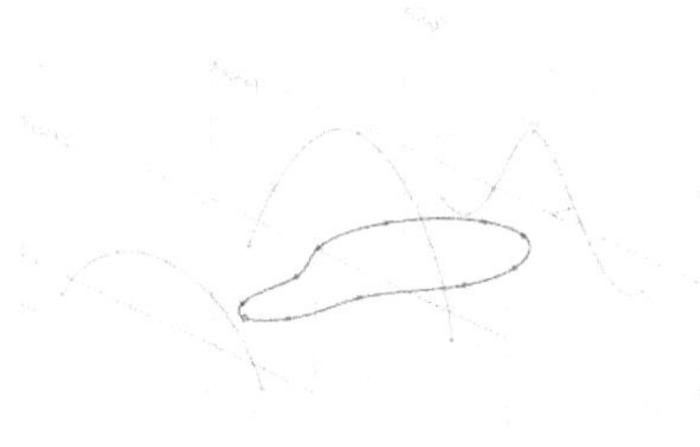

Then, recalling how to create a **Boundary Surface**, generate the surface seen in the figure below.

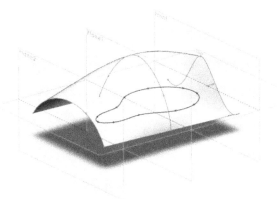

This next step is to use the **Project Curve** tool. This will map the closed sketch up to the surface. Be sure and use the **Sketch on Faces** command. Select the closed sketch on the top plane, then select the surface. The result will be a curve projected on to the surface.

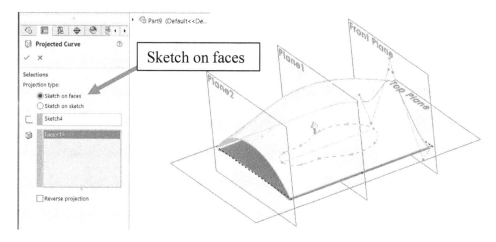

In the Surfaces Command Manager, select **Trim Surface.** In the properties manager, select Standard as the **Trim Type** and the curve as the **Trim Tool**. Make sure "Remove Selections" is selected and click on the surface inside the curve in the box below. Click **OK**. Your model should resemble the figures below.

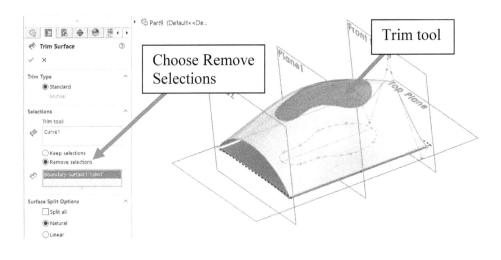

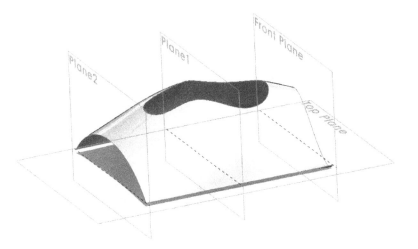

Exercise Complete

Exercise 75: Scale

This exercise is designed to show you how the Scale command allows you to perform a uniform or non-uniform scale.

To proceed, create a figure that looks like the one shown below. The dimensions are not important.

Next, select **Insert/Features/Scale**. The menu that appears has the option of **"Scale about"** on it. The default is Centroid. Input X=3, Y=1, Z=1.

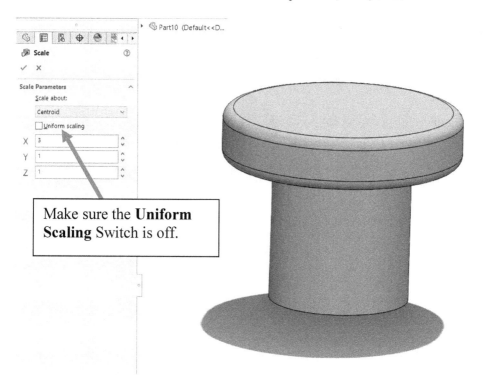

Make sure the **Uniform Scaling** Switch is off.

The result appears in the picture that follows.

When you want to scale geometry but don't want to scale it about the centroid, you may use a coordinate system. When you use a coordinate system you may have to position it using a sketch. As shown below, this sketch is placed on the bottom surface of the part.

The coordinate system is created using **Insert/ Reference Geometry/ Coordinate System.** Make the selections shown below.

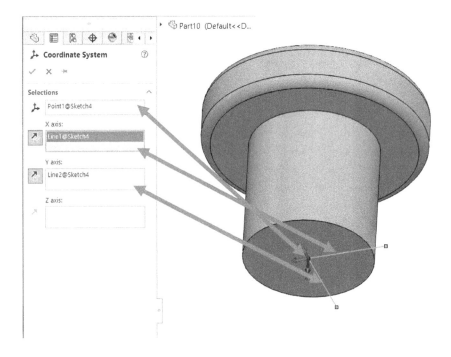

The coordinate system that results is centered on the bottom face of the solid with X and Y oriented to the sketch lines.

Next, Scale the shape one more time with X=.5, Y=.5 and Z=2.

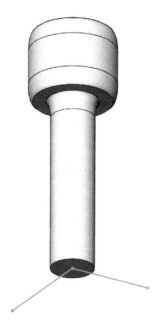

Exercise Complete

Exercise 76: Curve Through XYZ Points

In some instances, sketching a curve in the direction you want may not be that easy. SolidWorks incorporates a command that allows you to generate curves through points in space. In the Curves Command Manager, select **Curve Through XYZ Points.**

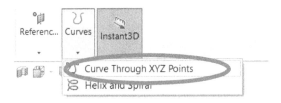

A **Curve File** window appears. Double-click each cell and enter the values shown in the figure below.

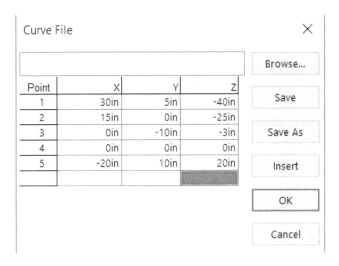

Point	X	Y	Z
1	30in	5in	-40in
2	15in	0in	-25in
3	0in	-10in	-3in
4	0in	0in	0in
5	-20in	10in	20in

A curve will appear in the graphics window. It should resemble the figure below.

Now, create a new plane that with the first reference as the curve and the second reference as the end point of the curve. This creates a plane normal to the curve. Sketch two concentric circles.

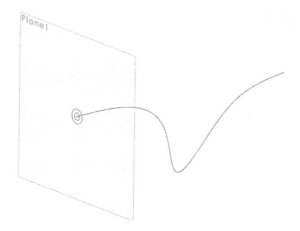

Choose the **Swept Boss/Base** Command in the Features Command Manager. Select the sketch with the two circles as the profile and the curve as the path. You should now have a tube that resembles the figure below.

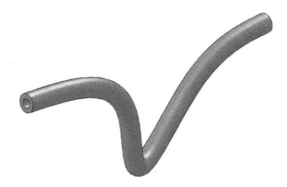

Exercise Complete

Exercise 77: Spline Control

Splines are sketch entities that offer the user the ability to create curves that will be used to create shapes of all types. Splines, difficult as they may seem to be to control at first, can actually be manipulated quite easily. In SolidWorks, spline tools were created to allow careful and almost accidental manipulation to achieve a variety of shapes.

In this exercise, splines are discussed rather briefly. The goal here is not to provide an exhaustive explanation of the potential of splines, but rather to allow you to see them in a bit more depth than what you've already experienced and to encourage you to explore and practice on your own.

Start by creating a spline on the Front Plane as seen in the figure below. *Note: Do not accept the sketch just yet.*

While still in the sketch, click on the curve. The Spline properties manager window appears to the left of the sketch. As with other curves, you can add relations, change the curve to a construction curve, and change parameters. In the Options box, check the **Show Curvature** box. A curvature scale/comb appears on the spline curve. This scale is just a graph of the curvature of the spline. See the figure below.

Curvature combs

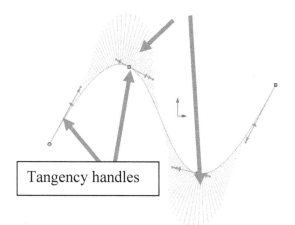

Tangency handles

The tangency handles are used to manipulate the tangency or angle of the curve as it goes through a given point, which in turn controls the shape of the spline. You can also add a tangent relation using the Spline properties manager. This is one method to control the shape. Another way is to add Spline points. To do so, click on **Tools/Spline Tools/Insert Spline Point**. You can now add points along the curve. Then, by dragging the point, you can manipulate the shape.

Another way to control the shape of your spline is to use a Spline Control Polygon. Click on **Tools/Spline Tools/Show Spline Control Polygon** to activate the polygon.

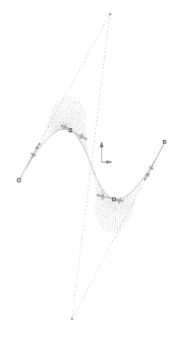

Dragging the points/nodes controls the shape and "smooths" out the curve.

There are other tools to manipulate splines and we encourage you to explore them at this time.

Exercise Complete

Exercise 78: Transition of Surfaces

When two or more surfaces need to be "connected" SolidWorks has a number of tools that allow you to bridge those surfaces together. If you recall from previous exercises, we used the Boundary Surface and Lofted Surface Commands to create somewhat complex and curvy surfaces. They can also be used to bridge other surfaces.

Start by creating a plane offset from the Front Plane and create the two sketches as shown in the figure below.

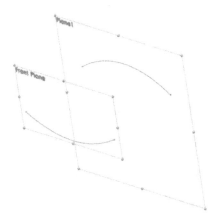

Select the **Extruded Surface** Command from the Surfaces Command Manager. **Extrude** each sketch away from each other as in the figure below.

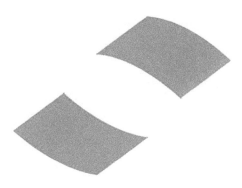

If you haven't noticed by now, there are a few ways to create surfaces when guide curves come into play. Choosing whether to use a loft or a boundary really depends on the amount of manipulation you want in your surface creation. It also depends on whether SolidWorks can actually create that particular surface.

Create a new **Sketch**, but this time, in the Sketch dropdown menu, select **3D Sketch.**

You are now in the 3D sketch mode. Select the spline command and click on each point on the two extruded surfaces, essentially creating a bridge between them. Then create a tangent relation between the curve and one edge and vice versa for the other edge. Do that for both curves. See the figures below.

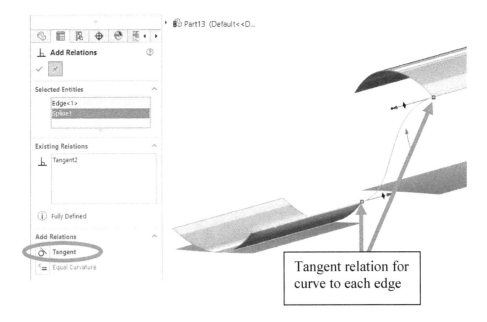

Tangent relation for curve to each edge

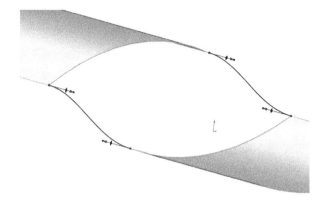

Select the Lofted Surface Command. The profiles are the edges and the guide curves are the two 3D splines. For the **Start/End Constraints**, select **Curvature to Face** for both conditions. Your model now has a surface with a smooth transition between two other surfaces. Your model should resemble the figure below.

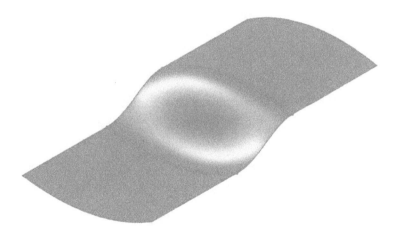

Exercise Complete

Exercise 79: Equation Drive Curves

There are occasions in a design where an equation is needed to develop the shape of the curve. Start a sketch on the Front plane. Click on the Spline dropdown menu and select **Equation Driven Curve.** The properties manager appears. Select an Explicit equation type. See the figure to add the values to create the curve.

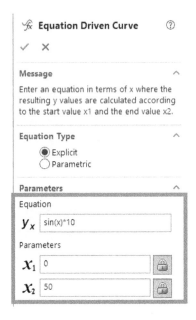

Also, create a construction line at the end of the curve. Your curve should resemble the figure below.

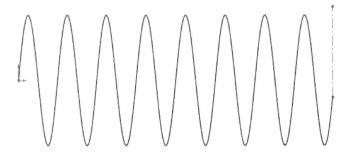

Use the Swept Surface Command to create a sweep feature. Using the construction line as the axis, revolve the curve **360 degrees**. Your model should resemble the following figure.

Exercise Complete

Exercise 80: Curved Surface, Delete Face, Ruled Surface

Manipulating surfaces can be frustrating at times. In this exercise you will learn some extremely useful techniques.

Start by creating the surface shown in the figure below. *Note: Use the **Swept Surface** Command to create the surface.*

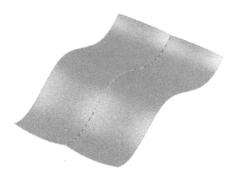

Now, create the closed curve on the plane above/below the surface. Now, project the line onto the surface as seen in the figure below.

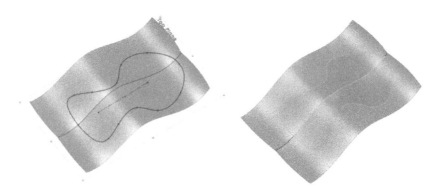

Now, use the **Delete Face** Command in the Surfaces Command Manager.

The **Delete Face** Command allows you to delete a face in a manner similar to the **Trim** Command. We will discuss the **Trim** Command later in another exercise. In the Delete Face Properties Manager, select the faces on the outside of the projected curve. In the Options box, select Delete. Your model should resemble the figure below.

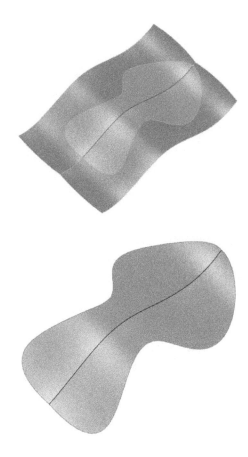

Now, you want to add some surfaces along the edge of the surface. The **Ruled Surface** Command is the answer. Select the command from the Surfaces Command Manager.

In the Ruled Surface Properties Manager, select Sweep as the Type. In the **Distance/Direction box**, insert a value of **0.50 in**. Make sure the Coordinate Input box is checked and enter a value of **-1 in** for the Y-direction. Select the two edges of the surface. Lastly, in the Options box, check the Connecting Surface box. Your model should resemble the figure below.

Exercise Complete

Exercise 81: Surfaces That Come to a Sharp Point

Often times, you may need to create some surfaces that are not necessarily on a 2D plane. That means creating curves that are in 3D space and using surface features to create some extraordinary shapes.

This exercise also leads into the idea of hybrid modeling (i.e. using solid and surface features). It is a powerful technique and one you will most definitely realize that is often needed in design.

Begin by creating the solid shape shown in the figure below. *Note: Notice that the model has a bit of a draft to it.*

Now, the next steps can get a tad frustrating, but keep in mind this is an essential technique to create complex shapes in any direction. Using a **3D Sketch**, create two curves that are perpendicular to the solid with each curve starting from the one end of the circular feature on the solid.

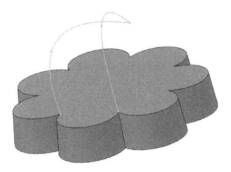

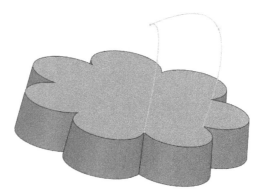

The best advice here is to continually reorient the model in the graphics window to get the appropriate direction when using a 3D sketch. You may also want to use the **Four Views** Command in the **Views Orientation** Command in the Heads-Up Toolbar. Once you've created the two curves, sketch a curve on the surface of the solid model that connects the two 3D curves. See the following figure.

Create a surface. The **Lofted Surface** command is recommended. The two 3D sketches are the profiles, while the curved sketch is the guide curve. Your model should resemble the figure below.

Notice: You must have two separate sketches as the profiles, or the operation will not work.

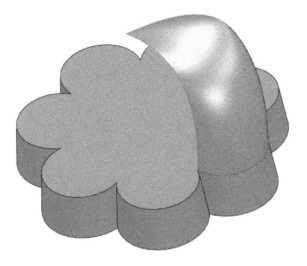

Now the fun part begins! Follow the same procedure around the solid model and you should come up with something similar to the figure below.

Exercise Complete

Exercise 82: Difficult Surfaces - Jellyfish

This next exercise follows a similar procedure to that of the previous exercise. Start by creating the 3D curves to create the body boundary of the jellyfish as seen in the figure below. *Note: The least frustrating approach is to create curves on two perpendicular planes. However, you will end up with only 4 curves and that may not look as pretty as say one with 5 or more curves evenly spaced about an origin. This exercise, for simplicity's sake, uses 4 curves.*

Now, select the Boundary Surface Command and create the body of the jellyfish. The boundary surface works best, but it takes some getting used to as to which curve to select first, second, and so on and so forth. Pick a 3D sketch as your starting point in the Direction 1 box. Then select the curve to the right of it until you've selected all four curves. Don't try to select the first curve again to form a closed shape. Instead, simply ensure that the "Closed" box is checked on in the property manager. This should build a nice surface similar to the figure below.

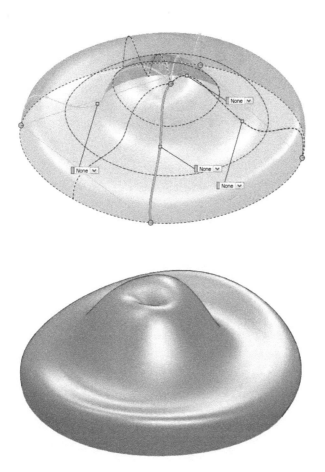

Now, we need to add a tentacle below the jellyfish bell, but nothing too fancy. Create a plane parallel to the bell and some distance below it. Select the Curves Command and select the **Helix/Spiral** Command. Sketch a circle on the new plane and construct a spiral upwards going inside the bloom. We used a Pitch and Revolution type spiral with a constant pitch of **30 in**. and **2 revolutions**, with a start angle of **315.00 degrees**. Your spiral should resemble the figure below.

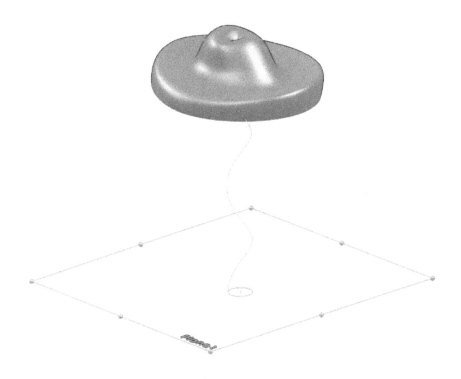

Accept the spiral. Now, on the new plane, create a new sketch and add a line that will create a tentacle ribbon. Don't make the line too long.

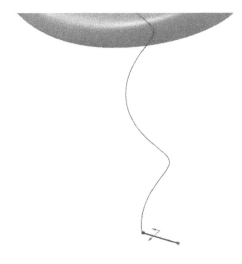

To create this tentacle-ribbon, use the **Swept Surface** Command. Use the line sketch as the profile and the spiral as the path. Your model should resemble the figure below.

Exercise Complete

Exercise 83: Surface Area Reduction

This exercise is designed to show that a loft can be created without the need for two geometric cross sections. One of them can be a point. You may ask, isn't a point a geometric entity? It is, but it has no cross-sectional area. The nice thing about Lofts is that you don't necessarily need to have actual area.

Start by sketching an arc on the Top Plane. Then, on the Front Plane, sketch another arc at the endpoint of the previous arc. See the figure below. *Note: One sure way to know that a sketch entity, in this case an arc, is centered and coincident with a point is to add a **Pierce** Relation. Just click on the point where you want the other arc to intersect and then on the other arc to create a **Pierce** relation with that line. Try it out.*

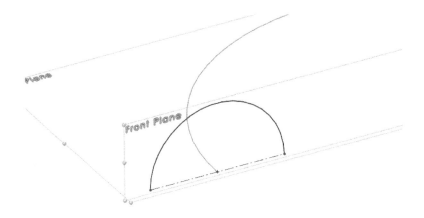

Create a new Sketch, again on the Front Plane, and add a sketched point to the other end point of the arc.

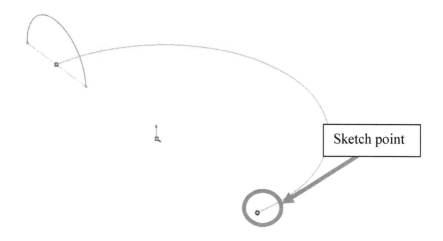

Sketch point

Now, create a **Lofted Surface**. Select the arc and the point as profiles. *Note: If you have trouble selecting the point, right click and use "Select Other."*

Instead of using a Guide Curve, select **Centerline Parameters.** Select the first sketch, the larger arc, as the centerline.

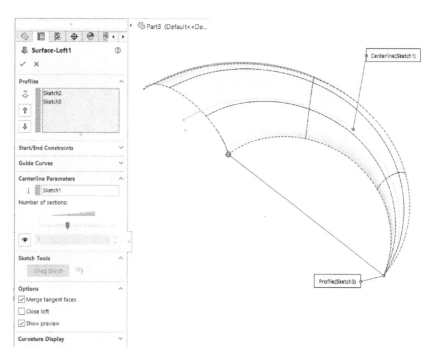

`

Click **OK**. Your model should resemble the figure below.

Exercise Complete

Exercise 84: Lofts - Two Sketches of Different Sizes

In this exercise we will be creating a **Lofted Boss/Base.** Start by selecting the **Helix/Spiral** Command (found under the Curves Command dropdown) and sketch a circle on the Top Plane when prompted. Dimension it to a diameter of **6 in**. For the "Defined By" section, choose **Spiral**. Specify an **8 in.** Pitch, **2 Revolutions**, and a start angle of **90 degrees** in the **Clockwise** direction. Your **Helix/Spiral** should resemble the figure below.

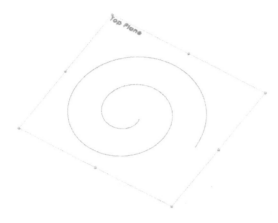

Now, create two planes, one at each endpoint of the spiral. We want these planes to be normal to the spiral, so define each of them by selecting the spiral and then an endpoint of the spiral. Repeat with the other endpoint to create the second plane.

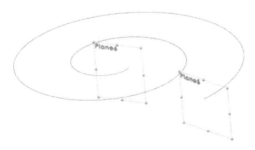

Now create a sketch on each plane. Sketch a **Center Rectangle** and add some fillets to the top corners. Dimensions aren't important, but make sure one rectangle is larger than the other. *Note: Recall the **Pierce** relation? This is a must to make sure the center of the rectangle is "touching" the end point of the spiral. Add this relation by selecting the center point of the rectangle and then, while*

*holding down the Shift key, selecting the spiral. The Relations property manager will appear with the **Pierce** relation shown. Select it and watch the rectangle attach to the end of the spiral.*

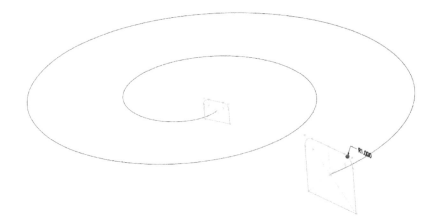

Now, in the Features Command Manager, select the **Lofted Boss/Base** Command. Select the two rectangular sketches as the profile, then, as in the previous exercise, use the **Centerline** Parameters and select the spiral as the centerline. Accept the changes. Your model should resemble the figure below.

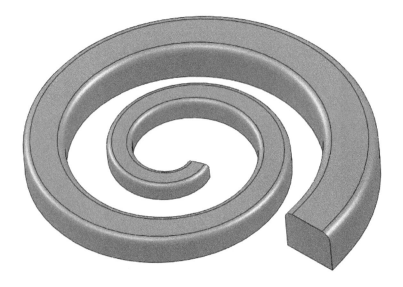

Exercise Complete

Exercise 85: Wire Creation

There will be times in design where wires or pipes need to be routed in an assembly. SolidWorks has a library for piping and electrical routing, but you might need something a bit more "custom." In this exercise, you will create two wires that are twisted around one another.

Something worth noting regarding wires:
It has been mentioned quite often that in CAD design, there are many ways to create the same part. That may be true, but it also depends on if it is done correctly. There is an "easier" way to create wires in SolidWorks, but it does not produce wires that are correct in the realm of reality. Each wire needs to be normal to the curve. You will notice this at the end of the exercise.

Start by sketching a spline on a plane of your choosing. In this case, we chose the Front Plane. Next, create a plane that is normal to the curve and set it at the end point of the curve as seen in the figure below.

On that new plane, sketch a line that is coincident with the endpoint of the curve. Be sure to evenly space this line across the endpoint. The length of the line is important, as it will dictate the spacing of the wires with the diameter you choose in your design.

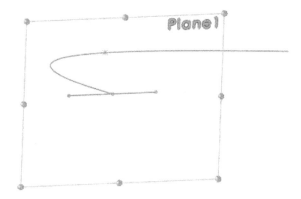

Next, create a Swept surface using the line as the profile and the spline as the path. In the **Orientation/Twist** type, under the Options box, change it to Twist Along Path and the Path alignment type to **Turns**. Put in **5** for the number of turns. Your model should resemble the figure below.

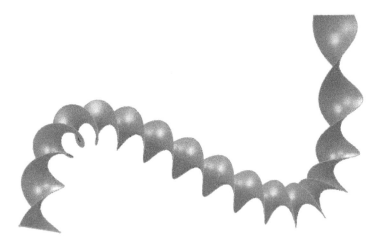

Now, create two planes on the edge where the line was created. Each plane should be normal to the edge of the Swept surface created. Start by selecting the edge of the Swept surface as the first reference, then select the endpoint of the edge of the surface as the second reference. Do this for each side.

On each plane, sketch a circle that is coincident to the endpoint of the curve. *Note: The diameter of the circle is important, but since we haven't used dimensions in this exercise, it's all about how it appears in the end.*

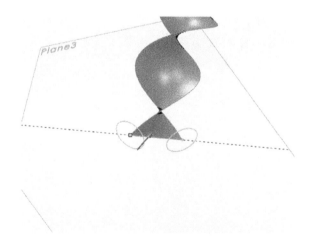

Now, create a Swept surface for each circle, using the edge of the previous surface. Your model should resemble the figures below.

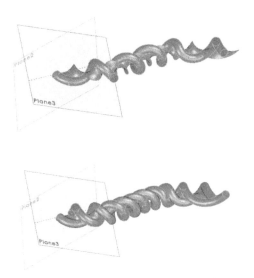

You can hide the first Swept surface to reveal the two wires twisted together. Notice how each wire is normal to the curve.

Exercise Complete

Exercise 86: Flex Feature Command

The Flex command allows you to manipulate the shape of a solid or a surface by **Bending, Twisting, Tapering** or **Stretching.**

Typically, this feature is used to give an audience a visual perspective of changes of state for a particular shape or material. Using it for manufacturing, such as for injection molded parts, is not recommended.

For this exercise, start by creating a sketch on the Top Plane as shown in the figure below.

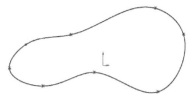

Sketch a construction line of some distance up on the Right Plane. Try to center the line inside the curve you created earlier.

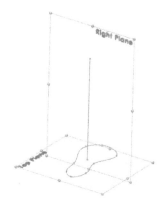

Now create a new sketch, again on the Right Plane, to add a sketch point on top of the construction line.

In the Features Command Manager, click on the **Lofted Boss/Base** Command. Create a loft. Use the curve and the point as the profiles. Your model should resemble the figure below.

Now, go to **Insert/ Features/ Flex**.

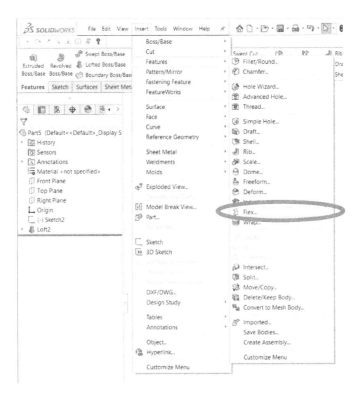

The Flex Properties Manager appears. Click on the solid. Two Trim Planes appear, one green and one red. These are the planes that dictate the change in the model's shape. They can be adjusted using the vector triad that appears in the center of the solid.

In the Properties Manager, select **Twisting** as the Flex Input. Right below that, in the angle box, insert a value of **90 degrees**. See the figures below.

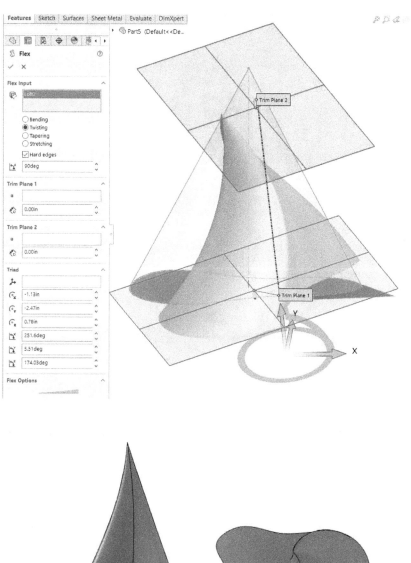

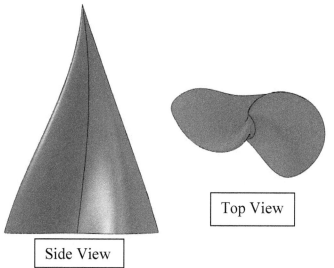

Side View

Top View

Finally, create a plane that is parallel to the Top Plane. Move it some distance up, to approximately ¾ the height of the solid model.

Now, navigate to the Surfaces Feature Command Tab. Select the **Cut with Surface** Command.

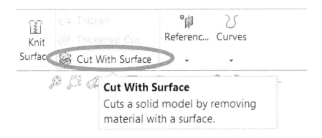

In the Properties Manager, select the new plane as the cutting surface. An arrow appears on the model. It should be pointing up. If not, click on the arrow to change the direction. Click **OK**. Your model should resemble the figure below.

Exercise Complete

Exercise 87: Draft Using a Parting Line

In many molded parts, a parting line is simply where two molded parts meet. In this exercise, you will create a single part, but create a parting line using a Split line then draft the body in two directions.

Start by creating a solid using the Top plane as the sketch plane and extrude up from it as seen in the figure below.

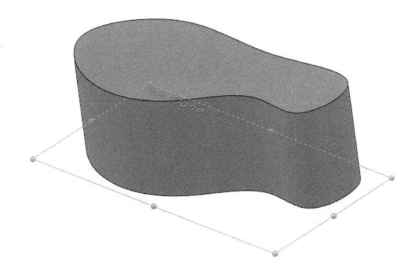

Next, sketch a spline on the Front Plane, perpendicular to the solid.

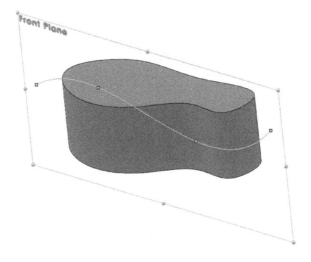

To create a parting line, use the **Split Line** Command under the Curves Command Manager. Make sure Projection is selected. Now select the spline curve as the sketch and the perimeter face of the solid. Your model should resemble the figure below.

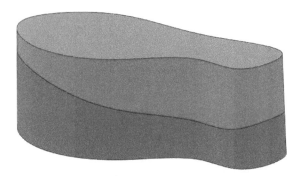

Because of the split line, the solid now has two faces around its perimeter.

To draft each face, select the Draft Command Manager in the Features Command tab. In the properties manager, choose the Top Plane as the Direction of Pull. Select the split line as the Parting Line edge. Indicate a draft angle of **10.00 degrees**. There will be two arrows, a gray one that indicates the direction of pull downwards from the Top plane and a yellow one, which should point downwards from the split line.

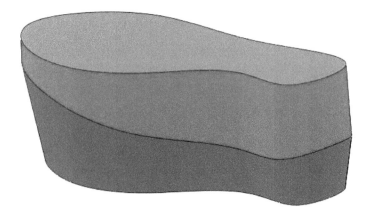

Follow the same procedure for drafting the top portion of the solid. *Note: Both arrows should be pointing upwards this time.*

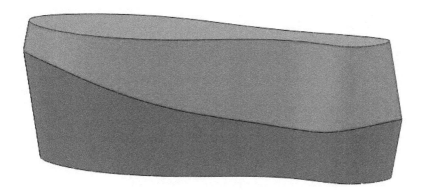

Exercise Complete

Exercise 88: Move Face, Offset Surface with Replace Face

If you recall previous discussions regarding Direct Editing, you know very well how powerful of a feature it is in SolidWorks. One of the tools in Direct Editing is the **Move Face** command. It allows the user to rotate, translate, or offset existing faces of a model within its facial boundaries.

There are limits to this command as there are with other commands in SolidWorks. For example, using **Move Face** may require that neighboring faces be trimmed or extended. If those faces cannot be changed, the feature cannot be maintained and it will fail.

This exercise will utilize both the **Move Face** Command and the **Offset Surface** Command on a single part.

Start by creating a plane parallel to the Top Plane and **3 inches** below it. Sketch a spline on the new plane and a spline on the Top plane as seen in the figure below.

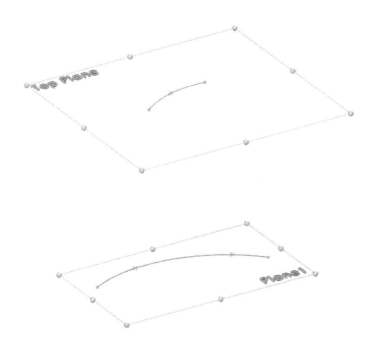

Create a **Boundary Surface** between the two curves to create the surface seen in the following figure.

Thicken the surface behind the front face to a thickness of **0.25 in**.

In the Surface Command Manager, click on the **Offset Surface** Command and choose the front face of the thickened surface to offset by **0.40 in** as seen in the following figure.

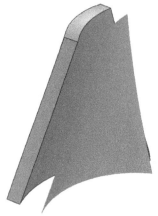

In the Surfaces Command Manager, click on **Replace Face.** In the Properties Manager, the first box is for the face to be replaced. Select the front face of the thickened surface. The second box is the face to replace it with. For this box, select the offset surface. Click **OK**.

Now move to the Direct Editing Command Manager. Click on the **Move Face** Command. Select the back face of the thickened surface. The triad appears. You can manipulate the face in different directions in different degrees of freedom (i.e. rotation or translation). In the properties manager, select **Translate.** Move the triad's arrow in the direction away from the surface, normal to it to whatever distance you choose. Click **OK**. Your part should resemble the following figure.

Exercise Complete

Exercise 89: Clam Shell

Take a look at your television remote, cell phone, or even video game console controller. What do you notice? You may see the two separate parts that create a clam shell or "solid" form factor. Designers use this type of design mainly for plastic injection molding because of the ease of manufacturability, the freedom to create complex geometries, and the overall rigidity when the two parts are secured together.

This exercise will make use of a great tool to create the lip and groove features of a clam shell as well as demonstrate the ability to create two distinct bodies in SolidWorks.

Create the sketch as seen in the figure below on the Top Plane. *Note: Dimensions are in millimeters.*

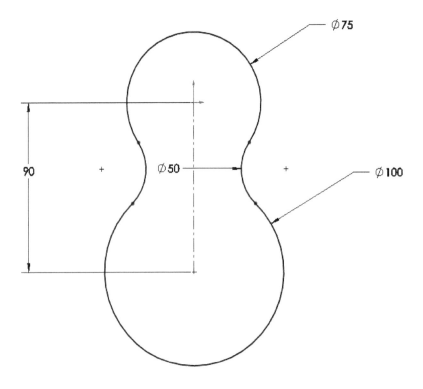

Extrude the sketch upwards to a thickness of **15 mm** and add an **8 degree** draft inwards.

Now shell the solid, selecting the bottom face. Shell inwards to a thickness of **4 mm**.

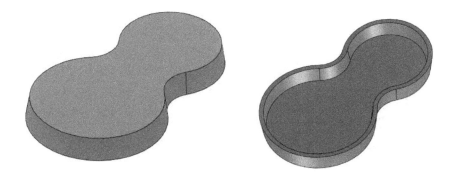

Now, in order to create a separate body, start by selecting the **Extruded Boss/Base** feature. Select the original sketch. **Extrude** in the opposite direction, with the same thickness and draft angle. Make sure to uncheck the Merge Results box.

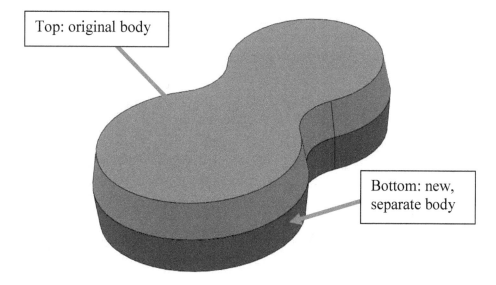

Top: original body

Bottom: new, separate body

Now, in the design tree, hide the original body. This will allow you to view the inside face of the new body to shell it. Take a look at the following figure to see a section view of the two bodies.

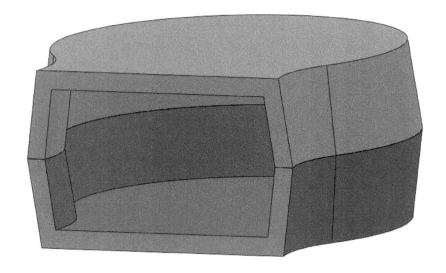

To allow you to create the lip and groove features of a clam shell, SolidWorks has a **Lip/Groove** Command. Navigate to **Insert/Fastening feature/Lip/Groove**. The Lip/Groove Properties Manager appears.

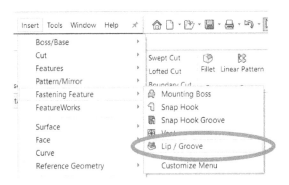

This feature allows you to create the lips and grooves with both bodies together. SolidWorks will automatically hide the body that is not being altered at that moment. You will notice this as you are creating the groove, then the lip. The shown part will switch as you progress with your selections.

Follow the steps in the following figure.

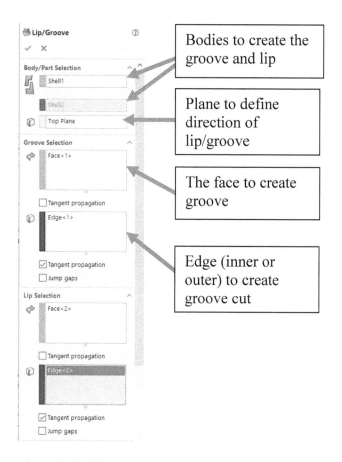

Bodies to create the groove and lip

Plane to define direction of lip/groove

The face to create groove

Edge (inner or outer) to create groove cut

For the top body, select the indicated features to create the groove. You will notice the body on the bottom is hidden as you select the features to use for the groove.

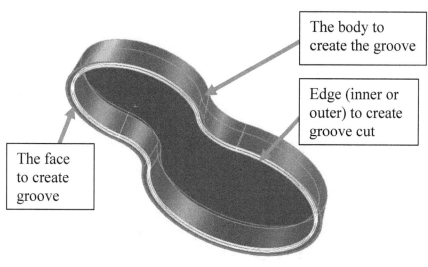

The body to create the groove

Edge (inner or outer) to create groove cut

The face to create groove

431

Now, select the first box in the "Lip Selection" section. Notice the top body will now disappear. Now select the features, following the same steps you just used to create the groove to create the lip. Add the dimensions as seen in the figure below to finalize the **Lip/Groove**.

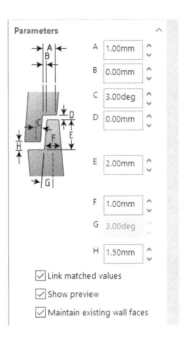

Click **OK.** Both models should now resemble the figure below. *Note: In the figure we used a section view to showcase the new lip/grove feature. Also, we intentionally added a **1.50 mm** gap to show the separation of the clamshell bodies more clearly.*

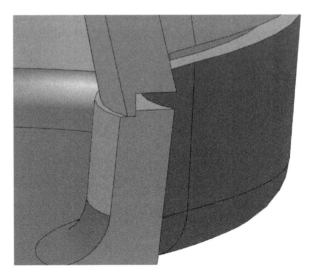

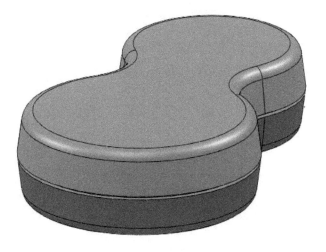

Exercise Complete

Exercise 90: Offset Face from a Solid

Create a solid model as shown in the figure below.

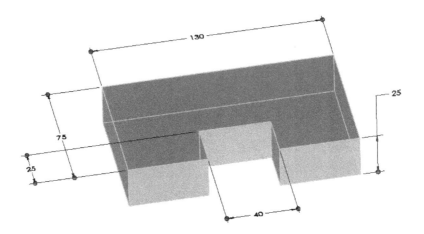

Go to the Surfaces tab and select the **Offset Surface** Command. Select the left, right, back, and bottom faces of the model, excluding the front faces that contain the notch. Set the offset distance to **10 mm**.

Click **OK**.

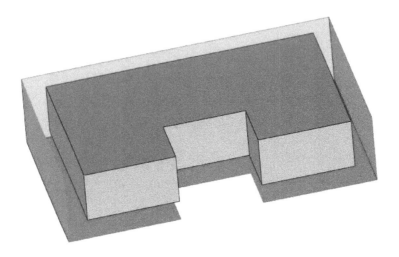

SolidWorks' Offset Surface feature is very simple. Varying the offset distance for one face at a time is not an option yet. However, SolidWorks does have **Direct Editing** and the **Move Face** command. To vary the offset distance of each face, start by selecting the **Move Face** command. Select the left offset face. You want a new distance of **5 mm**, but your initial offset was **10 mm**. So, in the property manager, select **Offset.** In Parameters, set the distance to **5 mm**, and flip the direction so the new face is offset inside the original offset.

Click **OK**.

Now, create a new **Move Face** feature and select the right face. Change its distance to **15 mm** by adding **5 mm** and offsetting outwards. Finally, create a new face for the bottom surface. Set its distance to **2 mm** inwards. Accept the changes. Your model should resemble the figure below.

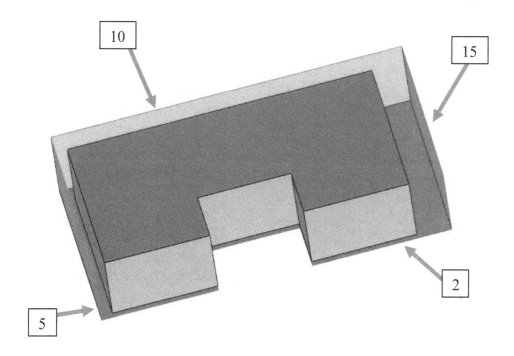

Exercise Complete

Exercise 91: Taper with Sweep

Create the sketches shown below. *Note: Use the **Center Rectangle** tool to easily place the center of the square on the endpoint of the first sketch. Dimensions are in millimeters.*

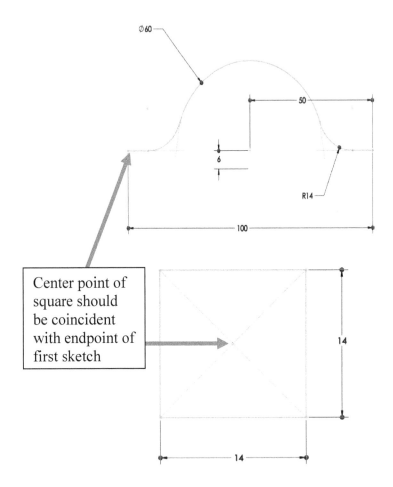

Create a **Swept Boss/Base** use the square as the profile and the curve as the path. Your model should resemble the figure below.

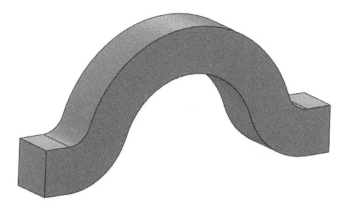

Generally, tapering or drafting a model to a certain angle works well. However, along a curved solid the taper is not uniform along the curve because it tapers from a single **Neutral plane**.

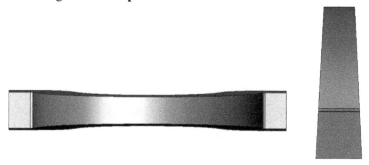

To prevent this, there is a quick method to use.

Create the sketch on the model as shown in the figure below. *Note: The sketch is on the right face of the solid.*

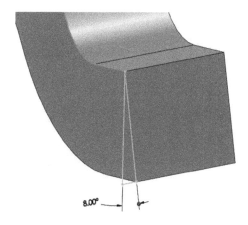

Create another sketch on the front face of the model. Using the **Convert Entities** tool (found directly to the right of Trim Entities), convert the top edge of the solid into a useable sketch as shown below.

Now, create another **Swept Boss/Base** using the right triangle as the profile and the converted curve sketch as the path. Your model should resemble the figure below.

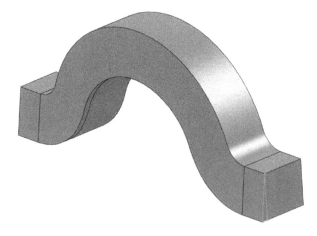

Notice the top view in the figure below. The draft stays uniform along the path.

Exercise Complete

Exercise 92: Curve Projection and Circular Pattern

Create the following surface and **Thicken** it to **0.20 in**.

Now, create a plane on the front curved face of the part. Start by selecting face as the first reference and then select the midpoint of the curved edge. See the figure below.

Next, create the following sketch on the new plane. Sketch three holes and pattern them individually around the center point as shown below. Use the **Circular Sketch Pattern** command and pattern the circles **360 degrees**.

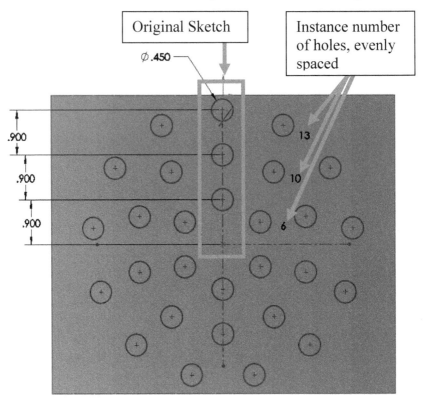

Next, using the **Split Line** Command, project the sketch onto the face of the thickened surface as seen in the figure below.

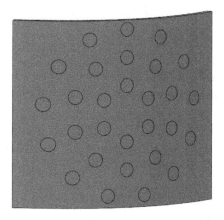

Finally, create the holes using the **Extruded Cut** command. Your model should resemble the figure below.

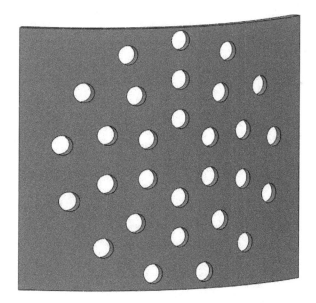

Exercise Complete

Exercise 93: Saddle Holes

Create the sketches as shown in the figure below. *Note: Be sure to constrain your sketches so they are symmetric. Dimensions are in inches.*

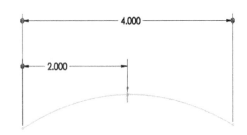

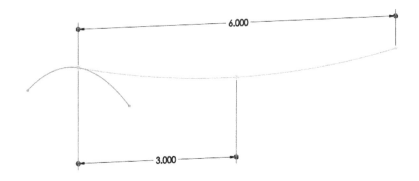

Create a swept surface as seen in the figure below.

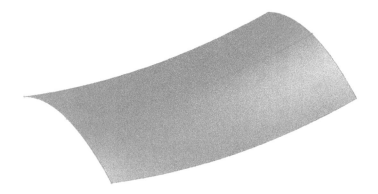

Now, **Thicken** the surface downwards to **0.50 in**.

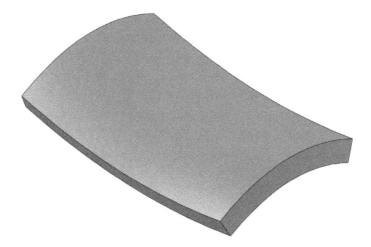

Start the **Hole Wizard** and create a counterbored hole, **size #6, ANSI inch**, with a **Normal fit**. Position the hole on the top surface of the solid then mirror the hole as seen in the figure below.

Exercise Complete

Exercise 94: Fit Spline

Often when creating solid geometry, you will notice parting lines between faces. Although the solid still acts as a single unit, there are times when it is necessary to have one continuous face.

A **Fit Spline** allows you to create a spline over an existing sketch by a user-defined tolerance. In this exercise, you will use **Fit Spline** to create a continuous face on an extruded solid.

Create the sketch as shown in the figure below. *Note: Dimensions are in millimeters.*

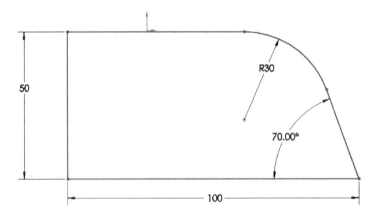

Navigate to **Tools/ Spline Tools/ Fit Spline.**

Now, select each line or curve on the previous sketch. The sketch has now been converted to a single, continuous curve. Click **OK**.

Extrude the new sketch to a depth of **100 mm**. Your model should resemble the figure below.

Exercise Complete

Exercise 95: Knobs

Due to the rectangular parameterized nature of surfaces, it is often difficult to create surfaces that resemble a knob, that is, any shape that is smooth and roundish but not a revolved body. Some examples include a hand hold for a climbing wall or an elliptical doorknob.

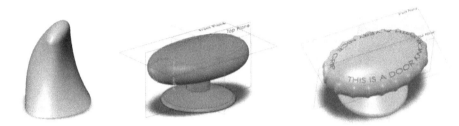

One of the best tools to help create these types of geometric forms is the **Filled Surface** Command within the **Curvature Control** Option Set to **Tangency** or **Curvature.** Using either one of these settings forces the newly created **Filled Surface** to have a smooth transition to the surface that it is being created on.

To practice, create the gray door knob shown above by starting with an elliptical sketch on the front plane. *Note: Units are in millimeters.*

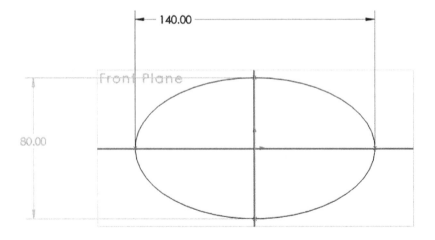

Next, create a point at the beginning of the ellipse using **Point** under the **Reference Feature** dropdown. Select the ellipse as the reference entity and then choose "Along curve distance or multiple reference point." Choose the **Percentage** button. Enter in **0 percent** and enter **1** for the number of points.

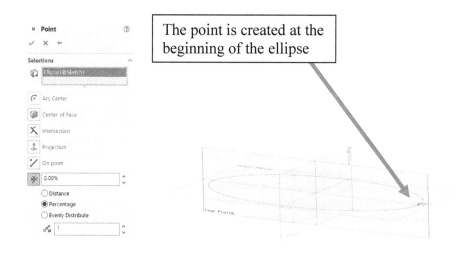

The point is created at the beginning of the ellipse

Next, create a sketch from the end of the ellipse and on the top plane.

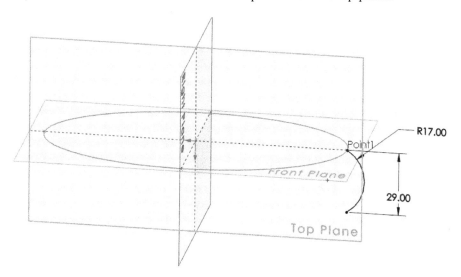

Once you have the two sketches use the **Swept Surface** Command to make an elliptical ring. The half circle is the section and the ellipse is the path.

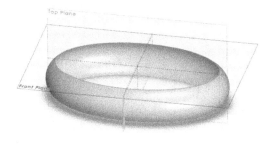

Next place a **Filled Surface** on top of the ring.

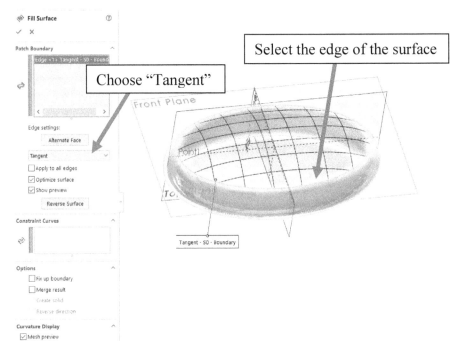

Create the same type of surface on the bottom.

You can now knit all of the surfaces into a solid and add a revolved body as shown in the following figure.

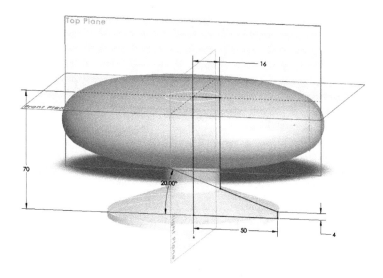

Create an offset surface **1 mm** from the top surface. This will serve to define the lettering later. Use **Insert/Surface/Offset**. Select the top surface and input **1 mm**.

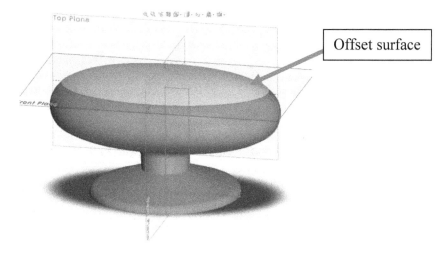

Offset surface

The next step of the exercise is to place letters on a sketch that is on the front plane. Select the ellipse from the first sketch and use the **Text** button (found next to the ellipse tool). A menu will appear that allows you to control the height of the letters and the spacing.

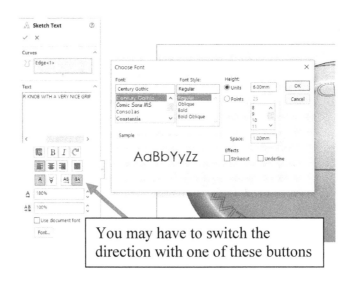

You may have to switch the direction with one of these buttons

The letters will appear as shown below.

Once you have the letters distributed on the ellipse you can extrude them with the **Up to Surface** option.

Up to Surface

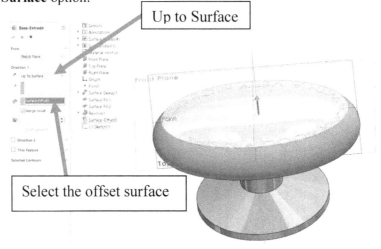

Select the offset surface

To make the bumps on the edge you may start with a sketch that is offset from the side sketch from the initial swept surface.

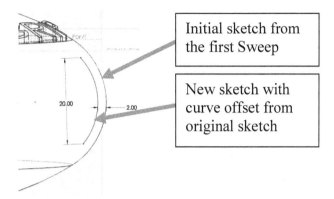

Initial sketch from the first Sweep

New sketch with curve offset from original sketch

Add a datum plane onto the end of the new sketch that is perpendicular and located at the end of the curve. Add a sketch at the end of the curve that has an **8 mm** diameter.

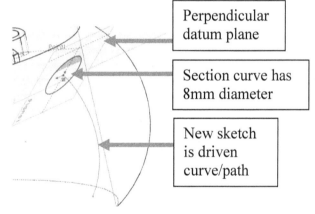

Perpendicular datum plane

Section curve has 8mm diameter

New sketch is driven curve/path

The next step is to create a Swept feature, but don't merge it. Fillet both of the edges with a radius of **4 mm**.

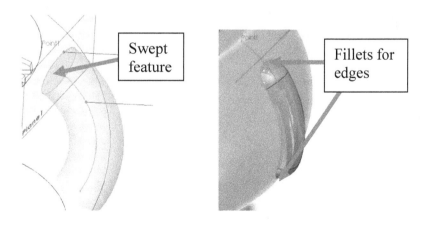

Swept feature

Fillets for edges

Once you've blended the edges of the small swept solid, you can pattern it all along the outside face. You will need to use **Insert/ Pattern-Mirror/ Curve Driven Pattern.** The menu below will appear. You will need to use the ellipse in the initial sketch as the Direction 1 drive curve, the number of instances is **18**, click on the "**Offset Curve**" button and set the **Alignment Method** to "**Tangent to Curve**".

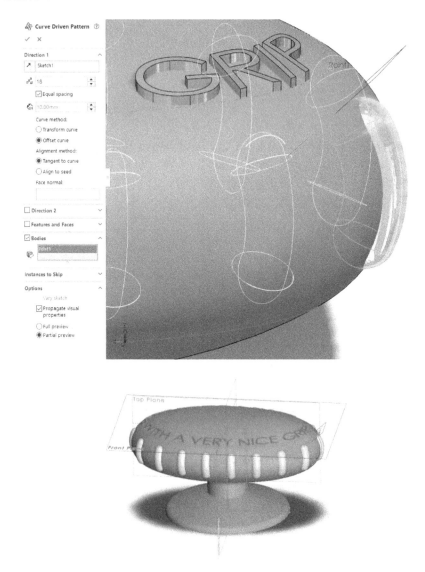

Once you have patterned the Sweeps you may combine them using **Insert/ Features/ Combine** check the **Add** button. Then blend all the edges to make the design smoother for when people grab the knob, or for when someone has to clean it. We do well when we remember to think about the experience that our customers will have with our product.

Apply a **10mm** radius all around the edges where the Sweeps meet the body of the knob.

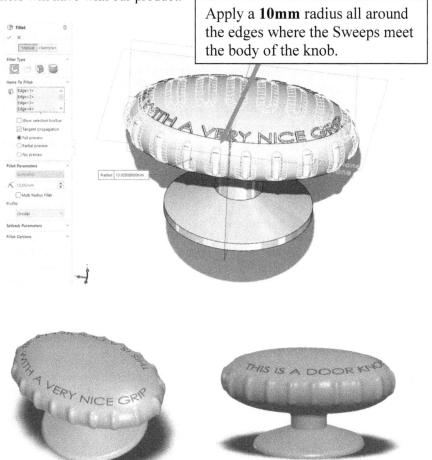

Exercise Complete

Exercise 96: The Lizard

In some ways, nothing teaches you more about how to use CAD than a job that's geometrically difficult. These jobs force you to go beyond what the software developers had in mind when they programmed certain commands. You are compelled to invent your own techniques – collections of commands that work well together, to fill in for the lack in software capability that these models reveal. The lizard model below provides a great example. The geometry is difficult because it has to be free flowing, it has to come to a sharp point at the end, bulge in the middle and maintain smooth continuity. It is also difficult because it's an art piece. There are no set numerical proportionalities that you can count on; you really have to do it by artistic eye and feel. The exercise that follows will illustrate.

To begin, it's good to think about the shape in terms of two orthogonal views coming together. To proceed, sketch the side view of the animal on the front plane starting with a spline that represents the spine of the animal, then two other curves that represent the top and bottom. The head is sketched in for reference.

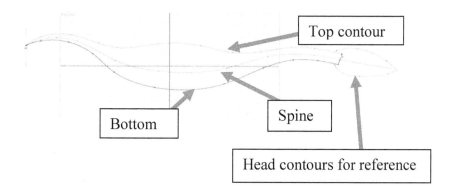

Top contour

Bottom

Spine

Head contours for reference

Next, sketch the top view of the animal on the top plane. It is important to sketch the spline representing the spine first, then splines to represent the left and right contours.

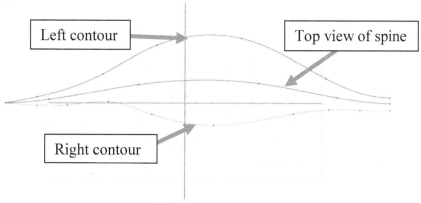

Left contour

Top view of spine

Right contour

Next, create one closed sketch out of the top contour, without the spine curve and one closed sketch out of the side view and extruded them toward each other with the "**Merge result**" Switch off.

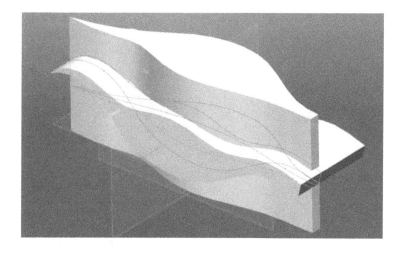

455

Next, using **Insert/ Features/ Combine** with the **Common** button checked, select the two shapes. They trim each other and you're left with a shape that has sharp corners but is getting closer to the overall shape of the animal.

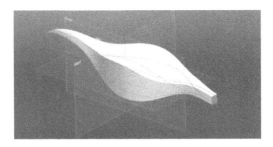

The next step is to superimpose the spine curve of the top view onto the spine curve of the side view so the result is a curve that starts at the point of the tail and goes right down the middle of the body.

First make a new sketch in the top plane and use the **Offset Entities** command to single out the spline in the center. Then do the same thing for the side view. Using the curve command **Projected/ Spline on Spline** you will get a curve that encompasses the curvature of the side view with the curvature of the top view. This is used to create a series of equally spaced points along the length so you can distribute orthogonal planes through each one.

The points are added using the **Point/ Along Curve Distance or Multiple Reference Point/ Evenly Distribute** command. Place **12** evenly distributed points on the curve so you can put datum planes through them that are all perpendicular to the curve at each point location. See the following figures.

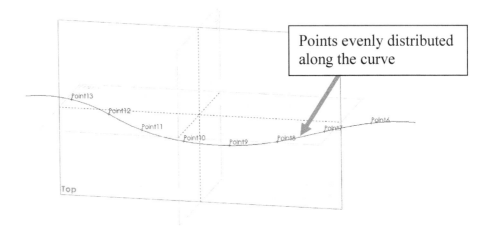

Points evenly distributed along the curve

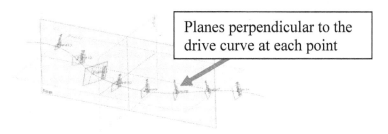

Planes perpendicular to the drive curve at each point

The next step in the overall technique is to intersect the datum planes with the solid body in order to create the cross-sectional geometry needed for the next step. To do this you may use the **Feature/ Split Line/ Intersection** command. The result is a number of squarish sections that are evenly distributed over the solid body that are all perpendicular to the drive curve.

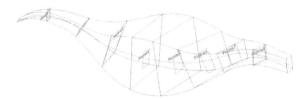

For each section, create a sketch that has an inscribed ellipse that is made tangent to the intersection curves. The figure below shows how the ellipse is made, with the four tangent constraints. It is important when you create the ellipse that the start point of the ellipse is made in corresponding locations for each ellipse.

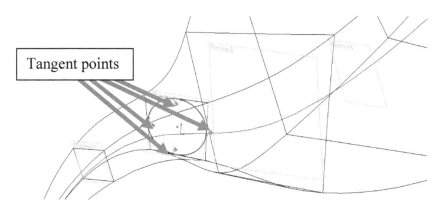

Tangent points

Once you have an elliptical sketch on each section, you are almost ready to use a **Bounded Surface**. The bounded surface is incredibly powerful because you get to control the shape with two sets of curves in two different directions. On each elliptical section there is a top point, a bottom point, a left and a right. You must now use the **Curve Through Reference Points** entity to create the second set of curves.

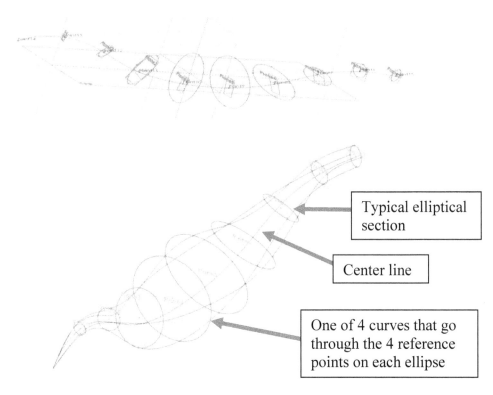

Typical elliptical section

Center line

One of 4 curves that go through the 4 reference points on each ellipse

When you create the **Boundary Surface** select the ellipses, starting at the end of the tail, one by one, all the way up to the head. These will satisfy **Direction 1**. Then select the curves through reference points as **Direction 2**. See the figure below.

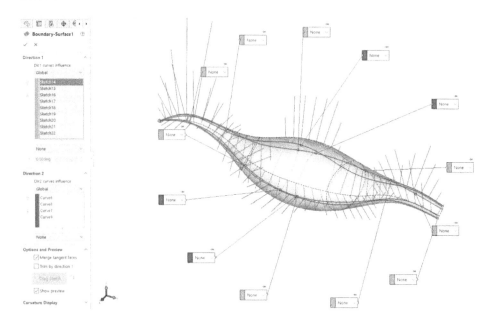

Once you have created the Boundary Surface it is an open surface not a solid. In order make it a solid, you need to close it on the end. Use the **Filled Surface** to close the opening at the end. Now use the **Surface Knit** entity with the "Create Solid" option turned on. You should now have a solid.

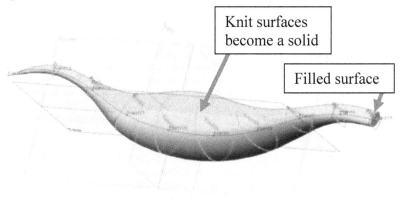

Knit surfaces become a solid

Filled surface

Once you have the main body you can now begin to think about how to place the appendages and the head. If you create a new sketch on the top plane you can locate the legs.

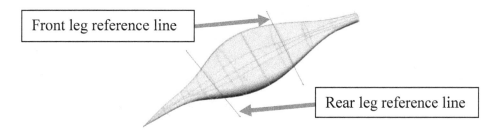

Front leg reference line

Rear leg reference line

In order to create a leg, you have to place a datum plane through the rear leg reference line and perpendicular to the top plane. Then create a sketch that represents the middle of the legs and create a Swept feature along the leg center curve.

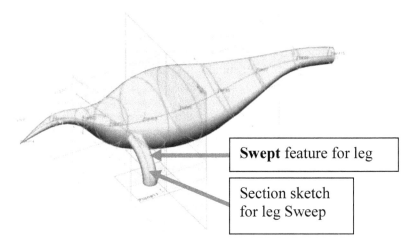

Swept feature for leg

Section sketch
for leg Sweep

Create all four legs, join them to the main solid body, and blend them.

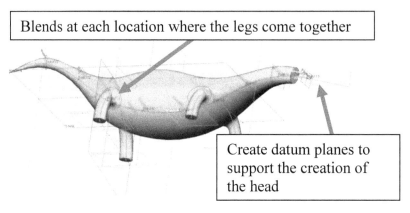

Blends at each location where the legs come together

Create datum planes to
support the creation of
the head

The head is made from four sketches: a top, a bottom, a left-hand sketch and a right-hand sketch.

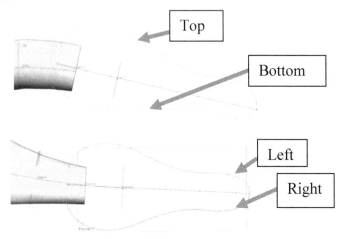

Top

Bottom

Left

Right

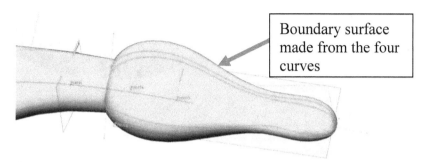

Boundary surface made from the four curves

Once the boundary surface is created, you may close it with a **Fill Surface**, **Knit** it together and **Add** it to the main body. Then it has to be blended where the head meets the neck. The eyes and eyelids are made with **Revolves**.

The mouth is made by creating a **Cut Extrude**, then driving a circular sketch around the edge.

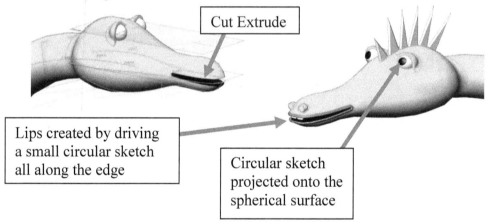

Cut Extrude

Lips created by driving a small circular sketch all along the edge

Circular sketch projected onto the spherical surface

The pupils in the eyes are created by projecting a circular sketch onto the revolved surface of the eyeball and then using a **Split Line/ Project** to create a separate segment of the spherical surface. In order to change the color, left-click on the surface you want to change then right-click on the **Appearances** tab. Then select the **Face** choice and left-click on the color palette. Finally, choose another color to apply. We used black. Now you have a pupil in your eyeball.

The feet are made from an extruded sketch. The sketched **Extrude** is shaped by subtracting a **Revolve** from it. Be sure to have the **Merge Result** Switch off.

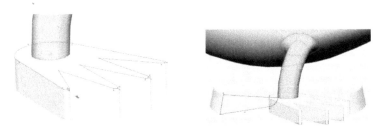

Once you have the first foot, use it to make the others. Since it's not merged, use **Insert/ Feature/ Move/ Copy.** When you see the triad appear, you can select the various axes and drag the foot to the site of the other foot. You can select the circle portion of the triad and you can also rotate it. You will also have to merge them once done. This is accomplished with **Insert/ Feature/ Combine/ Add.**

To finish your masterpiece, add some spines. To do this, add a datum plane at one of the point locations toward the end of the tail. The plane will have to be through the point and tangent to the surface. Then place a sketch on it with the point in the center of the sketch.

Extrude with **Taper** to make the fin. Pick the numerical values that best suit your project. Notice that the **Extrude** is in both directions.

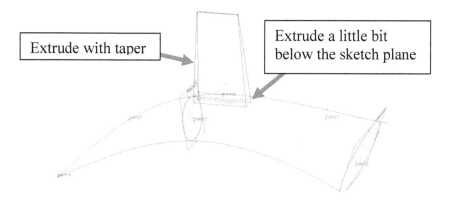

Extrude with taper

Extrude a little bit below the sketch plane

In order to shape the geometry, you can use a center datum plane to define a sketch shaped like a stegosaurus plate, extrude it, and use **Insert/ Features/ Combine/ Common** it as shown below.

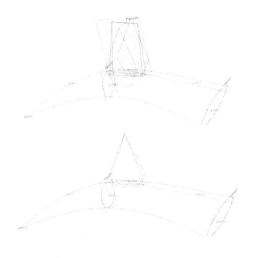

Now to place a number of fins all along the back of the animal you need to make a new spline that goes along the points that were previously distributed along the back and use the **Curve Driven Pattern** command.

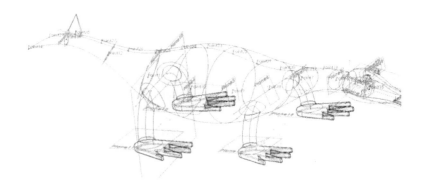

The pattern command needs to be used with the **Equal Spacing** Switch turned on with the **Offset Curve** method on and the Alignment method set to **Tangent to Curve.** You must select the fin, the curve and the face of the main solid for everything to work.

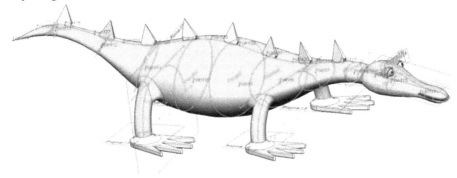

Add the spikes to the head with one well-placed sketch and a short extrude with built in tapers.

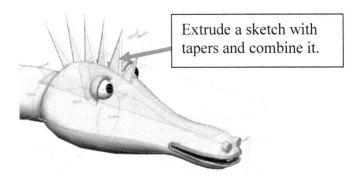

Extrude a sketch with tapers and combine it.

464

The final result is shown below:

Exercise Complete

Exercise 97: Hand Sketches into SolidWorks

Thus far, our CAD technology has not replaced the full advantages of a hand sketch. When you're designing a brand-new product you can solve many problems and advance the design very quickly just by using hand sketches. It doesn't matter if you have a tablet or a super duper whosey whatsit device, there's no substitute for a sketch that you can do on the back of a napkin. And while we're on the subject, there's no substitute for having a clear mental picture of what you want to build – hopefully that's where the sketches come from. That said, it's very important that when you've created that napkin sketch you can go forward in SolidWorks and translate it into product surfaces.

The first step is to scan the sketch or take a photo of it. Then you bring it into SolidWorks using the techniques outlined later in this chapter. From there you can use the scanned sketch to create curves and subsequent surfaces in SolidWorks. Once you've created the surfaces, you may knit them together and/or use the entire arsenal of modeling techniques to create the most creative models. In the example below these techniques are used to create a fully parametric model of an angler fish. Models of biological forms are often very difficult and a great way to learn new modeling techniques. This exercise serves two purposes; you will practice the technique of importing hand sketches into SolidWorks and you will also learn more advanced SolidWorks modeling techniques.

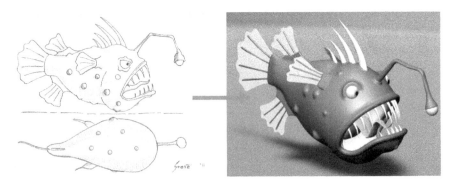

Hand sketch

Fully Parametric SolidWorks
Model

Create an outrageous hand sketch and scan it into a JPG. You can also use the one below which can be downloaded from the book's work files at *www.designviz.com/goodies*.

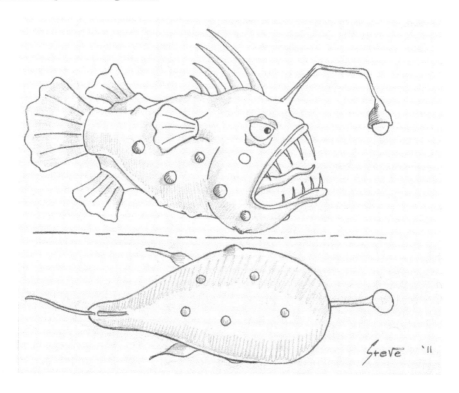

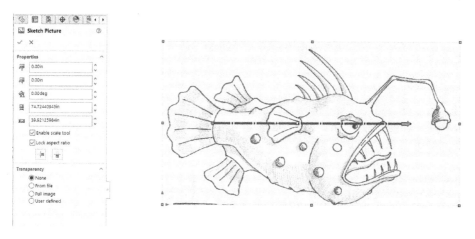

To insert the image into the part file, create a sketch on the Front plane. Then go to **Tools/Sketch Tools/Sketch Picture.** Choose the JPG from the work files titled "Angler Fish Profile." Click Open. The image is now on the sketch plane. Reposition the image as you wish.

Now create a sketch that follows the top of the fish and then one on the bottom as well.

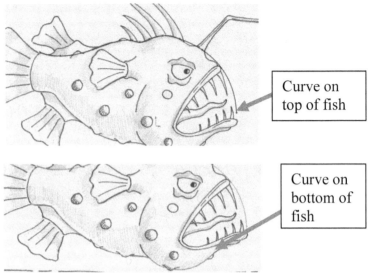

Curve on top of fish

Curve on bottom of fish

Create a plane upon which to place the bottom sketch of the fish as shown below.

Follow the procedure used for the first picture to insert the second image on the new plane. Center it on the front plane so that it intersects the first sketch. Now you may begin to trace this hand sketch as well.

Make two sketches tracing the image you just added. To simplify the following steps, you may create the curves of one side and mirror them to create a symmetrical figure. Then, create a boundary surface through all four sketches to form the body.

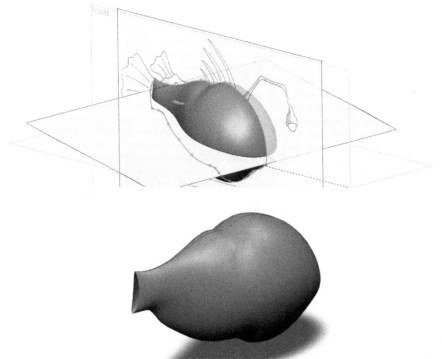

Use the **Split Line** command along the Front plane to create the curves that will be necessary for the next step.

Create a sketch at the tail of the fish and extrude it. The extrusion will allow you to create a loft with **Tangent** constraints.

A sketch is drawn on the front plane to give the back of the fish a smooth shape

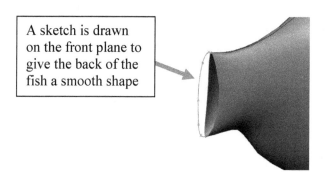

Create a lofted surface with end constraints turned to **Tangent.**

Mirror the lofted surface then **knit** all the surfaces together with **Create Solid** turned on.

Now add the mouth of the fish as shown in the following images.

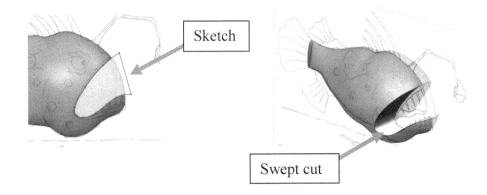

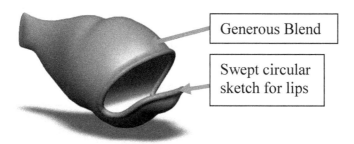

Generous Blend

Swept circular sketch for lips

The details shown below, such as the spines, teeth and tongue, are easier to create than they look. Follow the techniques shown on the next few pages to create them. As you work, bring back the hand sketch from time to time for reference.

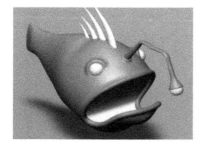

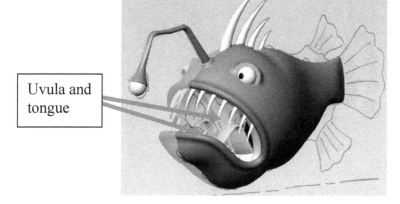

Uvula and tongue

To form the tongue and spines, all it takes is a drive curve, a perpendicular plane, a point and section. Using the **Loft** command, it will be quite easy to create these interestingly shaped objects.

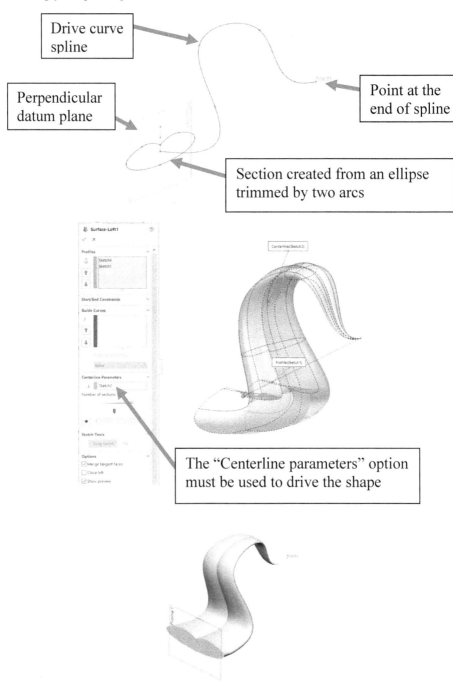

Drive curve spline

Point at the end of spline

Perpendicular datum plane

Section created from an ellipse trimmed by two arcs

The "Centerline parameters" option must be used to drive the shape

In order to create bumps on the surface of an existing solid, there is a neat technique that you can use. First create a datum plane that intersects the surface where you may want the bump or pimple. In this case, create a plane that intersects the fish body.

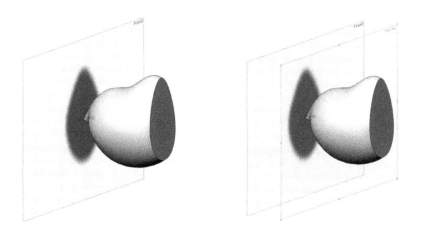

Next, create a sketch on that datum plane. In the sketch menu there is a command called **Intersection Curve** found in the dropdown under the **Convert Entities** command. Select it and choose the surface on which you want to make the pimple.

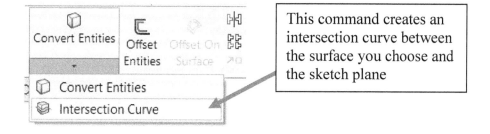

This command creates an intersection curve between the surface you choose and the sketch plane

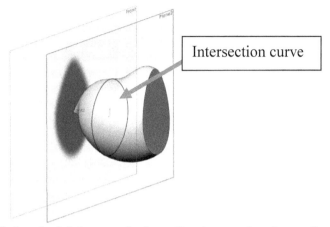

Intersection curve

Create a "D"-shaped sketch. Make sure its base lies just under the surface so that the straight line is close to the intersection curve. Also make sure that the straight line goes through the midpoint of the arc segment.

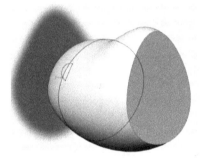

Revolve the section into a sphere. You may combine at this time with the body.

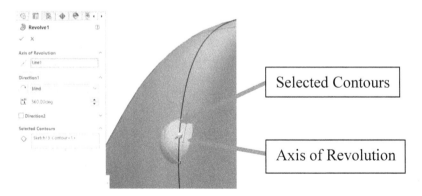

Selected Contours

Axis of Revolution

Finally, put a blend on the edge that meets the face by using the **Fillet** tool with the type set to **Face Fillet**. Make the feature the same color as the base surface and you have a finished pimple on the surface.

474

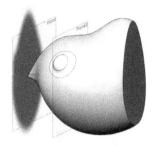 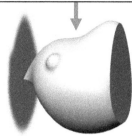

Continue to fill in details like the lure and fins until you have a completed fish. Feel free to get creative with the features and appearances to make it your own. Our completed example is shown in the following images.

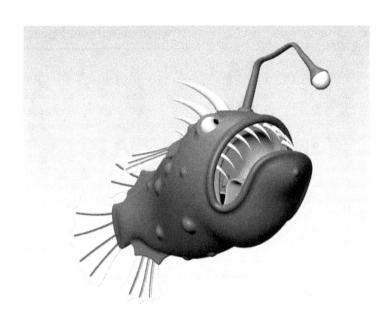

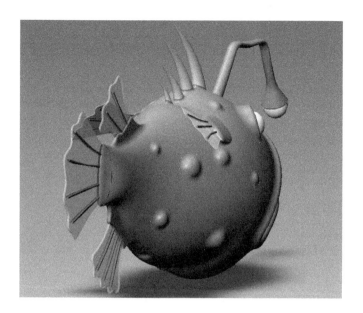

Exercise Complete

Exercise 98: More Advanced Curves from Equations

When you're trying to make certain types of difficult geometry, you need to use a parametric equation or set of parametric equations to create it. As seen below, an ellipse can be represented in terms of a parameter "t" and the equations "X_t," and "Y_t" that are functions of t. This enables you to define more complex geometry than you would if you were simply limited to explicit geometry with y as a function of x. The exercise below will teach you how to create a parametrically controlled curve. To proceed, create a sketch and choose **Equation Driven Curve** from the spline icon dropdown.

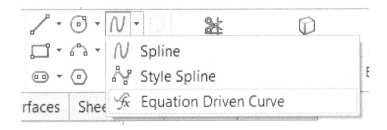

Choose **Parametric** as the equation type and enter the values shown below for X_t, Y_t, t and T_2. Notice π is represented as **3.1415 in X_t** and **3.14159 in Y_t**. Sine and cosine are measured in radians.

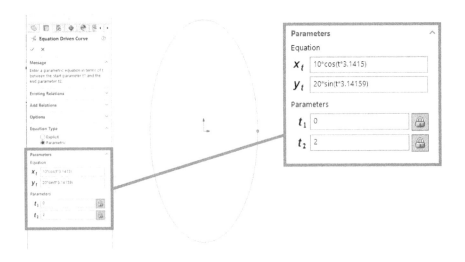

Exercise Complete

Exercise 99: Virus Model Using Equations

Building on the parametric technique for defining curves, let's try out an interesting application. Let's say a model of a virus is required for a study. The ripples of the cell wall can be represented by the equations in this exercise. For this example, instead of typing in a number for π we will use "pi".

Start by building the sketch depicted below on the top plane, with a curve defined by the equation shown and a line segment to close the section.

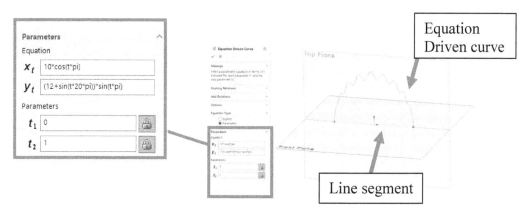

Next make a **Filled Surface** on the sketch. Once you have a filled surface, create a datum axis at the intersection of the top and front planes, then a **30 degree** angled plane as shown.

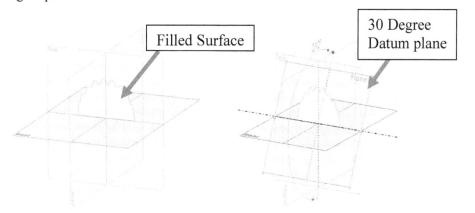

Next make another sketch on the **30 degree** plane. Create another curve by equation, but this time the equation is a little different. There's a negative sign before the first **sine** in the equation for Y_t, and the argument for the first sine is **(t*21*pi).** Close the shape with a line segment and create another filled surface.

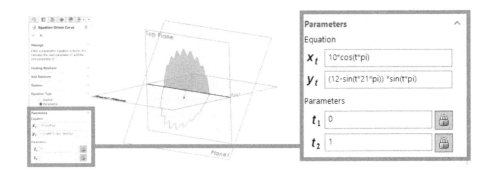

The two filled surfaces can be patterned about the axis one at a time. Be sure to select "Bodies to Pattern" rather than "Features and Faces." The "Equal spacing" switch must be turned on. The overall angle is **360 degrees** and the number of instances is **6**. You must repeat this for both surfaces until you have **12 sections** with alternating shapes.

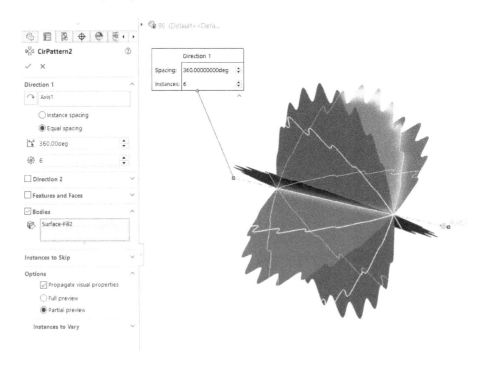

Once you have all the surfaces, you can create a **Lofted Surface** using the edges of all the sections as the definition. Remember to select "Closed Loft."

480

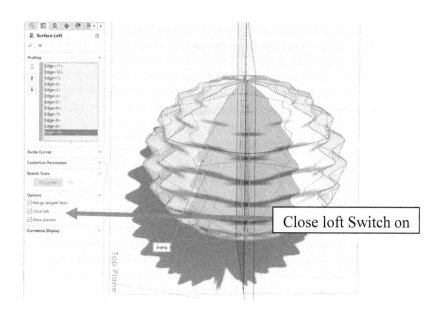

Close loft Switch on

Exercise Complete

Exercise 100: Configurations

When you have certain kinds of component parts that change shape based on where they are located in an assembly, there is a function called a configuration that can help you model the situation. For example, if you have a spring that starts out at **3 in.** high when it's purchased and **2 in.** high when it's assembled between two frame members, you can make the model with the two configurations. When you bring the component into the assembly, you will be able to **Configure** it. Based on your choice you will get the long one or the short one. To do this exercise we will create a very simple bar.

Create a new part and name it what you want. We called it "**Simple Configurations**". Once you have the part, select the **Configurations** tab.

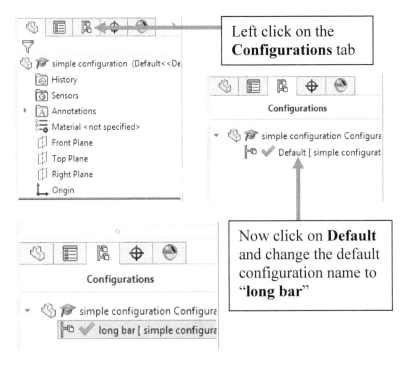

Once you've created the part and changed the name of the default configuration, it is time to create some geometry that will vary.

Create an extrusion that is a circle with a **2 in** diameter extruded up to **3 in**.

482

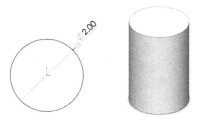

Now right-click on the part name and select **Add Configuration**

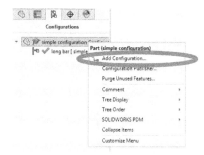

When you create the configuration, call it "**short bar**" and input the description shown.

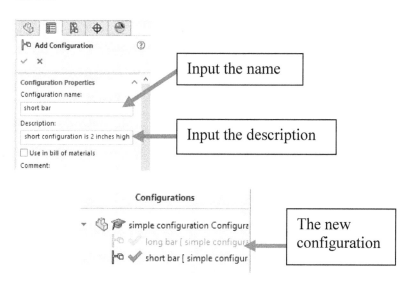

Next, double-click on the new configuration to make it active and edit the extrusion. You will notice there is a configurations choice box down below. Set the **Configuration** button to on. Change the height of the extrusion to **2 in**. The length of the extrusion is only **2 in** this configuration.

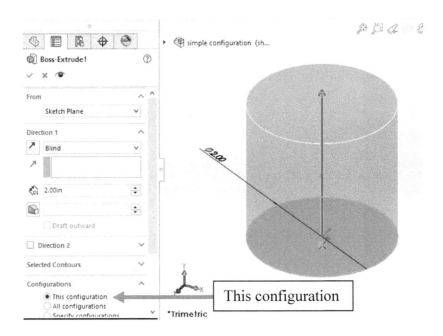

Now create an assembly and bring in two copies of the bar side by side.

Once you have the assembly, you can change the configuration of each component by right clicking the component within the Feature Manager, then selecting the **Configure Component** menu choice.

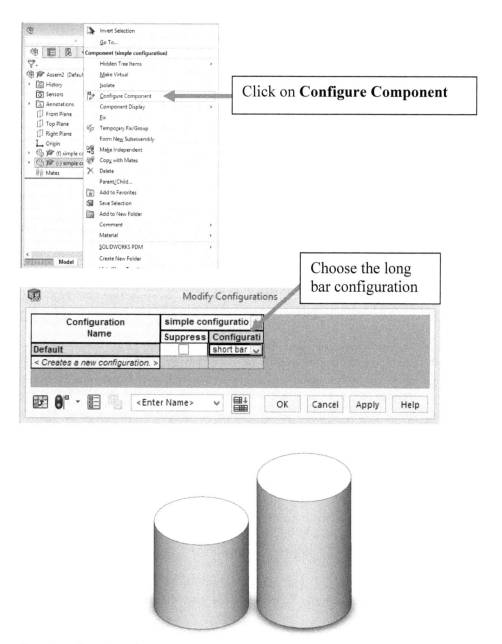

Click on **Configure Component**

Choose the long
bar configuration

Modify Configurations

Configuration Name	simple configuratio	
	Suppress	Configurati
Default	☐	short bar
< Creates a new configuration. >		

< Enter Name >   OK   Cancel   Apply   Help

Exercise Complete

485

Exercise 101: SimulationXpress

Engineers should be able to quickly calculate the stresses and deflections of their components before they spend a lot of time and money making prototypes or production geometry. The hand calculations that engineers perform are easy enough when the geometry is in the shape of something that is relatively simple, such as a beam or a pressure vessel, but when the geometry gets complicated we end up making guesses or even employ the "build 'em and bust 'em" analysis method. This can be very expensive.

However, SolidWorks provides a very nice and simple to use tool right within the main software package. It's called **SimulationXpress** and you can use it to perform many preliminary calculations as you are creating your design. There's a pretty extensive materials library that you can use to quickly apply the required material to the product you're designing. Then you place on the constraints and the loads and get a basic analysis.

To get our feet wet with this tool, let's try a very simple case. If you took an aluminum beam, welded it to the wall and hung a weight off the end, you would expect that the beam would deflect a bit. This is a cantilever beam, and it should deflect in a very predictable way according to the formula below where P is the load at the end, l is the length of the bar, E is the Modulus of Elasticity for the aluminum and I is the moment of inertia.

$$\delta_{max} = \frac{Pl^3}{3EI}$$

If we assume that the deflection curve for the material is linear in the range that we are analyzing we have the following calculations.

Put a 2000 Lbf load at the end of an aluminum 6061 cantilever beam that measures **30 inches** in length, **2 inches** wide and **4 inches** tall and it should deflect as calculated below:

P=2000lbf $L^3 = 27000$ in^3 E=10,000,000 Psi I=bh^3/12 = 10.666
Therefore, the theoretical max deflection is .169 inches.

Let's begin our exercise by creating a beam that is **30 inches** long, **2 inches** wide, and **4 inches** high.

Next select **Tools / SimulationXpress**

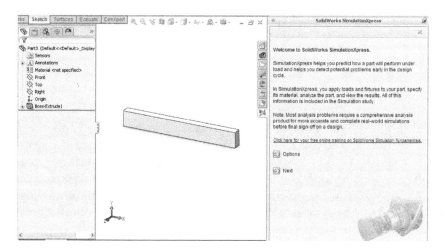

You may proceed with the simulation by selecting **Next** each time you finish a major activity. Select **Next** then select **Add a Fixture.**

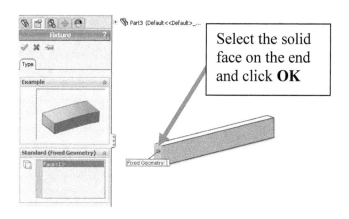

Once you have applied a **Fix** constraint to the end of the solid, select **Next** and **Add a Force**.

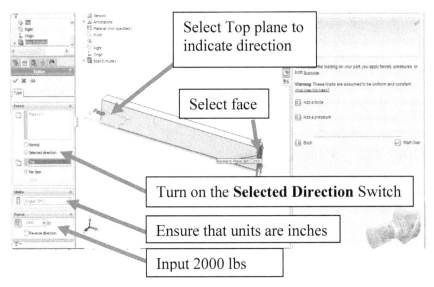

As shown above, you have to select the face on the right to apply the force, switch the direction to **Selected Direction,** select the Top plane, and switch the units to **English (IPS)** and input 2000 pounds. Once you click **OK** you can click on **Next** which will bring you to the **Choose Material** option. When you select the **Choose Material** option, you can scroll down to the **Aluminum Alloys** and select 6061-T6. Also click on the **English Units** Switch and select **Apply** then **Close**.

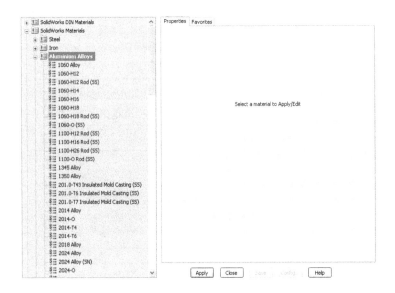

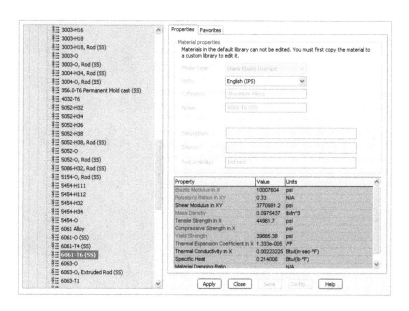

Finally, when you select the **Next** arrow you can then select the **Run Simulation** arrow.

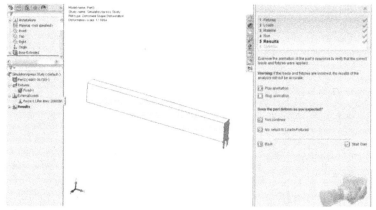

The system will ask "Does the part deform as you expected?" Hopefully the answer is yes and you can click the **Yes, Continue** button. You can now select the **Show Displacement** arrow in the SimulationXpress window.

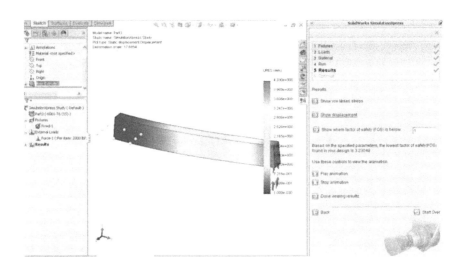

The result is displayed. The result in this case is **4.3 mm,** which is about **.17 inches**. This agrees with the theoretical calculations

Exercise Complete

Exercise 102: Creation of Automotive Geometry and Other Techniques

At some point we decided to purchase a truck for the purpose of putting a large advertising sign on it and parking it in a very conspicuous place so that people would read it as they drove by. We got the truck, made the bill board, and it sat in a paid parking space right off highway 101 in San Jose CA, all for about $2000.

It was about a year and a half before we decided we no longer needed it as a bill board. We went to retrieve it after all that time, put a new battery in it, and it started right up and ran strong. It now serves as the perfect vehicle for camping and hauling dirt bikes to an amazing park in Hollister CA. My daughter decided to give it a name. It was between Ermintrude, and Ephigene. Ephigene won. Now Ephigene makes frequent visits to Home Depot. This next exercise is a tribute to Ephigene. It provides an opportunity to really stretch your SolidWorks muscles.

The exercise begins with taking two pictures: a side view, and a front view. You can access the same pictures from the website *www.designviz.com/goodies*. The pictures are called **truck_side_view.jpg** and **truck_front_view.jpg**.

Next, we need a measurement of the actual truck. This is what is used to scale all of the model geometry. In this case, as shown in the previous diagram, the distance from the front of the truck to where the cab meets the box portion is **80 inches**.

To proceed, create a sketch with a line in it that is **80 inches** long so the picture can be scaled as it is brought in. Next, create a sketch on the same plane as the line and bring in a **Sketch Picture** using **Tools/Sketch Tools/Sketch Picture** as you did in Exercise 97. Scale the picture so the cab lines up with the **80 inch** line,

The image is scaled so that all dimensions are true

Now insert the front view on the right plane so that it is centered with the front plane. Use the same process that was used for the side view with the width dimension shown below.

Once you have both JPGs, you can sketch over them. First sketch the side view as shown below. The cab is done first.

Sketch of side view

492

As shown below the front view is used to create a sketch. Incidentally, the curvature of the sides of an automobile or truck is called the tumblehome.

Sketches are used to capture the tumblehome

Be careful because perspective shortens the dimensions

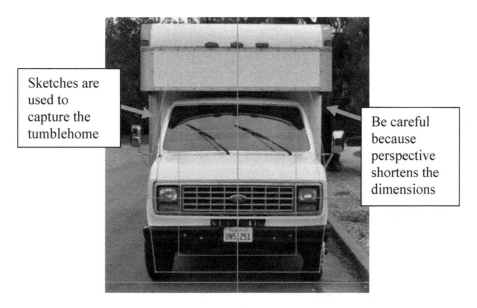

When you have a side view sketch and a front view sketch you can extrude them both with the **Merge Result** Switch turned off. Then you can use the **Insert/ Features/ Combine/ Common** command to keep only the portions that the two solids have in common as you did in Exercise 96.

The result is the main shape of the cab.

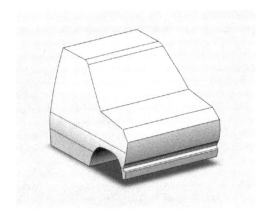

Next, a sketch is used to create an extruded cut, to give the roof some curvature.

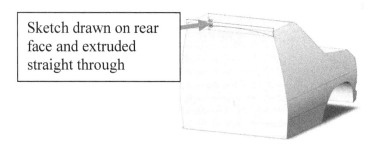

Sketch drawn on rear face and extruded straight through

The next step is to curve the windshield. Using **Insert/ Curve/ Split line/ Intersect**, select the "front" plane and the flat surface where the windshield is. A line is created down the center of where the curved windshield will be. This will be used as a drive curve for a Swept cut operation. Once you have created the drive curve, you may create a perpendicular datum plane at the end of it. Sketch an arc with a large radius on the datum plane at the beginning of the drive curve.

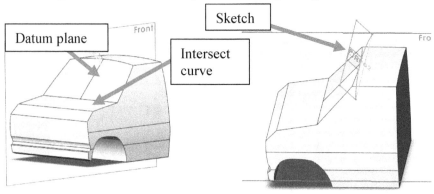

Datum plane

Intersect curve

Sketch

The new sketch and the drive curve are used to create a swept solid. The result is not combined (the **Merge result** switch is off).

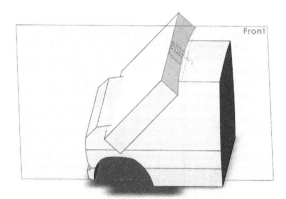

The bottom of the new solid is edited so as to conform to the shape of the hood. This is accomplished with the **Insert/ Cut/ With Surface** command.

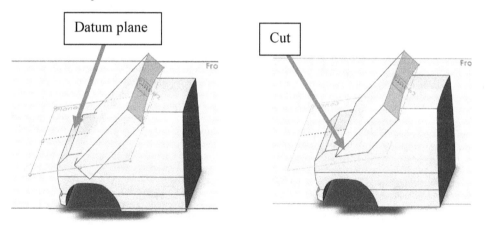

Finally, the trimmed cutter is subtracted from the model using **Insert/ Features/ Combine/ Subtract**.

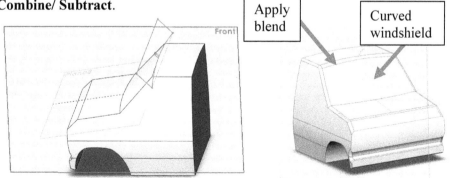

The hood has an indentation. Make a datum plane **20 inches** away from the mid plane. Create a sketch on that plane that contains an intersect curve and some geometry that dips below the intersection geometry. Turn the intersection geometry into reference entities so you can use geometry underneath to create a thin extruded surface. **Extrude** the sketch **40 inches** toward the center.

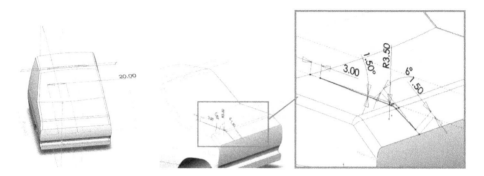

The surface is thickened into a subtract solid. The shape is subtracted and generous blends are applied.

Subtract solid and apply blends

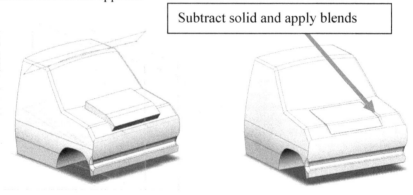

Details are often extremely important, especially when performing the industrial design function. In this case, the trim around the windshield really helps to define the shape of the windshield and bring it forward as a design element. In the same way that windows and doors are some of the most expressive features of a home, the windows, the grill, and the headlights are extremely important to the design of automotive geometry. In order to create the window trim, you need a datum plane that is roughly parallel to the window. This can be done by first creating a plane through three points as shown below, then creating an offset datum plane from that.

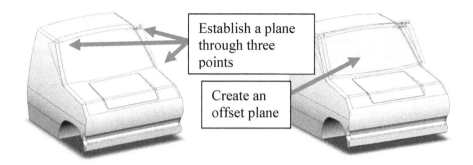

Establish a plane through three points

Create an offset plane

Once you have created a plane that is offset from the windshield surface, you may create a sketch on it and project the edges of the windshield surface onto the sketch plane. These are then extruded down past the windshield as a thin surface, blended on the corners and offset inward about **1 inch**. This creates two surfaces that intersect the windshield and define the inner and outer edges of the molding.

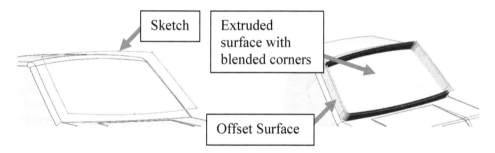

Sketch

Extruded surface with blended corners

Offset Surface

The surfaces are used with the **Insert/ Curve/ Split Line/ Intersect** command. This makes a region on the windshield that is then offset (**Insert/ Surface/ Offset**) with distance set to zero. Then the offset surface is thickened by about .**125in** (**Insert/ Boss/Base/ Thicken**). The result is a molding that is **.125 inches** thick and **1inch** wide. In general, when you add a piece of geometry (**Insert/ Features/ Combine/ Add**), its good practice to have some overlap. So, when you thicken the surface, you should probably thicken it by **.125 in** both directions. The small example below shows how two solids are "**Combined**" with a little overlap.

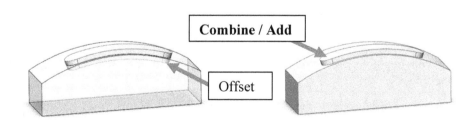

Combine / Add

Offset

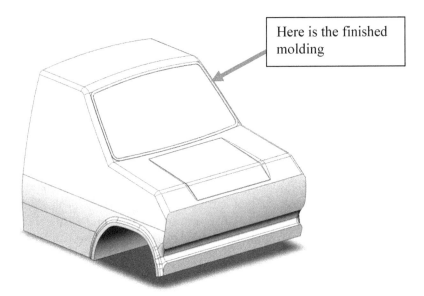

Here is the finished molding

The next step is to work on the grill and headlights using of the same skills used to make the molding. Create a datum plane that goes through the front surface, then an offset datum plane beyond that. Then add a series of sketches that represent the headlights, the turn signals, the grill, and the cool little ellipse-shaped emblem right in the center. Finally use a series of **Projects**, **Splits**, **Thickens**, **Extrudes**, **Patterns** and **Sweeps** to create the rest of the geometry.

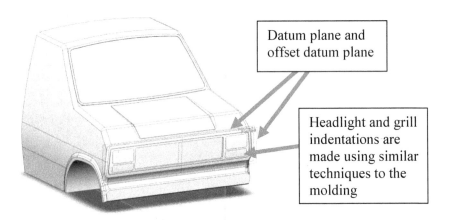

Datum plane and offset datum plane

Headlight and grill indentations are made using similar techniques to the molding

When you begin to color the various surfaces, the model starts looking very compelling.

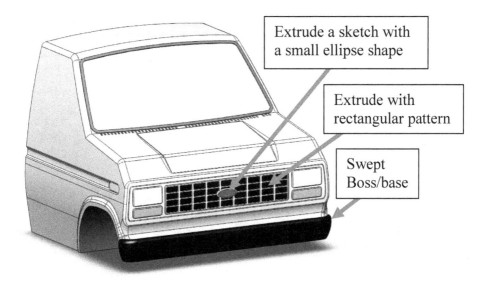

Extrude a sketch with a small ellipse shape

Extrude with rectangular pattern

Swept Boss/base

To create the side windows, create another sketch on the original surface representing the side view. In order to do so, temporarily make the side surface of the truck model transparent. This allows you to see the JPG underneath.

Make the surface temporarily transparent so you can see the shape of the window underneath and create the sketch for the windows.

Create a sketch that conforms to the shape of the window

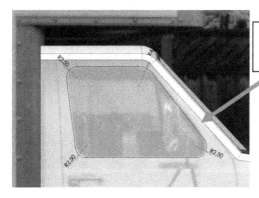

Sketch the window perimeter

Use the same technique that was used above to define the windshield molding. However, this time you will need to subtract the geometry instead of adding it. Before you subtract it, mirror it over to make the driver side window indentation. Make the indentation about **1 inch** deep.

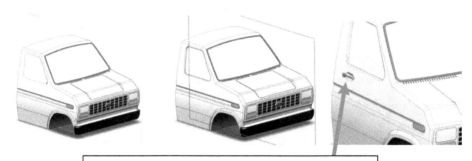

Handle indentation and handle geometry are created with a Revolve and a series of extrudes

Once you have the geometry for the cab pretty well defined, it's time to scoop it out so it has an inside. There is a technique that is very important for making interiors of things. Let's call it the ***Advanced Hollow Technique***. It's great for when you have an object that has a large cavity in it but it's too complex to use the usual **Shell** technique.

The way it works is to use the **Copy** command to create an exact duplicate of the object you want to hollow, and then **hide** the original solid while you operate on the copy. You can use a combination of offsets and cuts to make the copy smaller than the original. Once done you can **Insert/ Features/ Combine/ Subtract** the copied and operated on model, from the original. In essence the method allows you to model the interior space separately, then apply it to the original model. It's a very powerful technique that is extremely useful in the aerospace business, as well as for use with medical and consumer products. It is exceptionally good for injection molded geometry that has to be drafted and contains various ribs and bosses. Before we apply the Advanced Hollow Technique to the truck model, let's have a little practice. To proceed, create a simplified shape in a different part file that looks like a truck body, make it about **10 inches** high as shown in the following diagram.

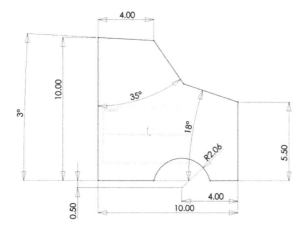

Extrude the profile **5 in** in both directions to create a solid that is **10 inches** wide.

Create the sketch shown below on the face where the windshield will go

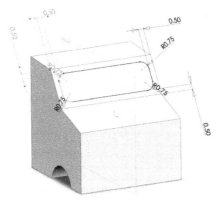

Extrude and cut the shape into solid. Create an indentation about **.5 inches** thick.

The tricky part is accomplished by making a duplicate of the part in the exact same location as the original using **Insert/ Features/ Move/ Copy.** When prompted, select the original solid. Make sure the **Copy** switch is turned on and the translate coordinates are all set to zero.

Copy Switch checked ON

X, Y, and Z are all set to zero

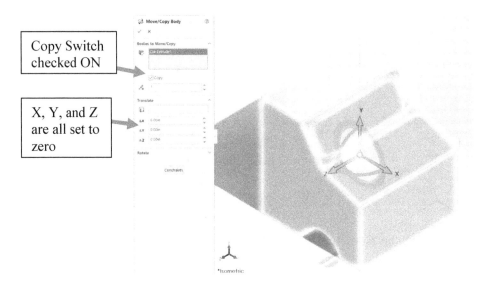

When you select **OK,** A small window will appear. You can ignore it and simply select **OK**.

You now have two identical copies of the solid. Now carefully select and hide the original.

Next, select **Insert/ Face/ Move** and select **Offset.** Set the offset value to **.25in** and flip the direction so that the surfaces are being offset in the inward direction.

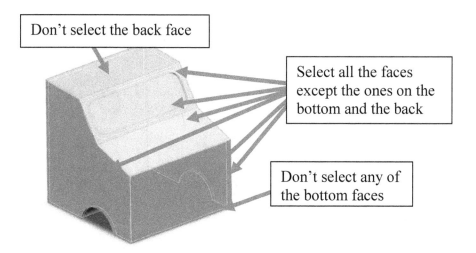

Don't select the back face

Select all the faces except the ones on the bottom and the back

Don't select any of the bottom faces

Once you have performed the offset, you will have a solid that is almost ready to be subtracted from the original.

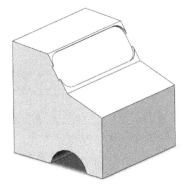

Make some more modifications to it. **Cut** out the bottom and make a contour that will represent the dashboard as shown below.

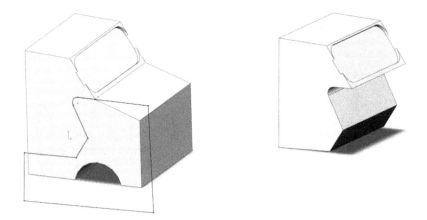

Now subtract the new solid from the original.

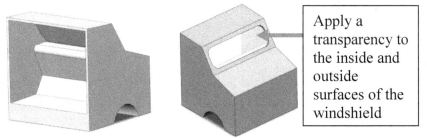

Apply a transparency to the inside and outside surfaces of the windshield

Now that you have had a bit of practice, do the same thing to the real model.

Once hollowed, add the steering wheel

The wheels are created using a **Revolved Boss/Base** for the overall wheel and hub, an extruded cut for the **4 slots**, a **Patterned Extrusion** for the lug nuts, and a series of wrapped, thickened, subtracted shapes for the treads around the outside.

The seats are also a series of extrudes, revolves, fillets, and coloring surfaces

In order to create the rear box portion of Ephigene, go back to the original side view sketch. The shape of the box section is simple as shown below in the new sketch.

Extrude the sketch about **88 inches** wide.

The rear tires are derived from the front tire, which is copied and moved out to the position of the rear tire. The center is modified, then the whole tire mirrored because the rear tires of Ephigene are doubled up.

Exercise Complete

Project 1: Drawer Assembly

It's nice to apply CAD skills to a real-life situation. This simple project is a drawer unit designed to lift a dryer so it's more convenient to get the clothes out. The model is sized as shown in the figure below.

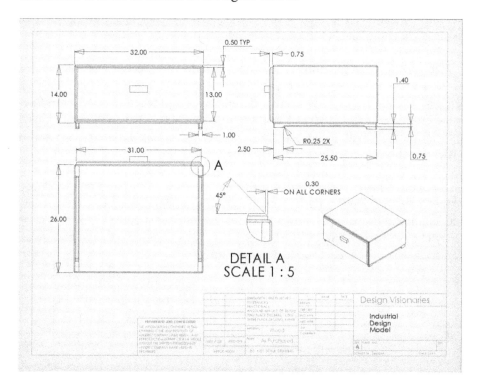

Begin by creating a series of extrusions and **Chamfer** all the edges by **.25**

The front face of the drawer is **.75 inches** thick and there are feet underneath as shown in the previous drawing. These are made of simple extrusions.

The model is used as the Industrial Design part file that drives the rest of the components. To proceed, select **File/New,** choose Assembly and click **OK.** This creates a new assembly file. Choose the Industrial Design Model to be assembled into the new assembly file then save the assembly by choosing **File/Save.** Give the assembly a name like "Drawer Assembly."

Now that you have an assembly file with the industrial design part file loaded into it as a component, you can create a new component and use the industrial design part file as the key associative definition. To proceed choose **New Part** from the dropdown of the **Insert Component** command. This will create a new component part file within the assembly. To begin creating geometry inside this new file, left click on it in the **Feature Manager** tool and choose **Edit part.**

When you edit the part, the objective is to steal the various surfaces you will need from the industrial design part to create a fully associated model in the new component part. For example, now that the new component is the in "Edit" mode you may choose **Insert/Surface/Offset,** set the offset value to **0.0,** and choose all the top surfaces of the industrial design **part file**.

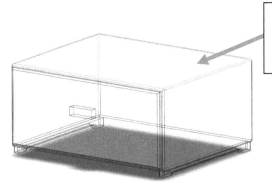

Select the top surface and the surfaces of the chamfer.

Now that you have associated surfaces in the new **part file**, it is time to use them to create the rest of the top plate model. Since the top surfaces comprise the actual top piece of the assembly, the surfaces have to be used to create the rest of the model. It is easier to model in the actual part file than by looking through the assembly, so left-click on the new part file in the Feature Manager and choose **Open Part.**

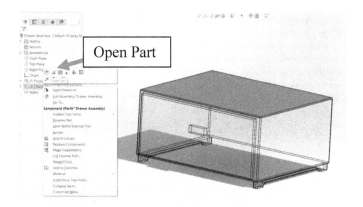

Open Part

The offset surfaces in the new part file are easy to use to build the rest of the solid. These surfaces are associated to the ID part file if and when you decide to change the entire design. This way, it's easy to change every component just by changing the ID part file.

Since you've opened the part file, you have access to the surfaces in the actual component part file. Use the **Surface Fill** command to close the shape and make it one piece.

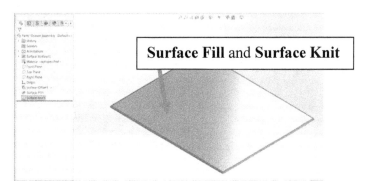

Surface Fill and **Surface Knit**

Create a plane that is offset .75

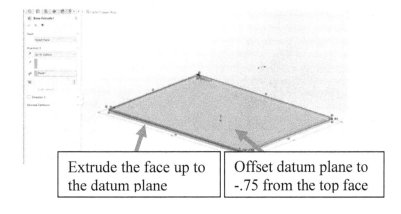

Extrude the face up to the datum plane

Offset datum plane to -.75 from the top face

When you go back to the assembly part file you will have the new Part in the assembly with geometry inside of it.

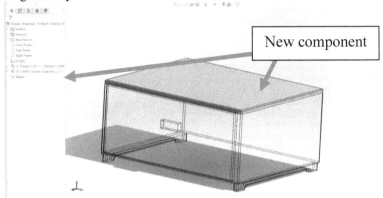

New component

The next step is to create the sides and the drawer cabinet. This is done by inserting a new part into the assembly, editing the part, and using the offset command to select the side surface. On the side surface you may draw a sketch and align its edges to the edges of the industrial design model.

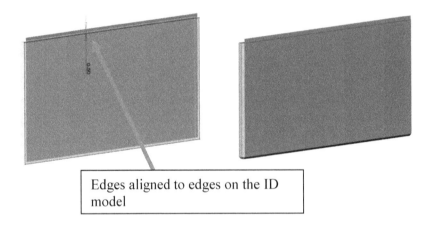

Edges aligned to edges on the ID model

Now that you have the side component, you can use it on the other side.

To create the rear plate, you may use the geometry of the top and the sides to define the shape of the plate. The modeling goes very fast if you create a new part in the assembly, edit the part, create a sketch directly on the back side of one of the sides and align the edges to the inside edges of the assembled parts. Then, simply extrude it **.75 inches** inward.

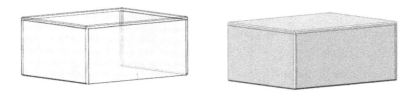

Make a new part file and use the same techniques to create the bottom plate.

The next thing we will do is get the drawer sliders into the assembly. The drawer sliders are a standard Home Depot part. At the printing of this book, these drawer sliders were available and we reverse engineered them. You can find them at *www.designviz.com/goodies*.

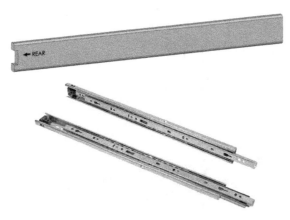

The sliders are placed in the assembly, with the little grooved portions to the rear and **5.5 inches** offset from the bottom plate.

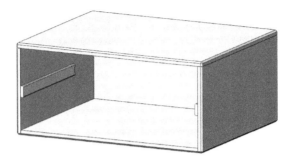

To create the feet, bring back the industrial design model, make a new part in the assembly and sketch on one of the side surfaces.

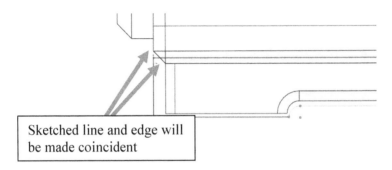

Sketched line and edge will be made coincident

The sketch is extruded to a thickness of **1 inch**. The new solid is a component that you can call **foot rail**. Bring in a copy of the rail component and assemble it using mating conditions.

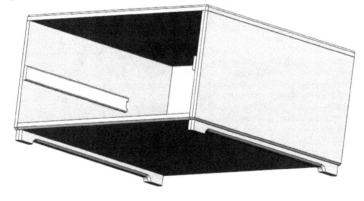

Now that you have all the components of the outer cabinet, you can create the drawer. As you did with the other components, you can create the drawer by inserting a new component into the assembly and selecting **Edit**

Part. Create a sketch on the outside face of the drawer and extrude it **.75in.** Then you may offset the inner surfaces of the sliders and the inner surface of the bottom plate. Sketch on the inner surface of the front plate of the drawer and relate it to the other surfaces.

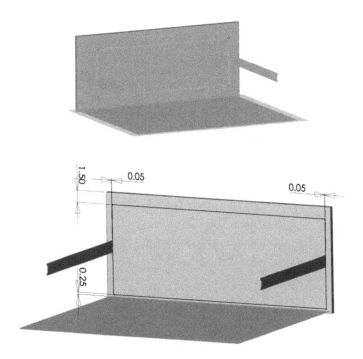

Next, extrude the sketch without adding it to the front plate. Extrude it out to **18 inches**.

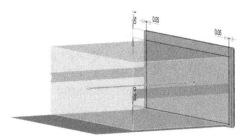

Shell the extruded portion of the drawer with a thickness of **.5 inch**. The plan is to build a **.5 inch** thick box out of plywood, then fasten a **.75 inch** plate to it. The drawer pull is added later. The drawer pull requires two **.2 inch** diameter holes that are **5 inches** apart, each **.25 inches** from the center.

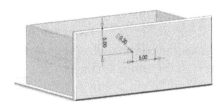

The drawer pull is another Home Depot part. The mount holes in it are **5 inches** apart and the screws that come with it require a **.2 inch** diameter hole. You may retrieve part files for the drawer pull and screws from the website *www.designviz.com/goodies*. The part names are **Drawer Pull.sldpt** and **Drawer Pull Screw.sldprt**.

To mate the pull to the front of the drawer, use **Concentric** mates between corresponding holes and a **Coincident** mate between the flat face of the pull and the front face of the drawer.

Once the entire assembly has been created, the holes in the sides can be added to provide a place for fasteners. The real-life assembly will be done with glue and screws. Now that the parts are all assembled, it is easy to place the holes. In the feature manager make the **Top Plate** the edit part.

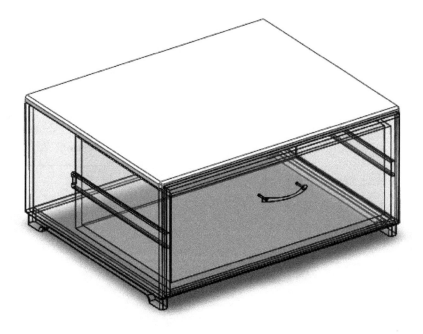

Now select the **Hole Wizard**. The Hole Wizard tool is very capable, but you must set it to the right values. Since we suggest putting the assembly together with bright brass sheet rock screws, you may set the hole values accordingly. That is, set the **Hole Type** to **ANSI Inch**, and the **Through Hole Diameter** to **.15**, and the **Countersink Diameter** to **.34**. *Note: For this exercise, we won't actually be adding these screws into the assembly.*

When you have all the values in place, you can save it all as a favorite hole type using the **Add to Favorites** button. Enter the name "Sheet rock screw 1.75 long". This will make it easier for subsequent projects.

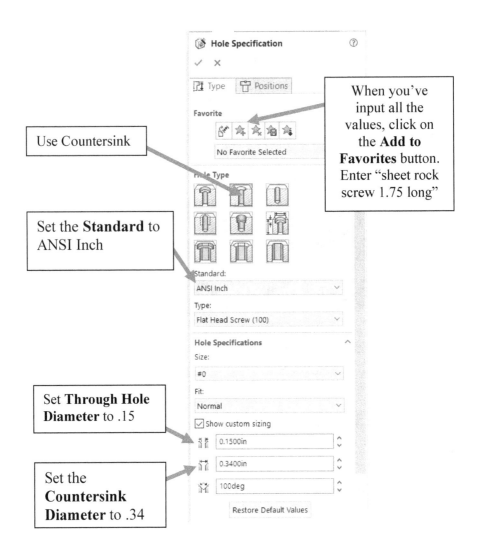

After you set all the values appropriately, click on the **Positions** tab. The positions menu prompts you to select the face on which you will be putting the holes before using the sketch tool. While in the sketch, a hole will be created everywhere you place a point entity. For this exercise, you can create all the holes on the left-hand side, position them as shown in the diagram to follow, then mirror them. You should end up having a number of holes distributed along the rear and side edges, all **.3875 inches** away from the edge and spaced out by **4 inches.**

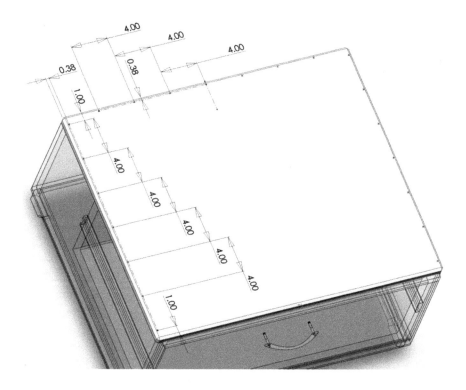

Once all the holes have been created, the **Top Plate** will appear as shown below.

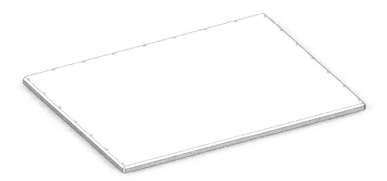

Let's say as you are creating the assembly, a design change suddenly becomes necessary. You suddenly realize that this project will be constructed of plywood. Unfortunately, the edges of the plywood don't really look very good when they are chamfered. It is much more desirable to cut the plywood sheets off straight and finish them off with a very thin molding. Therefore, the assembly needs to be changed and added to.

First, we can change the **Top Plate** by deleting the chamfer. Since the top plate was created by copying faces from the industrial design model, it may be a difficult and arduous task to delete the chamfers in the industrial design model. For that reason, let's make the change locally and see how it goes.

To proceed, Select the **Direct Editing** tab and use the **Delete Face** command. You can also select **Insert/Face/Delete**. Within the command select **Delete and Patch** and then select the faces at the corners to delete. It will not work if you try to select all the chamfer surfaces all at once.

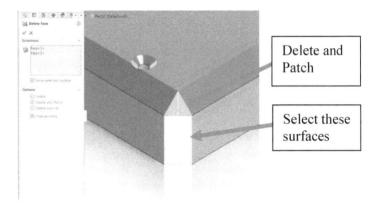

Delete and Patch

Select these surfaces

After the delete operation, all the vertical chamfers will be gone and the corners will appear as shown.

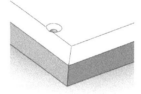

Now delete the rest of the chamfers. You may have to delete them one-by-one.

Front edge

Once the chamfers are all taken off the top plate, the molding needs to be added. Make a new component in the assembly by choosing **Insert/Component/New Part**. Next make the new part the **Edit Part** and click on the part once in the Feature Manger Design Tree so you can type over the default name to rename it. We called it "**Long Top Molding.**" Next make a sketch on the very end and perpendicular to the front face. You will also need another sketch on the front face.

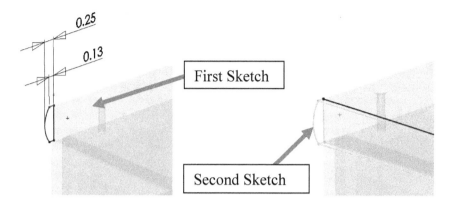

Next use the **Swept Boss/Base** command to create the molding.

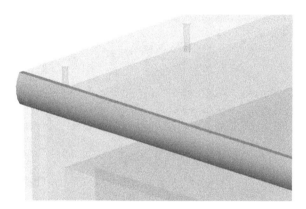

Similar methods are used to make the other piece of molding that goes on the short side of the top and the other pieces all around the assembly.

To finish off the geometry, holes must be added to the side plates and the back plate. The moldings will be glued and nailed. For this simple assembly, the fasteners don't need to be modeled.

In order to add the holes to the side plates it is best to use the **Assembly Features/ Hole Wizard.** This is because the side plates are match drilled when they are assembled. In other words, instead of pre-drilling the holes in the side plates which would make them mirror image parts, you can assemble them, attach them to the top plate, insert the bottom plate and drill all of it together. The **Hole Wizard** in the **Assembly Features** menu works in the same way the as the one in Modeling. Each side plate gets 7 holes along the bottom edge, and 4 up the back edge of the side as shown below.

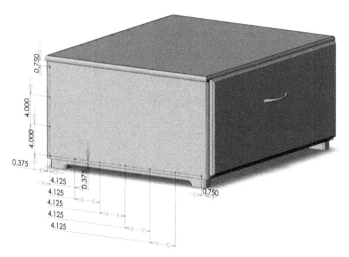

The holes in the rear plate will be placed as shown below. These holes can easily be placed using the regular hole wizard in the "rear plate" file. The hole dimensions should be the same as those on the top sheet.

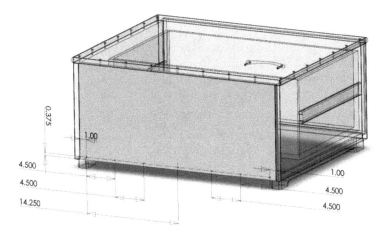

When the drilling of holes is all done, and all the components are present, one can create an exploded view. The exploded view is best done in a different "configuration". As you may recall from a previous chapter, a SolidWorks configuration is an alternate state of being for a SolidWorks component or assembly. In order to create and view a new configuration, you have to open the configurations manager, and through a series of clicks, create a new configuration and make it the displayed assembly. To switch back and forth, you just select which configuration you desire. You can name the various configurations representative names such as "exploded assembly" or "normal view".

To proceed, click on the configuration manager icon.

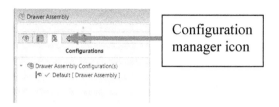

Configuration manager icon

Next right-click on the main configuration, in this case "**Cabinet assembly configuration(s)**" and left click on **Add Configuration**.

Click on **Add Configuration**

The Add configurations window will appear. You may now input a new name and a description. Enter **Exploded View 1.**

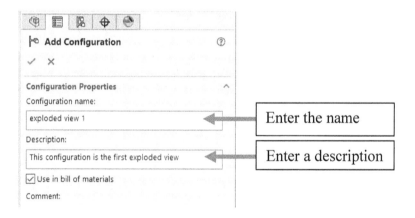

Enter the name

Enter a description

Now you will have two configurations. The new one is active. You can now create the exploded view.

To proceed, choose **Insert/ Exploded view.** The menu that appears allows you to select each component and drag it with the "manipulator handle".

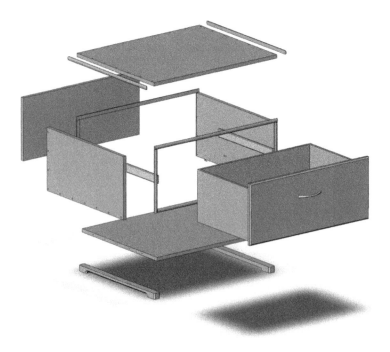

Once you are done creating the exploded view, you may switch between the Default view and the exploded view just by selecting the icon.

You may now create an Assembly Drawing. This is accomplished by selecting **File/ Make Drawing from Assembly.** You will get a good default drawing format.

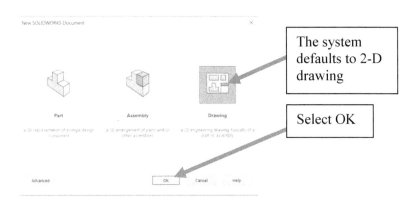

The system defaults to 2-D drawing

Select OK

Next, right-click in the middle of the sheet that appears and click on
Properties.

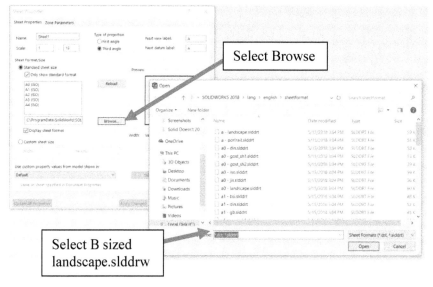

Next select **Insert/Drawing View/Model**. This is how you choose what model you will be creating the drawing for.

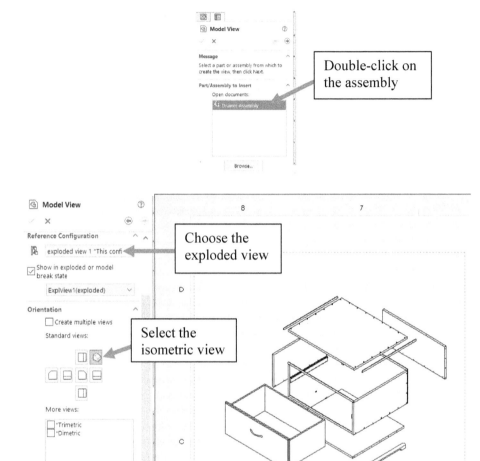

Once you have placed the view, you can place the Bill of Materials. Select **Insert/ Tables/ Bill of Materials**. If you accept the defaults and click on the drawing, the Bill of Materials will be placed.

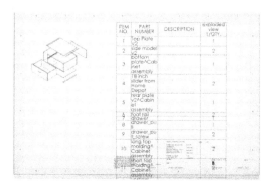

To size the text, you can left-click and drag over the entire Bill of Materials and a menu will appear that allows you to change the font and edit a variety of other attributes. You can also left-click in the upper left-hand corner to move the Bill of Materials around and size it.

Now select **Insert/Annotations/Auto Balloon.** The balloons come in according to the pattern of your choice, then you can move them around by clicking and dragging.

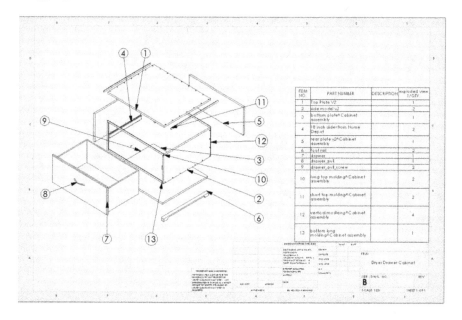

Exercise Complete

Project 2: Marshmallow Gun

This Marshmallow gun is a really cool project that you can make in SolidWorks to practice your skills, and then make it on your own at home with parts that can be found at your local home improvement store.

The SolidWorks Assembly of the Marshmallow Gun

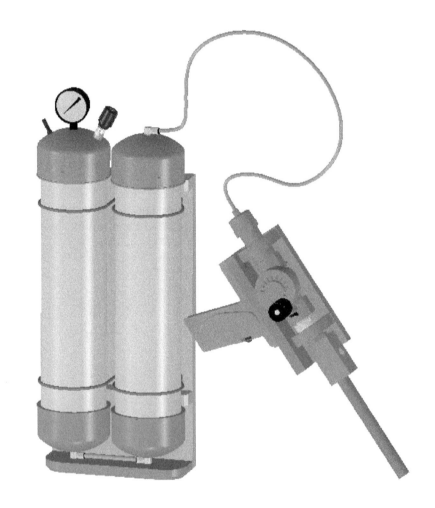

The "Real Deal" Marshmallow Gun

PC NO	PART NAME	QTY
9	3_4IN PIPE	1
8	3_4IN TO 1IN ADAPTER	1
7	1 IN MALE ADAPTER	1
6	1IN TO 1IN THREAD	1
5	SCREW	8
4	EXHAUST VALVE	1
3	HANDLE	1
2	HANDLE SUPPORT	1
1	MAIN PLATE	1

PC NO	PART NAME	QTY
19	1_16IN SCREW	4
18	BATTERY COVER	1
17	1IN ADAPTER BRACKET	2
16	9V BATTERY	1
15	SLEEVE - WOOD	1
14	ELECTRIC SWITCH	1
13	TRIGGER PLATE	1
12	HOSE FITTINGS	1
11	1 IN CAP	1
10	1 IN TUBE	1

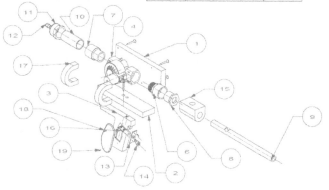

Above is the exploded view of the Gun Assembly. You can download the rest of the plans and part files at *www.designviz.com/goodies.*

A Few Parting Words About CAD

Speculating about any business that has to do with software and computer capabilities is always risky. The quantum leaps that occur over time are extremely difficult to predict. However, what is apparent is what CAD users want. Hopefully what CAD users want is what the industry will continue to provide sooner or later. CAD users all over the globe have difficulty finding the commands they are looking for especially as they do increasingly complex tasks. It is extremely important for solid modeling systems to get better at organizing and streamlining the user interface so various commands are easier and easier to find. To some degree the most powerful systems are at a disadvantage to the lesser ones due to the sheer volume of commands and abilities that they have over lesser systems. It can be confusing, especially for new users. Another general thrust in CAD systems comes from the fact that most design engineers would love to find some way to do away with the entire drafting process. Indeed, high end systems already have the ability to capture things like geometric dimensioning and tolerancing, surface finish call outs, and non-shape data right in the 3-D model. In the future this will undoubtedly be made easier and more common. Another controversial trend in CAD is the total abandonment of parametrics. There are a large number of engineers who never felt that the move to parametric modeling was a benefit. Commensurately there are a small yet growing number of CAD software designers who are determined to make a non-parametric paradigm as a productive and easy way to perform design iterations with parametric modeling.

The future may yield a solid modeling package that gives anyone at any time the choice to be parametric, non-parametric, or light weight. By and large all CAD modelers look at all the features and functions of all the other packages and make sure that somehow they have everything that everyone else has. In recent years, CAD software companies have bought each other out and made new programs that incorporate everything that the other programs had plus what they had originally. It's also a great way to increase the installed base of users. Going forward, it is the opinion of the authors that CAD systems of the future will be fewer, far more powerful, less expensive, more well known to users and engineers that just come out of school, and easier to use as an expert or a novice user. It is also the opinion of the author that the more powerful the systems become over time, the more exciting and fun they will be to use. They will have more computing power and capabilities, and we as designers will be asking them to do increasingly difficult geometry. To some degree designers limit the shape of their designs based upon the limitations of the CAD systems that they use. In the future we will all enjoy more freedom and better designs.

Training

There is only one way to learn the best methods of using CAD – use it for hours and hours and create difficult geometry. To some degree the memory of the various commands is in the fingers. You must spend the required amount of time using each command so you'll remember where it is. Hopefully reading books like this and doing the tutorials that you find all over the internet will help greatly. The best training you can have is when a good trainer who is a designer in his or her own right painstakingly leads you through exercises that resemble the kind of geometry that you are responsible for. The best trainer has a lot of things rolled up into one: mechanical engineering ability, creativity, excellent knowledge of CAD, an excellent way with people, and most importantly the will to share. These folks are difficult to come by. When you find one, keep 'em. If you don't have access to a good trainer or you don't have the budget, then by all means, keep challenging yourself to go beyond the tutorials. Keep creating difficult geometry and trying out commands that you've never touched before. It can be frustrating, but in the end it will bear fruit.

Glossary

3D Sketches - Sketches created in a 3D space rather than on a single plane

Arc - A segmented section of a circle

Assembly - A file type designed to contain multiple SolidWorks parts mated together in a specific arrangement (.SLDASM)

Bill of Materials - A list of all the parts used in an assembly that can be added to a drawing while drafting

Blend – Another term for a fillet, filleting an edge

Blind - The option to define a distance, such as the depth of an extrusion or extruded cut, by a numerical value rather than by relating it to a plane or other face.

Body - A 3D object in SolidWorks.

Broken View - A drafting tool that allows a long part entity to be represented more compactly in a view.

"Build 'em Bust 'em" Analysis - Where a concept is tested by building a model and testing to see if it holds up or breaks under stressful conditions.

CAD - Computer-aided design

Chamfer - A tool that replaces the sharp edge of an object with a flattened face

Child Features - Features that are related to and dependent upon a parent feature

Clam Shell - Two shells of material that clasp together to make a product's exterior

Coincident - Alignment along the infinite extension of a given line segment

Collapse - Reduces a view back to its original form from an exploded view

Collinear - A relationship between two line segments that are placed along the same theoretical line

Component - A part that is added to an assembly

Concentric - Circles centered about the same midpoint

Configurations - Variations of a part or assembly that can be created and exchanged as needed to capture different states of the model

Constraints - Restrictions placed on the position of sketch components or SolidWorks parts to create or maintain a desired shape or relationship

Coradial - Circles of equal radius and that are centered about the same point

Cosmetic Threads - Dashed lines added to a shank or hole to represent a threaded surface without using the excessive memory it would take to render actual threads

Curve - A nonlinear segment

Cut - A function that removes indicated sections of a body

Datum Plane - A plane that can be created or used as a reference or sketch base. Default planes are Top, Front, and Right.

Dimensions - Fixed numerical values placed on sketch components or 3D features to scale and relate them to real-world size

Draft - A tool that adds or adjusts the taper angle of the face of a solid

Draft Angle - A taper applied to a body, often to aid in the manufacturability of cast or molded parts

Drafting - The act of creating a drawing by arranging view orientations, dimensions, etc. on a single sheet of paper which can easily communicate a design.

Drawing - A file consisting of 2D views and information to represent a 3D part or assembly for easier viewing and comprehension (.SLDDRW)

Export - Brings files out of SolidWorks for storage or to save them in a format that can be used in other applications

Extrude - Creates a 3D component of a fixed or drafted cross-sectional profile from a 2D sketch as if by pushing the material through a die.

Extrude Cut - Carves out a 3D shape from a body by removing an area in the shape of and some distance from a 2D shape

Face - A surface that forms part of the boundary of a 3D shape

Fillet - A tool that replaces a sharp edge of an object with a rounded face that has a specified radius

Fixed - A constraint that locks an entity to its current position without relating it to another entity

Flange - A sheet metal face, often connected to others with bends

Flex - A command, used primarily to demonstrate properties rather than for manufacturing, that allows you to manipulate the shape of a solid or a surface by bending, twisting, tapering or stretching

Geometry - Lines, curves, shapes, etc. in a CAD model

Global Variables - Values that can be defined and used in more than one instance throughout a part to relate dimensions and values

Gussets - A bit of material added to a body to make it more structurally sound

Import - Allows you to bring outside files into SolidWorks

Industrial Design (ID) - A single model that represents the entire exterior of a product used to drive the shape of the actual components.

Isometric - An angled projection or viewpoint that showcases the 3D aspects of a part that would not be visible in a typical front or top view

Jog - A sheet metal tool that allows you to easily add in a section that bends the part as if it were going up and over or down and under something

Knit Surfaces - A tool that connects various surfaces together to create a single surface or a solid

Loft - A smooth surface created between profiles and shaped by optional guide curves

Louver - An angled slat often used for ventilation that is punched out of a sheet metal piece

Mates - Constraints that relate parts in an assembly

Merge - A relation that fuses two points into one

Midplane - A direction used for extrusions and similar tools that adds equal thickness on either side of the plane

Midpoint - The point equidistant from the endpoints of a segment

Mirror - A tool that reflects a feature, face, or body over a specified axis of reflection

Mirror Entities - A sketch tool that reflects curves across as specified axis

Model - A 3D part or assembly that represents a real-world object

Motion Study - A simulation that demonstrates how the pieces of an assembly will behave when a force is applied

Over Dimensioned - A sketch that has dimensions that are unnecessary or conflicting because they are already defined by a different dimension or constraint

Offset - A distance between one entity and another

Parallel - A relationship between lines such that they will never intersect

Parameter - One of a set of numerical values that defines and drives features and geometry

Parent Features - A feature upon which one or more dependent features rely. If changed, it will impact those child features as well.

Part - A 3D model created in SolidWorks that acts as a single component

Part File - The most basic type of SolidWorks file, containing one part (.SLDPRT)

Parting Line - A line that separates two sections of a body

Pattern - A sketch component or body that is repeated once on a linear, circular, or otherwise defined path

Perpendicular - A relationship between entities such that that they are at 90 degrees to each other

Product Coordinate System - A globally defined coordinate system that is used for all parts of the assembly

Projection – A process by which all points on a line or curve are plotted to where they intersect a surface or plane

Radius - The distance between the midpoint of a circle and any point along its curve

Rebuild - A command that updates a sketch, part, or assembly to fit the changes made to a certain feature

Reference Geometry - A plane, point, axis, etc. that is used to provide a position, create a relationship, or provide a surface to create a sketch

Revolve - A tool that creates a 3D body from a 2D sketch by rotating the sketch around a specified axis

Revolve Cut - Carves out a 3D shape from a body by removing the sections within the bounds of a 2D sketch rotated around a specified axis

Rips - Cuts in a bit of sheet metal created from a 3D part which allows it to be unfolded

Scale - Resizes an object according to specified proportions

Shell - Thins the inside of a 3D object so that all sides have the same specified thickness or are removed

Simulation - A calculated experiment of the reaction of a part to a force or pressure which is demonstrated in a digital space

Sketch - A 2D shape made in SolidWorks which is used to then create 3D objects

Snap - When a feature that is being moved through space automatically jumps to a defined point or edge signifying that the feature will be connected to it when applied.

Solids - A filled 3D body

Super Duper Whosey Whatsit - A whosey that whatsits

Surface - A flat 2D face that is defined in 3D space

Sweep - Creates a 3D component from a 2D sketch following the path of another sketch, edge, or surface

Symmetric - Mirrored on both sides of an axis or plane

Tangent - A line that touches a point on a curve without crossing over it at any other point along its infinite extension

Tangent arc - An arc that is tangentially related to a line

Taper - An angle that has been added to a flat face

Texture - The appearance applied to the surface of a solid object

Top Down Assembly - Also called *master modeling* or *template modeling*, this technique starts with a single model that represents the entire exterior of a product (the ID model) and uses it to drive the shape of the actual components

Trim - To delete selected segments of a sketch

Wireframe - View option where all faces are made transparent and all edges of the 3D body are made visible

Zip File - A file format used for lossless data compression that groups one or more files together

Index

www.ingramcontent.com/pod-product-compliance
Lightning Source LLC
LaVergne TN
LVHW062259060326
832902LV00013B/1968